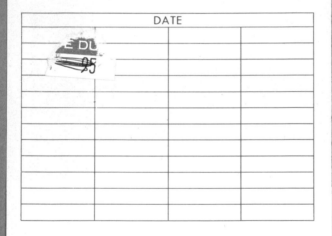

The Changing Workplace

Carl McDaniels

The Changing Workplace

Career Counseling Strategies for the 1990s and Beyond

J o s s e y - B a s s   P u b l i s h e r s

San Francisco   •   Oxford   •   1990

THE CHANGING WORKPLACE
Career Counseling Strategies for the 1990s and Beyond
  by Carl McDaniels

Copyright © 1989 by: Jossey-Bass Inc., Publishers
                    350 Sansome Street
                    San Francisco, California 94104
                              &
                    Jossey-Bass Limited
                    Headington Hill Hall
                    Oxford OX3 0BW

Library of Congress Cataloging-in-Publication Data

McDaniels, Carl.
    The changing workplace : career counseling strategies for the
1990s and beyond / Carl McDaniels. — 1st ed.
        p. cm. — (The Jossey-Bass social and behavioral science
series)
    Bibliography: p.
    Includes index.
    ISBN 1-55542-146-6 (alk. paper)
    1. Vocational guidance. 2. Professions—Forecasting.
3. Occupations—Forecasting. I. Title. II. Series.
HF5381.M39625 1989
331.7′02—dc19   88-46081
                                                       CIP

Manufactured in the United States of America

The paper in this book meets the guidelines for
permanence and durability of the Committee on
Production Guidelines for Book Longevity of the
Council on Library Resources.

JACKET DESIGN BY WILLI BAUM

FIRST EDITION

    First printing: May 1989
    Second printing: June 1990

Code 8921

The Jossey-Bass
Social and Behavioral Science Series

Contents

Preface

The Changing Workplace is about alternative futures for the workplace. It zeroes in on where people will be working in the future, that is, on the *settings* in which work will take place—and not specifically on the industries, occupations, or workers of the future.

There are scores of official government publications on the jobs and workers of the future. There exists an equal number of unofficial monographs, reports, and books on the same topics. Most of these prognostications share one trait; they present one point of view and argue that this is the way the future will unfold. *The Changing Workplace* recognizes other possibilities. It looks at alternative options on future places of employment and presents one particular option people can exercise in order to gain flexibility in the face of possible future changes in the workplace.

Intended Audience

The Changing Workplace was written specifically for the more than 150,000 counselors who help people with career development. The main concepts are directed to counselors in a wide variety of settings who work with teenagers, young adults, mid-career changers, pre-retirees, and senior citizens. In short, all counselors—whether they are in schools, in two- or four-year colleges and universities, in public or private employment/outplacement agencies, industry, or in government—need to have a sense of where the people for whom they provide assistance can find satisfaction and challenge in tomorrow's workplace.

Teachers, psychologists, adult and vocational educators, and others in the helping professions share these concerns with counselors; therefore, they also should find the book helpful in working with people throughout the life span—for instance, as they look for their first full-time job, or try to find a new direction after being displaced from a job, or just seek to prepare themselves for a different stage of life with shifting personal priorities.

Counselors and others in the helping professions need a balanced, carefully measured view of the future world of work and leisure. They need to be aware of alternatives in changing work settings in order to best serve the career development needs of the people with whom they work. *The Changing Workplace* presents some of these important alternatives and shows how they can be implemented and kept up-to-date in the years ahead.

Background

Every reader deserves to have confidence in the credentials and background of the person writing a book such as *The Changing Workplace*. My academic credentials are listed on the author's page, covering thirty-five years of teaching, counseling, and administrative work. This is the more personal background. I have been interested in work and workers since I sold *Liberty* magazines as a boy on the streets of Waco, Texas, in the 1930s. As a teenager, I had part-time and summer jobs as a paper boy and later as a messenger for the old *Evening Star Newspaper* in Washington, D.C.; as a bellman in a Pennsylvania resort hotel; as a summer day-camp counselor at the YMCA in Arlington, Virginia; and as a construction laborer and union member on the remodeling of the White House. All these jobs helped to shape my notions about work and workers. In my adult years, I have been employed as both a teacher and a counselor. In doing those jobs, I have always been concerned about people's career development over the life span.

The evolution of this book has taken place over the last twenty years, while I have been at Virginia Tech, the land-grant university for Virginia. Since 1979 it has been my good fortune to assist in the development of the career information delivery system called Virginia VIEW (Vital Information for Education and Work). This multimedia system is in over 1,000 locations around the Old Dominion. Our goal from the start has been to have the most accurate, up-to-date, usable, and economical system available to every citizen in Virginia without regard to ability to pay—which means at no cost to the user. The 6,000 + pages of career information we pulled together and then disseminated in a wide variety of forms sharpened my longstanding interest in the future of work and workers.

In 1986, in an article in a special issue of the *Journal of Cooperative Education,* I formulated what I felt were three general scenarios for the future of work. This article formed the basis for Part Two of this book. Later I realized that writers on the subject (including me) had paid scant attention to some of the emerging settings for work. So I developed the concept of the "Three Wild Cards in the Work Game"—entrepreneurship, small business, and work at home (described in Part Three of this book). The last part of the book (Part Four) is based on my twenty-five-year concern for the interrelationship between work and leisure throughout an individual's career (McDaniels, 1965). This book, then, is the culmination of a lifelong interest in work, workers, work settings, leisure, career development through the life span, career information delivery systems, and alternative futures.

A Caution

Conceivably, conditions in the United States or the world could change in such a way that some of the issues stressed here would take on more or less importance. For example, if the national unemployment rate continues on a downward trend as it has in 1987–88, it would have an effect on all three scenarios. Similarly, the resurgence of manufacturing and productivity in late 1987 and early 1988 also could affect the three scenarios. Nevertheless, the broad points made in all four parts of the book seem on solid ground—supported as they are by nearly 200 sources of reference. Certainly, the general principle of the emerging importance of entrepreneurship, small business, and work at home as expanded work settings for the future seems firmly rooted in the social, economic, and political trends of the time. And surely the concept of one's career as the interaction of work and leisure over the life span is not tied to economic conditions and deserves attention and discussion based on the evolving nature of all three terms.

Overview of the Contents

Each chapter in *The Changing Workplace* has a section on what counselors, teachers, psychologists, and others in the helping professions can do to keep up with local, state, national, and worldwide changes that will inevitably come about. Each chapter ends with an annotated listing of the books or articles that had the greatest influence on me in formulating the content of the chapter. For the person who is curious about where some of the ideas came from, this is a place to pursue further study.

The Changing Workplace is by no means the "final word" but is rather a starting point and a framework that readers can use to find information or concepts that will aid in assisting the people whose best interests we, as counselors, seek to serve. The sections on what to do to keep up-to-date or how to seek better local sources of confirming data are meant as suggestions or beginning points in the endless search of where the ever-changing world of work is going.

Part One introduces *The Changing Workplace* by looking at a variety of viewpoints on the future for the United States and for work and workers in particular. This part presents a framework for counselors and others reading the book.

In Chapter One I discuss the often mysterious-sounding process of forecasting the future of work (or anything else). This chapter analyzes some of the most frequent methods used in "future" writings and looks at examples of good and bad forecasts.

Chapter Two maps out the shape of the future work force and work setting. The chapter presents a detailed synthesis of the demographics of the past, present, and possible future makeup of the work force. Where will the young workers come from? Will there be more women and nonwhites in the work force? Also, what are the future prospects for full-time, shared, part-time, and flexible work? A number of figures and tables from the Bureau of the Census and the Bureau of Labor Statistics are included.

Part Two describes three possible scenarios for the future of work. It groups the main ideas in this field around three main themes (using a traffic light metaphor), each highlighting a different prospect for the changing workplace.

Chapter Three examines for counselors a future workplace full of high technology and exotic occupations. The writings of Cetron, Cornish, Feingold, Naisbitt, Toffler, and others whose work appears regularly in *The Futurist* (published by the World Future Society) are discussed. Many of these writers envision revolutionary, dramatic changes in the future world of work. The pros and cons of this vision are examined, and I present some suggestions on how counselors can keep current on this viewpoint.

Chapter Four presents a different scenario. Based largely on publications of the Bureau of Labor Statistics and the writing of Sar Levitan and others, it visualizes a future not dramatically different from the present. Workplace changes, according to this view, will be evolutionary rather than revolutionary. I analyze the strong and weak points of this scenario and show how counselors can stay up-to-date on the subject.

Chapter Five discusses a generally pessimistic view of the future of work—emphasizing the decline of manufacturing, the downscaling of jobs, and high unemployment. Again, I evaluate this scenario and show how to remain timely on this topic.

In Part Three I describe a different way of approaching the future of work: by *setting* rather than by occupation or industry.

Chapter Six examines why entrepreneurship is growing so fast. I present entrepreneurship options in this chapter and highlight programs such as those advanced by the Association of Collegiate Entrepreneurs as well as Drucker's new book, *Innovation and Entrepreneurship*.

Chapter Seven discusses the growth of small business. It shows that most new jobs are being created in businesses that employ less than 250 people, often in those businesses employing less than 100 people. I examine employment opportunities such as franchising in a variety of small businesses. Profiles of several prosperous small businesses are presented, along with tips on how counselors can stay fully informed on the subject.

Chapter Eight takes a look at the estimated ten million people working at home today and reports that the work-at-home trend will continue. Several work-at-home options are examined, such as the fabled "electronic cottage" with networking connections to a mainframe computer, crafts people, direct salespeople (Amway, Mary Kay), and service people (accountants, locksmiths). Since this is a relatively invisible place of employment, I present suggestions on how counselors can learn more about this emerging work setting.

Part Four focuses on the work-leisure connection by emphasizing that one's career is made up of the interaction of work and leisure throughout the life span.

Chapter Nine is an overview chapter for Part Four. It establishes the definitions of work, leisure, and career and looks briefly at some of the main issues regarding the future of both work and leisure. I discuss how work and leisure can interrelate and examine some of the unresolved work-leisure issues. The chapter concludes with proposals for changes in institutions to better support the work-leisure connection.

Chapter Ten is really the heart of Part Four. It goes from theory (Chapter Nine) to practice. First there is a challenge: Why not encourage people to do what they enjoy? Then there are twenty illustrations of people from various age groups who have actually taken the leap to put their leisure to work. I discuss the pros and cons of this and suggest occupations and jobs that directly relate to a variety of leisure activities.

Chapter Eleven looks at a six-stage view of work and leisure development over the life span, emphasizing crucial differences and similarities in each epoch. Then a case is made for a broad-based approach to career counseling (CC = LC + WC), as opposed to leisure counseling or work counseling alone.

Finally, the chapter lists and discusses seven principles that should help point counselors toward a unified career counseling approach over the life span.

Acknowledgments

This book, like most others, represents the combined efforts of a great many people.

First, it took a magician to make sense out of some of my scribbles and scratch-outs. Somehow my incomplete thoughts and unfinished sentences were brought into meaning, shape, and form on the proper pages and with the right references. All the credit for typing and formating the various stages of the drafts, redrafts, and final drafts goes to the wonderful Virginia Tech Counselor Education Program Area secretary, Julia H. Moore. Without her quick and efficient work, this book could not have been completed. Special thanks to her.

Second, the effort would not have been possible without the encouragement of family and friends. My wife, Ann, and our three daughters, Lynn, Lisa, and Diane, postponed many activities and left me alone because of "the book." I could not have completed this effort without their understanding. My colleagues here at Virginia Tech, especially those on the staff of Virginia VIEW, assisted in many ways—by providing thoughtful comments or passing along an article or a clipping about a new book or study or newly reported enterprising work setting. They provided valuable feedback when my ideas were in the formative stages begging for refinement.

To all the above, a sincere note of thanks and appreciation.

Blacksburg, Virginia   Carl McDaniels
March 1989

To my wife, Ann

The Author

Carl McDaniels is professor and program area leader of counselor education at Virginia Polytechnic Institute and State University (Virginia Tech) in Blacksburg, Virginia. Since 1979 he also has been project director for the Virginia Career Information Delivery System (Virginia VIEW). He received his B.A. degree (1951) in psychology and history from Bridgewater College (Virginia) and his M.Ed. (1957) and Ed.D. (1964) degrees in counseling from the University of Virginia at Charlottesville. He is a Licensed Professional Counselor (LPC) in Virginia, a Nationally Certified Counselor (NCC), and a Nationally Certified Career Counselor (NCCC). He has had the following professional experience: as a teacher and counselor in the public schools of Virginia; personnel man in the U.S. Navy; staff member of the American Association for Counseling and Development; and, for the past twenty-five years, a counselor educator at George Washington University and Virginia Tech. He has been a visiting professor and lecturer at more than a dozen other colleges and universities.

McDaniels's main research interests are in career information systems and their use in a wide variety of settings for people of all ages. In addition, he has written extensively on the interrelationship of work and leisure in career development over the life span. He is on the editorial board of the *Journal of Career Development* and has served as guest editor of special issues entitled "Leisure and Career Development Through the Life Span" and "A Decade of Career Information Delivery

Systems: 1977 to 1987.'' He has published articles in professional journals such as the *Occupational Outlook Quarterly, Vocational Guidance Quarterly, Personnel and Guidance Journal,* and *Counselor Education and Supervision.* He is the author of *Developing a Professional Vita and Resume* (1978), *Finding Your First Job* (1981), *Unlocking Your Child's Potential* (1982, with D. Hummel), and *Leisure: Integrating a Neglected Component in Life Planning* (1983) and the editor of *Vocational Aspects of Counselor Education* (1965).

In 1988 McDaniels was recognized by the National Career Development Association with its highest honor, the Eminent Career Award. He was president of the National Career Development Association in 1973–74 and also served as president of the following organizations: the National Capitol Personnel and Guidance Association, the North Atlantic Association of Counselor Educators and Supervisors, and the Virginia Vocational Guidance Association. In addition, McDaniels has served as a consultant to a wide variety of organizations, associations, government agencies, local school systems, and community colleges, primarily in the mid-Atlantic and southern states.

The Changing
Workplace

PART ONE

What to Expect
in Tomorrow's Workplace

Counselors and others in the helping professions have a deep and abiding interest in the future, as well as a crucial need to know what the world will be like five or ten or twenty years from now. Part One therefore first examines, in general terms, how forecasts about the future are made and then turns the spotlight on what we might expect in the work settings of the future. This part is a general introduction to the topic of the changing world of work and how counselors can best understand these changes and interpret them to their clients.

The chapters in this section of the book examine some of the broad, general factors having to do with tomorrow's workplace. Chapter One looks at the research methods used by leading forecasters such as John Naisbitt, George Gallup, and Willis Harman and then goes on to review some studies of the accuracy of forecasts made by the Bureau of Labor Statistics over the past several decades. It points out that even the best methods can produce flawed results under certain conditions, such as the outbreak of large-scale hostilities, significant changes in worldwide economic patterns, major alterations in health conditions (for example, the proliferation of AIDS), or related shifts in food or water supplies. Examples of predictions in the areas of health care and manufacturing and among different states and regions highlight the uncertainties that render accurate

1

predictions difficult. Finally, as an example of "a forecast gone bad," the chapter focuses on the prediction that college enroll- ments would drop in the 1980s. (Instead, at most institutions, enrollments increased.) Some lessons learned from that inac- curate prediction are analyzed.

Chapter Two discusses the specific changes expected in the work force and work settings over the next decade. Five major work-force changes predicted in a government-sponsored study, *Workforce 2000* (Johnson, 1987), are highlighted, along with Bureau of Labor Statistics projections for occupations and industries in the year 2000. Also examined are the attitudes and ethics of the workers themselves, as revealed in the writings of Bernard Lefkowitz, Daniel Yankelovich, Perry Pascarella, and others. As examples of the changing workplace, the chapter ex- amines work sharing and job sharing, flexible schedules, and the emphasis on worker training.

Chapters One and Two (as well as the other chapters in this book) conclude with (1) a section on what counselors can do to deal with the conditions presented and stay up to date in their own work and (2) an annotated listing of five or six major references that can be pursued for more detailed analysis of the major points covered in the chapters.

1

Forecasting
the Future of Work:
A Cloudy Crystal Ball

Do you want to read about the future? There is certainly no shortage of forecasts about the future of work, leisure, education, the family, and virtually every other aspect of life. The magazine shelf in any newsstand will give you all the predictions you need for the year 2000 and beyond. The same is true of local bookstores, which often have a separate section just for "Books on the Future."

Probably the two best-known current writers about the future are Alvin Toffler and John Naisbitt. Their books, *Future Shock, The Third Wave, Megatrends,* and *Re-Inventing the Corporation,* have sold in the millions. In the professional literature for counselors, the biennial publication of the *Occupational Outlook Handbook (OOH)* has entrenched itself as one of the best-selling books put out by the Government Printing Office. In most editions a lead chapter, called "Tomorrow's Jobs," provides an every-two-year update on where the future labor market is headed. The *OOH* makes use of numerous charts and graphs for clarity and ease of understanding. The September 1987 *Monthly Labor Review* has a series of articles on the Bureau of Labor Statistics' preview of the economy for the year 2000. The World Future Society's periodical, *The Futurist,* and its monographs and books focus on all aspects of the future. So there are plenty of popular and professional books and magazines out there to satisfy even the most intense curiosity.

But what does all this talk about the future, and specifically the year 2000, have to do with counselors and others in the helping professions? First of all, our students and others with whom we work have a natural curiosity about the future. After all, that is the world they are going to be living in. Second, we as professionals instill a sense of confidence if we are alert and concerned about the future—not dwelling on the past or nonchalant about the present. When we focus on the future, we demonstrate a sense of direction for ourselves and those with whom we work. Third, by showing a genuine concern for our collective future here on spaceship earth, we reflect a seriousness of purpose. For all these reasons, counselors and other helping professionals should want to learn as much as they can about what the prospects are for the future for which we are helping people get ready. This chapter attempts to provide a perspective on forecasting, so that counselors can determine whom and what to believe.

Of course, there has never been a lack of fortune tellers, palm readers, astrologers, and self-proclaimed seers. But today the methods of forecasting are much more sophisticated. Computers, Delphi techniques, and holistic models are brought into play. People using such techniques are respectfully referred to as futurists, futurologists, and forecasters. They are expected (often for a large fee) to predict general or specific conditions for the next month, the next year, the next ten years, or the next century. The trick for us as counselors is knowing whom and what to believe.

The present chapter attempts to provide a sense of perspective on that problem. It first examines some of the general forecasting methodologies, making suggestions for more detailed investigation and giving four examples of specific methods used. Second, it discusses factors that can cloud anyone's crystal ball and gives three illustrations of potential uncertainties. Third, it describes what counselors and others can do to deal with uncertainties about the future, given their need to know more about tomorrow's workplace.

Forecasting Methodologies

This section attempts to provide a framework for the methodologies used in forecasting the future. While the brief discussion that follows cannot do justice to the larger efforts in this highly complex field, it does suggest additional readings on various futures research methodologies, and then gives four examples of how individuals and groups or organizations can set about making forecasts and projections.

For the reader who wants to know more about the entire matter of "future" research than we can cover here, there are ample suggestions in each issue of *The Futurist Bookstore,* a catalogue of new and older books available from the World Future Society. A brief list of significant titles might include: *Long-Range Forecasting* (Armstrong, 1985), *The Study of the Future* (Cornish, 1977), *Looking Forward* (Helmer, 1983), *Creating Alternative Futures* (Henderson, 1980), *The Futurists* (Toffler, 1972), and *Futuristics* (Wehmeyer, 1986).

John Naisbitt, whose book *Megatrends* (1982) has sold over 6 million copies, uses only newspapers in spotting trends, not magazines, books, journals, or radio and television. He argues in an interview in *The Futurist* (1985) that there are more newspapers in the United States in the 1980s than there were in the 1960s. Certainly, his point is supported by the rapid rise of *USA Today* to the top of the newspaper circulation list—it had achieved a daily circulation of 5.5 million by its fifth birthday in September 1987. Naisbitt contends that newspapers are the first draft of history, collecting information quickly and getting it out to readers just as quickly. Calling himself a forecaster, not a futurist, Naisbitt attempts to determine what is going on now, in the present, and from that systematic analysis to project trends (mega and otherwise) into the future. After seventeen years of conducting this type of trend analysis, he brought it all together in *Megatrends.* He writes about what he thinks is going on without insisting that his analysis is necessarily true. What he really wants to do is encourage a sharing of views on the future.

To produce the book *Forecast 2000* (1984), George Gallup, Jr., relied on a four-part research approach. First, through extensive use of the Gallup poll data, he determined the general public's opinion of various events. Researchers at the Gallup organization think that the public sees and senses things before organizations and governments do and often are far ahead of political and legislative leaders. Second, he used present trends to predict future actions (Naisbitt seems to use this same methodology). These key major trend indicators provide a basis for predicting what may happen in the future. Third, he conducted wide-scale surveys of the opinions and attitudes of young people. Gallup argues that the youth of today will carry these opinions and attitudes into their adult years, and that it is therefore important to listen to tomorrow's leaders, not just today's, when forming the basis for future forecasts. Fourth, Gallup secured the opinions of experts through the Delphi technique; that is, he conducted three surveys of the same experts (1,346 leaders in government, science, business, education, the arts, and other professional fields) to determine their priorities on certain issues. Gallup put these four methods together in coming up with a list of "Future Forces" that are carrying current conditions into the year 2000. This four-part method clearly takes more items into account than does a method that watches trends alone, and it thus represents a holistic approach to futures research methods.

A third example of forecasting is reflected in Willis W. Harman's book *An Incomplete Guide to the Future* (1979). Harman devotes a chapter to various methods of futures research. After looking at the pros and cons of these methods, he concludes that it comes down to *which futures* are feasible and which are not. He thinks that the responsible forecaster must take six principles into account:

1. *Continuity.* Above all else, societies exhibit continuity. Even in times of significant disruptions, such as wars, revolts, and economic and natural disasters, the larger elements of social roles and institutional structures tend to remain intact. Because of these slowly changing mega conditions, the future will be forecast to resemble the present, and current conditions will be altered in an evolutionary, not revolutionary, way.

2. *Self-Consistency.* Futures research obviously requires internal self-consistency, which means that there should be harmony in forecasts of future events. An illustration of failure to be consistent would be forecasting higher unemployment when smaller and smaller numbers of young people are coming into the labor market, as will be the case in the 1990s. This principle demands that future forecasts "make sense" when balanced against a variety of internal and external conditions.

3. *Similarities Among Social Systems.* This principle implies that, because individuals and social systems are more alike than unlike, they will behave in reasonably predictable fashion in similar circumstances. The disciplines of history, sociology, and anthropology use this type of approach for futures forecasting.

4. *Cause-Effect Relationships.* This principle implies that there must be an understanding of larger economic, social, political, and technological conditions as causal changes that will have an ulitmate effect on other conditions. For example, if labor is to be in short supply (*cause*), the yield (*effect*) probably will be a rise in wages to attract more and better workers to enter the labor force.

5. *Holistic Tending.* This principle requires that we look at the largest units possible—whole systems of ideas. How do more—rather than less—people think about a topic. The Gallup poll, for example, uses systematic sampling to get at collective opinions. This principle attempts to avoid the difficulties produced by individual bias.

6. *Goal-Seeking Societies.* Individuals, cities, states, and nations all have goals. These goals may not be stated explicitly, but they are almost always there and must be understood and taken into account by those conducting futures research. For example, if the United States has a goal of producing the lowest unemployment rate possible, then that will infer a certain type of future for education and adult training (and retraining).

Harman warns, however, that no matter how closely futures research conforms to these six principles, there is still more art than science to the process. Moreover, certain conditions tend to work against the best of forecasts—for instance, an incomplete knowledge of present and historical conditions, as well as the unpredictable nature of random events and of human choice and behavior.

Approaches Used by the Bureau of Labor Statistics

The U.S. Department of Labor's Bureau of Labor Statistics (BLS) has been projecting occupational employment trends for about forty years. The bureau emphasizes that its figures are *projections, not predictions;* that is, they are based on the assumption that *past trends will continue.* (For many readers the differences among the terms *forecasts, predictions, future estimates,* and *projections* are hard to discern.) The BLS has in the past used its own tracking system (through regional offices) and data collected by the Bureau of the Census every ten years for making these projections. In recent years it has instituted a new survey, called the Occupational Employment Statistics (OES), which is taken every three years and has more specific definitions for all the occupations. The BLS has also started to use three alternative versions of occupational projections (high, medium, and low growth), each based on a different set of economic assumptions. Previously, only a single projection figure was used; as a result, users tended to attribute too much precision to the accuracy of the figures.

Periodically, the BLS goes back and reviews its own projections. A review of its 1980 employment projections, which had been made in the early 1970s (see Bureau of Labor Statistics, 1982a), turned out to be quite favorable. They were generally about on target. A comparison of projected employment change and actual change between 1970 and 1980 showed that the BLS had correctly projected the *direction of change* in employment in each major occupational group except nonfarm laborers and operatives. The projections also correctly established that professional and technical workers, service workers, and clerical workers would be the three fastest-growing occupational groups.

Generally, differences between projected and actual employment levels were quite small for each of the groups for which the direction of change was projected correctly. An exception was managers and administrators. Employment levels for this group grew twice as rapidly as projected, resulting in a 1.4 million underestimate of employment in 1980, which turned out to be 10.9 million. Analysts were misled by the slow increase of the group during the early 1960s. Analysts also thought that the number of nonfarm laborers would decline slightly between 1970 and 1980 and that the number of operatives (comprising occupations such as machine tenders and assemblers) would grow. They were wrong on both counts. Laborers increased by almost 20 percent. As was the case for managers and administrators, projections for this group were too strongly influenced by trends in the employment of laborers during the 1960s, when growth was at a standstill.

The 1.6 million overestimate of operatives was the largest numerical error for a major occupational group. Still, the rationale behind the projections was sound. Operatives are concentrated in manufacturing industries, which are sensitive to economic fluctuations. After the economy recovered from the recession of the mid 1970s, employment of operatives grew steadily and might have reached the projected level if the economy had continued to improve. Employment was up to 14.5 million in 1979 but dropped back to 13.8 million in 1980, as the economy felt the effects of the 1979 oil-price shock.

An analysis of projection data on the sixty-four occupations revealed the following patterns:

1. The larger the occupation, the more accurate the projection was likely to be. Less than one-sixth of the occupations with more than 50,000 workers in 1970 had projections that were in the wrong direction, while more than one-third of the smaller fields had that mistake. Sampling errors diminish relatively as employment size increases, so the historical data for large occupations would be expected to provide more reliable trends to use in developing the projections.

2. Target-year employment usually was underestimated in the fastest-growing occupations and overestimated in those with the slowest growth. Occupations with the most rapid growth generally had the largest projection errors.

3. Many of the larger errors in the size of the projected employment change in an occupation resulted from poor esti-

mates of industry-occupational staffing patterns. The decline in the ratio of telephone operators to total employment in the telephone industry, for example, was greater than anticipated; consequently, the demand for workers in this occupation was overprojected. Staffing-pattern estimates also led to large errors in the projections for locomotive engineers' helpers, psychologists, credit managers, lawyers, and roofers.

4. Poor estimates of industry employment totals, rather than staffing patterns, however, were the primary causes of large errors for some occupations. If an industry is growing faster than anticipated, employment projections for occupations in the industry probably will be too low. The banking industry, for example, grew much more rapidly than expected, resulting in an underprojection of the demand for bank tellers. Projection errors for cooks, bartenders, and aircraft mechanics also were largely a result of poor projections for the industries in which those workers were concentrated.

So even the group that spends more time, money, and effort than any other person or organization falls short on its ten-year projections. The Bureau of Labor Statistics evaluates its work closely and often and is constantly trying to improve. Nonetheless, it does not make perfect projections every time. In short, the crystal ball is cloudy even under the best of circumstances.

What Can Cloud the Crystal Ball?

What can happen to throw forecasts off? The answer is "A great many things!" As a result, some writers in this field believe that predictions for more than five to ten years ahead are simply too risky. Just think back to 1971. Would anyone have predicted that by 1983 oil would be $30 per barrel and that the Japanese would lead the world in the production of automobiles, steel, and computer memory chips? Not many, and fewer yet would have believed these predictions and acted accordingly. Sometimes even two- to five-year predictions can go wrong. The forecasts that the double-digit inflation of the late 1970s would continue into the 1980s were not borne out;

oil became more plentiful, energy prices went down, the economy steadied, and inflation was lowered. In the labor market area, few could foresee the rapid influx of women into the workplace in the 1970s and 1980s. The usually cautious and reliable Bureau of Labor Statistics underrepresented the number of women expected to enter the labor force by some 6 million for the 1980s. The rapid rise of women in the labor force has been called the most significant change in the makeup of the workplace in the twentieth century. But in the 1940s and 1950s few saw it coming. The years between now and the year 2000 contain similar hidden pitfalls. What can we say about the growth of the United States and global economy and productivity, family formation, fertility, level of support for education and training, the labor-management balance, and many other factors?

So any forecast farther out than five to ten years is bound to be very speculative. Nevertheless, there is no lack of people and groups willing to take the risks of such speculation. What is more, there is a large audience anxious to buy the speculators' books, attend their seminars, and hire them as consultants to forecast the future.

In certain areas specifically related to the topic of this book, forecasting at present is especially hazardous. The following three examples highlight the uncertainties that we must take into account when we look at tomorrow's workplace. To illustrate these points even further, a familiar case of forecasting college enrollments for the 1980s will close this section. Although this illustration is not directly related to work and work settings, it does have a major bearing on the educational level of the labor force and clearly shows how a forecast that became conventional wisdom in the 1970s has proved to be wrong for some very good reasons.

Health Care Forecasts. Kabl and Clark (1985) point out some of the problems in making predictions about employment in the area of health care. For example, while there appears to be a clear shortage of registered nurses and no relief to that shortfall in sight, oversupplies of physicians are predicted. It is quite unusual to find a shortage *and* surplus situation in the same field.

Moreover, forecasters in this field must also ask themselves whether the rapid growth in health care technology over the last few decades will finally begin to slow down. Some signs that this is happening are already evident. For example, there are new and different kinds of patient care, many hospitals have made changes in their organizational structures, and increased attention is being given to the medical problems of an aging population. In short, there are some conflicting signals regarding employment in the health care field.

Therefore, predicting specific changes and their impact on health-care occupations is next to impossible. Nonetheless, if cost control remains a central focus of health care policy, the consequences for hospital workers in particular can be broadly identified:

- Slower job growth (because of the shift of much diagnostic and nonemergency care to outpatient facilities)
- Loss of some jobs (because of hospital closures, consolidations, mergers, and shared-service arrangements)
- Reduction in the number of hospital workers in administrative, clerical, food service, and housekeeping jobs (because of corporate restructuring and management efficiencies such as contracting out and more centralized record keeping, purchasing, marketing, and planning)
- Reduced hours and restraints on wages (through practices such as voluntary time off without pay)
- Shifts in staffing patterns, such as eliminating positions for licensed practical nurses or nursing aides
- Increases in the use of temporary workers

Forecasts About Manufacturing. There is little doubt that the long-term trend of increasing employment in the service sector and decreasing employment in manufacturing will continue. But where and when will the decline in production work bottom out? There are plenty of guesses but few certainties. According to the conventional wisdom, the decline will continue until only 5 to 10 percent of the work force is employed in manufacturing jobs. The Bureau of Labor Statistics sees a stabilization at around

10 percent of the work force, with output share of the nation's factories holding steady—signaling a continuing increase in productivity. Another view is that—because of the decline of the dollar in world markets; the return of some industries to plants in the United States; and the increasing profitability of previously declining industries, such as steel—there could well be a leveling off of the decline and even a modest upswing. This view is especially held by those who believe that small manufacturing companies will emerge as a new driving force in the rejuvenation of the manufacturing section of tomorrow's workplace (see, for example, Birch, 1987).

A promising prospect for manufacturing is the growth of "mini steel mills" such as the Nucor Corporation in Charlotte, North Carolina. Using nonunion labor and modern equipment, mini mills make products from steel scrap and often undersell major companies and importers as well. Nucor is now planning to expand, with two new mills to turn out larger construction products and make steel sheets for autos and appliances. The same story can be told about the growth of small manufacturing operations in textiles and printing. (Part Three of this book highlights the possible impact of the growth of small business in both production and service industries.)

Among the unknown factors that would affect predictions about manufacturing are the following: How strong is the will of government, labor, and management to stabilize the large existing industries at or near the current level? What will be the impact of smaller mills and factories on any stabilization or increase in employment? What will be the impact of larger "megaforces" such as the world economy, trade, the value of the dollar, the international balance of payments, and federal deficits? The trends are clear, but the cloudy crystal ball does not say where the trends will lead.

Regional and State Versus National Forecasts. Reports that give only a general national figure fail to tell the whole story of what is happening in the workplace. A mid 1987 economic report by *USA Today* shows unemployment at a 3.7 percent low in the New England states (New Hampshire has been below 3 percent since September 1985) to a high of 9.4 percent in the West South Central states of Arkansas, Oklahoma, Texas, and Louisiana. The East South Central states of Alabama, Kentucky, Tennessee, and Mississippi were not far behind, with a regional unemployment rate of 9.1 percent.

Even within New England, where the regional unemployment rate is the nation's lowest, there are variations. Maine, for example, has lost almost 8,000 of 20,000 jobs in the shoe industry since 1984, and double-digit unemployment figures are common in northern counties, far from the southern New England centers of prosperity. In the East South Central area, Nashville, Tennessee, and Huntsville, Alabama, have unemployment rates below the average for the area. Half of the region's population, however, lives in rural areas; and there the unemployment rate often runs far *ahead* of the 9.1 percent average. So even regional figures do not tell the entire story. Averages are just that: they may include pockets of extremely low unemployment but also areas where large numbers of people are out of work because of problems in the agricultural, energy, or manufacturing sectors.

These vast regional, state, and intrastate differences mean that the crystal ball may give bright and rosy forecasts for most, but not all, of New England but very dim and dismal ones for wide reaches of the West South Central and East South Central parts of the United States. Forecasting the future of tomorrow's workplace will surely be greatly complicated by the existence of these wide differences.

Forecasts of College Enrollments. National and state number crunchers have been forecasting a decline in higher education enrollments since the 1970s, when the last of the baby boomers reached college age. High school graduates, they predicted, would drop by 500,000 from 1977 to 1986. That estimate did hold roughly true. However, as Edmondson (1987) and Harrington (1987) have shown, the predicted low-enrollment crisis for colleges and universities never materialized. The figures are enough to induce caution in any future forecaster:

- Between 1980 and 1986, the number of young people aged 18 to 24 dropped by 2.7 million (9.2 percent), but the institutions of higher learning *actually* increased their enrollments by 300,000 (2.5 percent).
- Between 1985 and 1986, the number of high school graduates declined by 68,000, but the number of college freshmen increased by 150,000.

As a result of these figures, only a bit of the gloom and doom came to pass. Fewer than 10 percent of the 3,389 accredited colleges and universities have closed their doors in the last decade. Only four closed in 1984–85. Many seem to have closed because of regional, religious, or ethnic changes rather than national demographics—which set off the underenrollment panic in the first place. The analyses by Edmondson and Harrington suggest three general reasons for the almost total failure of the predictions.

1. Increased recruitment by colleges and universities certainly played a big part in the projection mismatch. Edmondson uses Oberlin College in Ohio as an illustration. Oberlin's new president created a fresh spirit of optimism and enthusiasm about local college enrollments. The college's staff conducted an extensive marketing study of their students, faculty, and alumni and decided to seek the best and brightest students from a national rather than a regional base. They used direct-mail materials, secured volunteer alumni as recruiters, moved their efforts from a regional to a national base, and attempted to ''sell'' Oberlin's merits in a very assertive fashion. As a result, applications have jumped 72 percent since 1982, and the number of National Merit Scholars in the 1986 freshman class was larger than the number in the entire student body in 1983. Alumni giving has doubled, and a $31 million capital improvement program is under way. So much for gloom and doom at Oberlin.

2. Growth in the number of female and older students was not anticipated. Female enrollment in higher education rose from 39 percent of total enrollments in 1965 to 51 percent in 1985. Women now constitute a majority of college students. The

college enrollment forecasters apparently failed to notice this trend, which had been building for the past several decades, just as the labor force predictors underestimated the number of women entering and staying in the work force over the same period. A further complication was the growth in nontraditional students—those over 25—which also seemed to catch the experts by surprise. While those making the forecasts were counting the decline in high school graduates, the enrollment of older college students was growing steadily, from about 15 percent of total enrollments in 1965 to nearly 30 percent in 1985. No one seemed to be including this group in the projections.

   3. The improved job market for college graduates was not expected. That is the main reason for the continued increase in college enrollments, according to Harrington (1987). In the late 1960s and 1970s, he points out, the competition among baby boomers in the labor market augured an unpromising outlook for college graduates. However, the improving prospects for high-paying jobs for college graduates, especially in engineering, business, and computer science, dramatically changed this outlook and made high school graduates more interested in attending college.

   The predictions of gloom and doom in college enrollments apparently were based mainly on one dimension—*demographics* of high school graduates. Certainly, no one took into account the *will* of colleges and universities to go out and seek students from new and productive sources. Whatever the reason for this erroneous prediction, it serves as a classic example that estimates by ''experts'' can go wrong for several very logical reasons that they never seemed to consider.

What Should Counselors Do?

   Most of us cannot be experts on the future of work, education, energy, or anything else. We can, however, be well-prepared consumers of what is being said and written by others. As the brief analysis set forth in this chapter shows, there are no perfect projections—no sure things in future forecasting; there are only best estimates, based on the most comprehensive methods and the most complete information. All forecasts are educated guesses by some individual or group—some good, some not so good, and some bad. Surely we need to take a look at them and not close our minds to what is being predicted. The following suggestions will help counselors as they attempt to appraise other people's vision of tomorrow's workplace.

Be Skeptical. So-called authorities who write articles or books, or come into your area for a seminar or speech, do not necessarily have a corner on truth. They may be full of hot air and have very little research or analysis to back up what they are saying. Be sure to examine their evidence before accepting their views of the future.

Seek Multiple Sources. Read as widely as you can on the subject of this book. Review the biennial projections in the Bureau of Labor Statistics' *Occupational Outlook Handbook* and subscribe to the *Occupational Outlook Quarterly* for periodic updates. Compare all other forecasts to those of the BLS. It has no built-in bias and no "axe to grind" and has been in the business longer than anyone else. Read other sources as well. The six references at the end of this chapter might be a place to start. Finally, read beyond the headlines. Often the newspaper writers look for the most eye-catching aspect of a story, not the essential facts. Get the entire story. Request full reports when reading summaries that do not seem to fit with your experience or best judgment.

Confirm Credentials. Check out the people or organizations that are making the forecasts. Who are they? What are their credentials? How accurate and up to date are their references, if there are any references? What are the sources of funding they use? What are their professional credentials to write on the subject? How long have they been studying the subject? Keep in mind the old-fashioned warning "consider the source."

Keep an Open Mind. Consider all the legitimate sources on the subject of future forecasts. Do not let your own preconceived ideas stand in the way of looking at all reasonable materials.

Look for Regional and State Reports. Most of what is reported in the press and on television is national in scope. That is well and good, but there are increasing regional and state differences. By all reports, the job outlook in the Great Lakes region is different from the outlook for New England. States within a region also can vary widely. West Virginia's economic condition is far different, for example, from Virginia's. National reports may be off for both states. Each state's career information delivery system (CIDS) and public employment service and some type of regional body, such as the Appalachian Regional Commission, should be the best sources of information for your area.

Seek Local Sources. Some think that local sources of future forecasts are really the best ones. After all, everybody works in a local job! Find out from the local public employment service what it expects over the next five to ten years. Ask the same question of the local chamber of commerce, union leaders, or educational and civic leaders.

Suggested Readings

Casale, A. M. *USA Today: Tracking Tomorrow's Trends.* Kansas City: Andrews, McMeel & Parker, 1986.

Written by the director of news research of *USA Today,* this book draws from more than one hundred public opinion polls conducted by *USA Today* since 1982, when the paper started. It covers a wide spectrum of topics, such as "Working in the 80's" and "USA at Play," as well as general issues. It also takes a broad look at the future. If you like *USA Today,* you will probably like this book and its style and format.

Gallup, G., Jr. *Forecast 2000.* New York: Morrow, 1984.

A first-rate book written by the head of one of the top opinion research firms in the country. Gallup has some interesting observations on what he calls the nine "future forces" that control our future: (1) wars, terrorism, and the nuclear threat; (2) overpopulation; (3) economic pressures; (4) the double-edged sword of technological progress; (5) the environmental emergency; (6) the curse of crime and violence; (7) the faltering family; (8) the high hope for good health; and (9) a prognosis for American politics. Gallup also suggests what people can do to increase their understanding of these forces.

Gillespie, G. A. (ed.). *Leisure 2000: Scenarios for the Future.* Columbia: Department of Recreation and Park Administration, University of Missouri, 1983.

An excellent collection of writings by outstanding leisure professionals and leisure educators concerning what they anticipate for recreation and leisure in the year 2000. They discuss the possible world economic, environmental, sociological, and technological changes that society will deal with by the year 2000 and explain how these conditions may affect recreation and leisure services in the future.

Harman, W. W. *An Incomplete Guide to the Future.* New York: Norton, 1979.

In this book a broad-based professional who understands both social and technological systems describes several possible future routes for the United States and the rest of the world. Primarily, Harman believes that the industrialized world is undergoing a metamorphosis to what he calls a "transindustrial society" and that the essential characteristics of that society can already be identified. Since we know that this change is under way, he alleges, we have an opportunity to reduce the social disruption that usually accompanies such dramatic changes. His newest book, *Global Mind Change* (1988), updates his earlier ideas.

Johnson, W. B. *Workforce 2000.* Indianapolis: Hudson Institute, 1987.

Research that led to this book was conducted under the auspices of the highly respected Hudson Institute, and was funded by the U.S. Department of Labor. The book describes the general forces shaping the American economy of today and in the future.

Kiplinger Washington Letter. *The New American Boom*. Washington, D.C.: Kiplinger, 1986.

This book, by the staff of the Kiplinger Washington Letter, predicts that America is on the threshold of a new kind of economic boom. This one will lead to sustained prosperity through rising productivity, brought on by extraordinary advances in computers, robotics, biotechnology, communications, and new materials. Especially good sections on the future of work and leisure in the United States.

2

How Workers
and the Workplace
Are Changing

What changes are most likely to take place in the work force and in the workplace over the next decade or so? This chapter focuses on the new projections toward the year 2000 in both of these areas. Although we noted in Chapter One that forecasts longer than ten years can be risky, the Bureau of Labor Statistics (1987) has made extensive occupational and industrial projections to the year 2000. In addition, some interesting demographic factors have been generalized by Johnson (1987) into five broad categories concerning the possible makeup of the future work force.

Over the next ten to twenty years, certain age groups in the population will increase in numbers, and other age groups will decline. Much is known about the pure numbers, but little is known about how the individuals in *all* the age groups will respond to these expected changes. Nor is much known about how political institutions in general and the workplace in particular will respond to the changes in the work force.

This chapter will also discuss some of the changing conditions in the workplace—not the technological aspects of various systems but the "humanizing of the workplace," as some have called it. This new workplace will encourage employee involvement and be responsive to the problems and concerns of workers.

It will be a flexible workplace with new forms of work schedules and locations as options, at least for a sizable number of employees. In addition, the workplace of the future will most certainly include more training and retraining programs than it has in the past. The framework for this change is already in place with what the American Society for Training and Development (1986) estimated at $120 billion spent for training and development in 1985.

Coming Changes in the Work Force

Five major changes in the makeup of the work force seem destined to become realities, according to the best demographic analysis available from U.S. government sources and to the study sponsored by the Department of Labor that resulted in *Workforce 2000* (Johnson, 1987). At the same time, however, we cannot predict how individuals or institutions will react to these five factors or what other political, economic, or social changes may take place to balance them off, and so a large element of uncertainty persists. Some discussion of these reactions appears briefly in the next section of the chapter, and it is followed by a summary of the projections to the year 2000 recently released by the Bureau of Labor Statistics.

A consensus on these final changes is possible because most of the people in the USA who are going to be working in the United States in the year 2000 have already been born. Those who began first grade in the fall of 1988 will be in the high school graduating class in the spring of the year 2000. We already know the approximate number of students in that first grade, as well as the approximate number in the class of 2000. What we are not sure of is how the world of work will change technologically or politically in response to the changing demographics described here. Consider the following possibilities:

1.   The minimum wage will be raised.
2.   The age at which children can work will be lowered to younger than 16 years.
3.   The cap of earnings for Social Security recipients will be removed.

4. Child-care facilities in the workplace and in the community will be expanded.
5. There will be major shifts toward labor-saving systems in the workplace—systems that do not seem economically feasible at the present time.

The other big unknown is how entry-level workers and some members of the current work force will respond to the changes expected in tomorrow's workplace. The increasing diversity in the adult population has been described by Yankelovich (1981) in *New Rules* and Lefkowitz (1979) in *Breaktime*. More recently, Pascarella (1984) has studied the changing attitudes of the people in the work force whom he calls "the new achievers." He feels that many of today's workers are more interested in personal fulfillment at work than in money and titles. According to Pascarella, people no longer believe that toil and self-denial eventually bring rewards or that accumulating material possessions gives life meaning. Instead, today's new achievers seek intangibles in the workplace, such as self-development, creativity, participation, freedom, and a sense of wholeness and commitment. Responses by managers and executives to some of the ideas and challenges set forth by Pascarella will have much to do with the attractiveness or unattractiveness of tomorrow's workplace.

William B. Johnson—project director for a study conducted by the Hudson Institute and funded by the U.S. Department of Labor—served as the principal author of *Workforce 2000*, the book that grew out of this study. The book includes many interesting tables and charts as well as a keen analysis of what is expected to happen between now and the year 2000. What follows is a summary of some of Johnson's (1987) ideas about expected changes in the makeup of the work force over the next decade or so.

1. *Growth in the population and in the work force will proceed more slowly than in the past half century.* Bureau of the Census figures clearly show that the population of the United States will grow more slowly over the balance of the century than has been the case since 1950. (For Bureau of the Census and Labor Statistics figures, see Figure 1.) It is not a question of population growth

Figure 1. Growth of Population and Labor Force, 1950–1990.

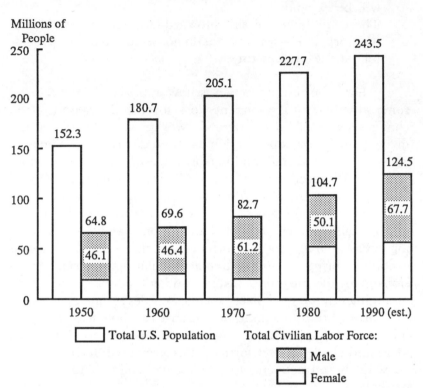

Source: Bureau of Labor Statistics, 1988b, pp. 74–75; Bureau of Labor Statistics, 1988c, pp. 91–92; and Bureau of Census, 1988, p. 7.

entirely, but of *rate of growth*. The estimated 1 percent population growth per year during the 1980s and three-fourths of 1 percent per year during the 1990s is below the average for the 1960s and 1970s. Similarly, the rate of growth in the labor force is slower in the 1980s than in the 1960s and 1970s. These two factors may contribute to a slower economic growth than in the past two decades, with a more limited population to draw from. Spot labor shortages may exist over the next decade or so.

2. *The population and the work force will both be older, while the pool of young workers will become smaller.* The baby boomers (those born between 1946 and 1965) will be getting older over

and the work force steadily upward. The number of people over 65 in the work force will decrease as the "depression-era" generation moves toward eventual full retirement. For employers who depend on young workers to fill high-turnover, entry-level jobs, the news is that this age group (16–24) will drop from 41 million in 1980 to 34 million in 2000 (Supple, 1986). These figures have led Supple to write about "The Coming Labor Shortage." Indeed, the impending shifts in the population and the labor force may well challenge employers to do some serious thinking about traditional approaches to hiring and keeping employees.

3. *Women will continue to enter the work force in significant numbers, but the rate of increase is expected to slow down.* Economist Eli Ginzberg (1979) calls the feminization of the work force the biggest change in the world of work in the twentieth century. From all indications, that participation will continue to increase at least through the year 2000; however, the pace of the change will slow considerably (see Table 1). One of the indications of the slowdown is directly related to the point just covered— namely, that fewer young people are entering the work force. Also, if women continue to retire relatively early, the aging of the baby-boom generation will mean a significant drop in the percent of women in the labor force after ages 45–54. Of course, employers may be able to arrange changes in the workplace (wages and working conditions—see a later section in this chapter) to make it attractive for these women to stay in the work force longer than anticipated.

Table 1. Women in the Work Force, 1950–2000.
(Numbers in thousands, except percentages.)

	1950	1960	1970	1980	1990	2000
Women in the work force	18,389	23,240	31,543	45,487	57,230	66,670
Female labor force participation rate	33.9%	37.7%	43.3%	51.5%	57.5%	61.1%
Female share of the work force	29.6%	33.4%	38.1%	42.5%	45.8%	47.5%

Source: Adapted from Johnson, W. B., 1987, p. 85.

4. *Minorities will be much more of a factor in the entry-level labor market until the year 2000.* Over the next decade or so, blacks, Hispanics, Pacific Asians, and other minorities will make up a larger and larger share of the new entrants into the labor market. As the following Bureau of Labor Statistics figures (1988c, pp. 18–26) show, minorities are growing as a percentage of the total population *and* the labor force.

	1970	1985	2000 (Estimate)
Percent minorities in the population	10.9	13.6	15.7
Percent minorities in the labor force	11.1	13.6	15.5

Said another way, it is estimated that 29 percent of the new entrants into the labor force will be minorities. Minorities are expected to make up 15 percent of the labor force in the United States with much higher percentages in certain regions and metropolitan areas.

5. *Immigrants will make up a growing share of the population and the labor force.* If present trends continue, immigrants will represent the largest share of increase in the population and the work force since early in the twentieth century. In the period between 1970 and 1980, immigrants accounted for about 4.5 million in the growth of the United States population. The figures for the 1980–1990 period will not be available for several years, but indications are that the number will be higher than the 4.5 million in the previous decade. In the West and the South, the number of non-native-born Americans grew by nearly 100 percent in the period 1970–1980. More than half of all immigrants are concentrated in California, Texas, and New York. The Los Angeles area alone accounts for one-fifth of all recent immigrants. Although forecasts of legal and illegal immigration are difficult to make, conditions in the late 1980s suggest no immediate end to the new wave of immigrants into the population and the labor force.

In summary, the changing work force is likely to contain a smaller percentage of young people and a larger percentage of older people, females, minorities, and immigrants.

Bureau of Labor Statistics:
Projections for the Year 2000

This section summarizes the Bureau of Labor Statistics' projections for the year 2000. Five articles presenting changes projected over the period in more detail were published in the September 1987 issue of the *Monthly Labor Review* (see "Suggested Readings" at the end of this chapter).

Employment. The United States economy is projected to add more than 21 million jobs during the 1986–2000 period. Of this increase, 20.1 million are projected to be nonagricultural wage and salary jobs, and 1.7 million will be nonagricultural self-employed or unpaid family jobs. These gains will be somewhat offset by a projected decline in agricultural employment. The projected employment increase—over 19 percent for the period and 1.3 percent a year—represents a slowing of employment growth, due in large part to the slowing of labor force growth. In absolute terms, nonagricultural wage and salary workers increased by nearly 26 million between 1972 and 1986—an expansion of nearly 35 percent, or 2.2 percent a year. Between 1979 and 1986, however, nonagricultural wage and salary jobs grew only 1.5 percent a year.

    Goods-producing industries will show almost no aggregate employment change over the 1986–2000 period. Service-producing industries will, therefore, account for nearly all the projected growth. Among the goods-producing industries, only construction is expected to increase, adding almost 900,000 jobs. Although agriculture will show growth in wage and salary jobs, that increase should be more than offset by a decline in self-employed workers. Manufacturing employment is projected to fall by over 800,000 jobs, although output in that sector is projected to grow 2.4 percent annually. But productivity (efficiency of output) in manufacturing is expected to grow even more rapidly.

    Within manufacturing, many industries are projected to experience employment growth—some quite rapid. The sector will provide over 18 million wage and salary jobs—employment for 15 percent of the wage and salaried work force. In general, the manufacturing industries expected to decline in employment are those that have experienced job loss for years, such as basic steel, leather goods, shoes, tobacco, some of the textile and basic metal-processing industries, and many of the food-processing industries. Projected employment gains in manufacturing are in printing and publishing, drugs and pharmaceutical products, computers, and instruments industries.

Large growth in jobs is projected for wholesale and retail trade. The expected expansion of over 6 million wage and salary jobs is in line with the long-term trend of these industries, which are growing at the same or a slightly faster pace than the economy. Finance, insurance, and real estate also are forecast to grow, adding over 1.6 million jobs during the projection period. Over 10 million jobs are projected to be added to service industries, with health and business services important contributors. Government is expected to expand by about 1.6 million jobs, with virtually all the increase at the state and local levels.

Occupations. The projected growth in employment can be viewed not only by industry but also by occupation. Five occupational groups are projected to exceed the average growth in employment: technicians and related support workers; service workers except in private households; sales workers; executive, administrative, and managerial workers; and professional workers (See Table 2 for details.) Only two occupational groups are projected to show absolute declines over the period: (1) farming, forestry, and fishing workers and (2) private household workers. In addition, below-average growth is projected for administrative support workers (including clerical workers) and for precision production, craft, and repair workers. Virtually no change is projected for operators, fabricators, and laborers.

A comparison of projected employment growth by major occupational group with those jobs currently held by blacks and Hispanics shows that neither group is well represented in the fast-growing occupations; both are overrepresented in slow-growing or declining occupations. A similar analysis for women yields comparable results, although the disparities are not nearly as great as for blacks and Hispanics.

Table 2. Employment by Broad Occupational Group, 1986–2000.
(Numbers in thousands.)

Major Occupational Group	1986	Projected, 2000	Percent Change, 1986–2000
Total employment	111,623	133,030	19.2
Technicians and related support workers	3,726	5,151	38.2
Service workers, except private household workers	16,555	21,962	32.7
Sales workers	12,606	16,334	29.6
Executive, administrative, and managerial workers	10,583	13,616	28.7
Professional workers	13,538	17,192	27.0
Precision production, craft, and repair workers	13,924	15,590	12.0
Administrative support workers, including clerical	19,851	22,109	11.4
Operators, fabricators, and laborers	16,300	16,724	2.6
Private household workers	981	955	– 2.7
Farming, forestry, and fishing workers	3,556	3,393	– 4.6

Note: Estimates of 1986 employment, the base year for the 2000 projections, were derived from data collected in the Occupational Employment Statistics surveys.

Source: Bureau of Labor Statistics, 1987, p. 4.

The projections also show a growth in the share of jobs requiring at least one year of college, a slight decline in the share of jobs requiring high school completion, and a sharp decline in the share of jobs requiring less than a high school education. In general, occupations in which current participants have the most education are projected to grow the most rapidly—although many jobs should continue to be available for those with only a high school education, despite their relatively slower growth (see Tables 3 and 4). However, those with less than a high school education face increasing difficulty in their job search and less opportunity for good pay and advancement. These labor market problems frequently stem from a lack of education or training needed to adapt to the employment effects of changes in technology and the structure of demand. The continuing large number of high school dropouts clearly signals that an important problem remains. Given that blacks and Hispanics are disproportionately represented among those with less education and are projected to account for an increasing share of workers,

Table 3. Fastest-Growing Occupations, 1986–2000.
(Numbers in thousands.)

Occupation	Employment		Change in Employment, 1986–2000		Percent of Total Job Growth, 1986–2000
	1986	Projected, 2000	Number	Percent	
Paralegal personnel	61	125	64	103.7	.3
Medical assistants	132	251	119	90.4	.6
Physical therapists	61	115	53	87.5	.2
Physical and corrective therapy assistants and aides	36	65	29	81.6	.1
Data processing equipment repairers	69	125	56	80.4	.3
Home health aides	138	249	111	80.1	.5
Podiatrists	13	23	10	77.2	0
Computer systems analysts, electronic data processing	331	582	251	75.6	1.2
Medical records technicians	40	70	30	75.0	.1
Employment interviewers, private or public employment service	75	129	54	71.2	.3
Computer programmers	479	813	335	69.9	1.6
Radiologic technologists and technicians	115	190	75	64.7	.3
Dental hygienists	87	141	54	62.6	.3
Dental assistants	155	244	88	57.0	.4
Physician assistants	26	41	15	56.7	.1
Operations and systems researchers	38	59	21	54.1	.1
Occupational therapists	29	45	15	52.2	.1
Peripheral electronic data processing equipment operators	46	70	24	50.8	.1
Data entry keyers, composing	29	43	15	50.8	.1
Optometrists	37	55	18	49.2	.1

Source: Bureau of Labor Statistics, 1987, p. 56.

the recent decline in college enrollment of blacks reported by the Department of Education is unfortunate.

Despite the faster than average growth in employment for occupations requiring a bachelor's or higher degree, the surplus of college graduates that began in the early 1970s is expected to continue through the end of the century. However, the gap between supply and demand for new college graduates is expected to narrow considerably as we move into the 1990s,

Table 4. Occupations with the Largest Job Growth, 1986–2000.
(Numbers in thousands.)

Occupation	Employment		Change in Employment, 1986–2000		Percent of Total Job Growth, 1986–2000
	1986	Projected, 2000	Number	Percent	
Salespersons, retail	3,579	4,780	1,201	33.5	5.6
Waiters and waitresses	1,702	2,454	752	44.2	3.5
Registered nurses	1,406	2,018	612	43.6	2.9
Janitors and cleaners, including maids and housekeeping cleaners	2,676	3,280	604	22.6	2.8
General managers and top executives	2,383	2,965	582	24.4	2.7
Cashiers	2,165	2,740	575	26.5	2.7
Truck drivers, light and heavy	2,211	2,736	525	23.8	2.5
General office clerks	2,361	2,824	462	19.6	2.2
Food counter, fountain, and related workers	1,500	1,949	449	29.9	2.1
Nursing aides, orderlies, and attendants	1,224	1,658	433	35.4	2.0
Secretaries	3,234	3,658	424	13.1	2.0
Guards	794	1,177	383	48.3	1.8
Accountants and auditors	945	1,322	376	39.8	1.8
Computer programmers	479	813	335	69.9	1.6
Food preparation workers	949	1,273	324	34.2	1.5
Teachers, kindergarten and elementary	1,527	1,826	299	19.6	1.4
Receptionists and information clerks	682	964	282	41.4	1.3
Computer systems analysts, electronic data processing	331	582	251	75.6	1.2
Cooks, restaurant	520	759	240	46.2	1.1
Licensed practical nurses	631	869	238	37.7	1.1
Gardeners and groundskeepers, except farm	767	1,005	238	31.1	1.1
Maintenance repairers, general utility	1,039	1,270	232	22.3	1.1
Stock clerks, sales floor	1,087	1,312	225	20.7	1.0
First-line supervisors and managers	956	1,161	205	21.4	1.0
Dining room and cafeteria attendants and barroom helpers	433	631	197	45.6	.9
Electrical and electronics engineers	401	592	192	47.8	.9
Lawyers	527	718	191	36.3	.9

Source: Bureau of Labor Statistics, 1987, p. 57.

in part because the population decline in numbers of college-age individuals will reduce the number of college graduates.

Occupations generally filled by young workers—such as food service, retail sales, and construction labor—are projected to continue to generate many jobs, and the declining numbers of young workers could improve the youth labor market situation. At the same time, given the expected sharp decline in the number of youth, employment opportunities may arise for others seldom employed in those jobs, such as the recently retired who want to work part time. This development also could increase the labor market participation of some groups, such as black males, who currently have much lower participation rates than white males of the same age.

Women, blacks, and Hispanics have traditionally been highly concentrated by occupation. Although this occupational segregation has lessened in the past decade, the future offers a chance for further improvement because of the rapid growth in many occupations not traditionally filled by Hispanics, blacks, and women.

The Changing Workplace

In giving a brief overview of the changing workplace, the following discussion will emphasize the overall *changing conditions of work,* not the *changing technology of work.* These changes are emerging because employers—in order to secure and retain the best people as a way of improving productivity and efficiency—are becoming attentive to the "quality of worklife" (QWL). Greenberg and Glaser (1980, p. 19) define QWL as "the opportunity for all employees at all levels in an organization to have substantial influence over their work environment by participating in decisions related to their work, thereby enhancing their self-esteem and satisfaction from their work."

Increasing productivity from the employers' point of view seems agreeable to employees as long as (1) the productivity increases are not achieved at the expense of the workers (that is, through layoffs, loss of overtime, stress, and pressure), (2) the rewards of increased productivity are shared with those individuals who helped bring about the improvement, and (3) the true goal of improved productivity is to make the organization more competitive in the external marketplace and thus to make it a better and more secure place in which to work.

In short, "quality of worklife" programs provide concrete and ever-present opportunities for individuals or task groups at any level in an organization to influence their working conditions. But this necessitates an open style of management in which ideas are shared and genuinely considered. This is not a top-down arrangement. Rather, it calls for a partnership between management and nonmanagement people that will allow them to work together in all kinds of cooperative arrangements, as well as for straightforward employee involvement in the process.

Another way of approaching the changing workplace is from the perspective of employees. Two well-known books— *New Rules* (Yankelovich, 1981) and *Beyond Boredom and Anxiety* (Csikszentmihalyi, 1975)—have reported workers' concerns, while Applegath in *Working Free* (1982) has pointed out some of the alternatives to the typical 9-to-5 job. Applegath, in fact, wants to empower readers to feel that there are choices to earning a living in a traditional fashion. He includes numerous descriptions of people who have broken loose from accepted work patterns and gained a sense of freedom in new ways to work— some of which will be detailed in the following paragraphs. Applegath believes that changes in the workplace will come about, at least in part, because of the changing priorities of the American people as they seek freedom and meaning in all aspects of their lives—including work, leisure, and family life.

Work Sharing and Job Sharing. Work sharing and job sharing are two of the visible changes in the workplace that symbolize some of the underlying openness to different options in the workplace. Both have potential benefits to employers and employees. In *Work Sharing* (1981) and *Flexible Life Scheduling* (1980), Best deals with many of the issues, policy options, and prospects currently under consideration in this field. He discusses two types of work sharing. The first type is usually restricted to specific firms, which use work sharing as a short-term strategy to prevent layoffs and dismissals by temporarily reducing worktime;

for instance, these firms may keep all employees on the payroll in slack times by cutting the workweek from forty to thirty hours. The second type is usually used to combat longer-term problems at work. Firms may, for instance, reduce worktime among employees across the board to create jobs for the unemployed, thus distributing work more evenly among the available work force. Best indicates that work sharing has been around in various forms for quite a few years. He sees it coming into play mainly as a tool for combating unemployment by sharing and distributing jobs. McCarthy and Rosenberg (1981), in their book *Work Sharing Case Studies,* cite many examples of work sharing in places such as Fieldcrest Mills, Ideal Industries, and Black & Decker.

Job sharing, in contrast, is viewed as a new pattern in the "quality of worklife" formula. Meier (1978) details all the options in her book *Job Sharing.* She defines the term as an arrangement whereby two (or more) employees hold a position together, as a team jointly responsible for the whole or separately responsible for each half. Four conditions usually prevail under the best of conditions: (1) The arrangement is voluntary for all concerned. (2) It involves the splitting of a normally full-time position. (3) Both workers must perform a 50 percent share of the work involved. (4) Provisions for fringe benefits are included. Meier provides interesting illustrations of where and how job sharing is succeeding in all types of work settings. Olmstead and Smith (1983) offer a practical guide to carrying out Meier's ideas through flexible work schedules.

The Administrative Management Society (AMS) conducted a survey in 1986 to see how job sharing had changed from an earlier 1981 study. In 1986, the AMS found, 16 percent of companies in the United States allow job sharing, and another 5 percent are considering it. In the 1981 study, only 11 percent had such arrangements. The AMS also found that 80 percent of the firms pay workers at a rate equal to the salary/wage level assigned to the full-time job equivalent. In general, larger companies were somewhat less likely to have job sharing than smaller companies were. Medium-sized companies (1,001–10,000 employees) had the highest level (21 percent allowing job sharing). Firms in the West (18 percent) and in the West

Central region (32 percent) were more likely to allow job sharing than firms in the South (5 percent). The employers surveyed attributed significant benefits to job sharing:

1. Availability of a talented pool of people who want something more than a conventional part-time job
2. A wider range of abilities and skills brought to a job when two people, instead of only one, work at it
3. Greater productivity, perhaps through a shorter workweek that would stimulate workers to produce more
4. Better retention of valued employees and reduced turnover
5. Greater flexibility in work scheduling, reduction in absenteeism, and continuity of job performance

In addition to work sharing and job sharing, several other, perhaps more familiar, types of less than full-time work still have substantial impact on the workplace: part-time work, with 13.5 million people working fewer than thirty-five hours per week; temporary work, with an estimated 700,000 people not permanently employed; and multiple jobs, with 5.7 million workers estimated as holders of a second job. Indeed, members of this last group represent a significant and growing portion of the total work force. For example, between 1970 and 1985, the number of multiple jobholders (better known as moonlighters) jumped by almost 2 million.

Flexible Schedules and Compressed Workweeks. These two relatively recent changes in the workplace show considerable promise as options for employers and employees. There are several kinds of so-called flexitime, including "flextour," "gliding time," "variable day," and "maxiflex," but the central idea is that an employee gets to select a starting and quitting time during the workday within limits set by the employer. Most flexitime plans require employees to be present during certain established hours—known as "coretime." Flexitime, which does not change the number of hours worked, can be used in full-time and part-time situations. The AMS survey found the following growth in flexitime among American companies:

	Percent of Companies
Survey Year	*Allowing Flexitime*
1977	15
1981	22
1986	28

Interestingly, 42 percent of the firms in the survey expected the use of flexitime to increase, and 90 percent of the firms using flexitime indicated that the program was developed internally by corporate employees, not by outsiders. The following advantages were reported by companies in the AMS (1986) study:

1. Improves employee attitude and morale
2. Accommodates working parents
3. Results in fewer traffic problems since workers can avoid congested streets and highways
4. Increases production
5. Decreases tardiness
6. Accommodates those who wish to arrive at work before interruptions begin
7. Facilitates employee scheduling of medical, dental, and other types of appointments
8. Decreases absenteeism
9. Accommodates the leisure-time activities of employees
10. Decreases turnover

Flexitime was reported in firms of all sizes, but was present in over half of the large companies (those with more than 10,000 employees).

Another type of flexible scheduling, the compressed workweek, comes in all shapes and varieties. Basically, the idea is to permit employees to work full time (that is, a forty-hour week) in a shorter-than-usual workweek. Simply put, this arrangement reallocates worktime over the week, although it does not change the total time worked. Some typical patterns include: four days (ten-hour days), three days (thirteen-hour days), and alternating five-day workweeks and four-day weekends (nine-hour days are worked). A great deal has been written about this option, but the AMS survey found that only about 5 percent of the firms permitted any of these compressed work schedules. These plans have obvious advantages, such as improved morale, avoidance of morning and evening rush hours, and substantial chunks of leisure time to be used as the worker sees fit.

Worker Training. All these changes in the workplace open up a number of promising opportunities for the time available through flexible worktime. Meier (1983) believes that the flexibility will lead to much greater worker participation in company-sponsored and company-supported (by tuition assistance) programs. The American Society for Training and Development (ASTD), in its report entitled *Serving the New Corporations* (1986), notes that training and development is already big business, with over $210 billion per year expended on formal and informal programs. Of that figure, an estimated $180 billion is spent on adult job-related training. More than 70 percent of all executive, professional, and technical workers take part in these training programs. According to a recent report by the Center for Education Statistics (1987), there were over 40 million adult education courses in 1984. Between 1969 and 1984, enrollment in these courses increased by 79 percent, and the number of courses more than doubled. Most people who took these adult education courses did so to get ahead on the job. Clearly, the changing American workplace is enabling employees to take advantage of job-related training programs and other forms of adult education.

What Should Counselors Do?

To keep abreast of the actual and projected changes in the work force and the workplace, counselors need to work together in developing an information search network. Such a network will help them discover and acquire relevant materials. Here are some ways to begin:

Read the Major U.S. Government Sources. The two leading agencies for reporting changes in the workplace and the work force are the Bureau of Labor Statistics (Department of Labor) and the Bureau of the Census (Department of Commerce). Both have a variety of publications that can assist counselors in staying up to date. The periodicals from the Bureau of Labor Statistics are especially helpful. The *Monthly Labor Review* publishes data when they are first reported. Eventually, the *Occupational Outlook Quarterly* publishes the data in summary form, and every two years the *Occupational Outlook Handbook* summarizes research findngs and projections for that period.

The Bureau of the Census publishes the yearly *Population Profile of the United States,* which summarizes the most significant information in an easy-to-read and understand format. The yearly *Statistical Abstract of the United States* is a national data book and guide to sources. Most of us cannot keep up with all of these publications on a regular basis, but we can work together to find reliable sources and share key information in our work settings.

Read Relevant Magazines. A growing number of national, regional, and local magazines contain a storehouse of useful information for counselors. For example, *American Demographics* is less than a decade old, but it represents the interesting, well-written, and graphically attractive magazine of the future. It carries regional and national notes as well as interesting articles that are almost certain to be of interest to counselors in the area of career information. The same is true for the spate of regional, state, and local magazines that carry quality articles about major employers and changes in work and working conditions in the area of coverage. Some of these magazines are a worthy professional investment.

Keep Up with New Books in the Field. Most professional association periodicals and newsletters carry reviews and ads for new books. Exhibitors at professional meetings have similar information available. In addition, commercial newsletters such as the *Career Opportunities News* (published by Garrett Park Press, Garrett Park, Maryland 20896) summarize new reports, studies, surveys, and books. The *Career Planning and Adult Development Network Newsletter* (San Jose, California) serves a similar function for a more specific adult counseling–oriented readership. There are many new and not well-known publishers around today as the field has proliferated nationwide. So do not be put off by the name of an unfamiliar publisher. Remember, who ever heard of Ten Speed Press before Richard Bolles's *What Color Is Your Parachute?*

Suggested Readings

Applegath, J. *Working Free.* New York: AMACOM, 1982.

A handbook of alternatives to the 9-to-5 job routine. A wide variety of alternatives are highlighted as well as illustrations of people who are "working free." This book, in the mold of Lefkowitz's (1979) *Breaktime* and Yankelovich's *New Rules,* provides encouragement for those who are not happy with the status quo working arrangements.

Best, F. *Flexible Life Scheduling.* New York: Praeger, 1980.

A comprehensive review of the flexible hours/place notion. Best points out that not everyone can or should pursue alternative life patterns but that a growing number of people would be better off with institutional options for more flexibility. He calls for supportive social policies to allow more flexibility in the workplace.

Bureau of Labor Statistics. Special issue of *Monthly Labor Review,* Sept. 1987.

This special issue contains the latest BLS projections for the economy, labor force, and occupational change to the year 2000. Almost every issue has at least a couple of good articles on the topic of this book. For instance, the November 1986 issue is devoted to the topic of time spent at work and has nine articles dealing with moonlighting, flexitime, temporary workers, and other related topics.

Greenberg, P. D., and Glaser, E. M. *Some Issues in Joint Union-Management Quality of Worklife Improvement Efforts.* Kalamazoo, Mich.: Upjohn Institute for Employment Research, 1980.

A good state-of-the-art book on quality of worklife (QWL) issues. In addition to the authors' comments and insights, there is a summary of conference proceedings on the subject, involving union and management representatives.

Olmstead, B., and Smith, S. *The Job Sharing Handbook.* Berkeley, Calif.: Ten Speed Press, 1983.

The authors are cofounders of the San Francisco–based organization called New Ways to Work. The book is essentially a practical guide for anyone who wants a flexible working schedule and job/life satisfaction. It contains numerous forms to fill out and follow as well as sixteen profiles of people who are sharing a job. A solid book for putting the job-sharing theory into practice.

Pascarella, P. *The New Achievers: Creating a Modern Work Ethic.* New York: Free Press, 1984.

A good description of some of the changing attitudes toward work by a growing minority of employees who are looking for more than a pay check and a title. The new achievers want meaningful tasks that promote or at least permit self-development, self-esteem, creativity, participation, freedom, and a sense of wholeness and commitment. Pascarella offers an agenda for United States firms to follow in harnessing the full potential of these seekers of career fulfillment.

Three Scenarios on the Future of Work: Implications for Career Counseling

This part of the book attempts to help counselors and others understand that there are alternative futures for work in the United States. What should be emphasized here is that there is not *one* best view of the future or work—there are many. In fact, so many different views of the future of work have been advanced that counselors and other people probably find it difficult to comprehend them all. To simplify that task, I have grouped these views around three main themes or scenarios: the "Green," "Yellow," and "Red" Scenarios. The three colors are meant to be parallel to traffic lights—Green for Go, Yellow for Caution, Red for Stop. The scenarios sketched out in the following three chapters provide a framework for the more elaborate descriptions that are easily accessible through the literature in this field.

Counselors should realize that each of the alternatives is based on the rationale of fairly stable conditions in the nation and the world. Even within the United States, conditions vary by states and region, depending on a host of economic, social, political, and geographical factors. For example, the rise and fall of interest rates has an impact on many business and industrial plans. Likewise, peaks and valleys in world oil prices significantly affect various regions of the nation. Certainly, the current debate over mandatory retirement ages will have an impact on work and workers. Likewise, political action to change the minimum wage or to create a subminimum wage could have a major impact on any of these possible alternative futures. It goes without saying that an outbreak of armed conflict on an international scale would radically reshape the future of work, and there are a great many other conditions that could quickly throw off even the most logical scenario.

This part of the book emphasizes first of all how important it is for counselors and others to understand that there are at least three alternative futures for work. Second, it points out some of the pros and cons for each of the scenarios. Third, it suggests what counselors and others can do to stay up to date and current on each of these three scenarios.

Overview of the Three Scenarios

Chapter Three examines the position taken by authors such as Alvin Toffler, John Naisbitt, Marvin Cetron, Norman Feingold, and Edward Cornish. Many of the articles in *The Futurist,* published by the World Future Society, reflect this point of view. All these writers point to dramatic and revolutionary changes in the workplace, as a result of new technologies.

Chapter Four focuses on the material mainly coming from U.S. Department of Labor sources, such as the *Monthly Labor Review,* the *Occupational Outlook Quarterly,* and the biennial *Occupational Outlook Handbook.* Several independent writers who share this more centrist view also are discussed. These writers emphasize a future somewhat like the present, with changes occurring in an evolutionary—not a revolutionary—fashion.

Chapter Five concentrates on the more pessimistic view of writers such as Eli Ginzberg, Bob Kuttner, and Barry Blueston and organizations such as the AFL-CIO, United Auto Workers, and the congressional office of Technological Assessment. According to this view, the loss of jobs in the manufacturing sector and increases in lower-paying service jobs will lead to a two-tier work force (with some highly paid workers and a great many poorly paid workers), a dwindling middle class, and high joblessness.

3

The Green
or Go Scenario:
Fast Track and High Tech

Advocates of the "Green" Scenario look forward to a fast-paced future with a high-technology, high-touch, highly visible, computer-driven work force and a highly robotized industrial workplace. In the future envisioned here, the United States will pass from the Postindustrial Age to an Information Age and perhaps eventually to a Postinformation Age. A period of rapid job change and emerging occupations also is forecast.

Certainly, counselors hear a great deal about this scenario. It appears on newsstands and in bookstores and is broadcast over the radio and television. Many of its advocates publish their views in *The Futurist,* the official periodical of the World Future Society. An analysis of the articles there and in various books raise a variety of themes relevant to this scenario. After a brief introduction about the early trend setters, Chapter Three focuses attention on five of these themes: (1) New Age work settings, (2) the changing workplace, (3) robots in the workplace, (4) the changing job mix, and (5) emerging careers. Other themes could be selected, but these five represent the core of the Green Scenario. The chapter also includes a brief section on the popularization of this scenario, as well as a section that weighs its pros and cons.

Early Trend Setters

Alvin Toffler (1970), in his book *Future Shock,* envisioned a fast-paced, throwaway society where the workplace is dominated by temporary groups that come together to solve a problem or produce a product and then disband to wait for another call to work. Some evidence for this point of view appears in the growing number of "contract workers" who really work for temporary employment organizations such as Kelly Services and Manpower Temporary Services. They may work for two days or two weeks or two years at an office or other work setting but never become permanent employees. Toffler also forecasts that work will move out of factory and office complexes into the community and the home as the world moves into a "superindustrial era."

Another popular futurist writer, John Naisbitt (1982), has also forecast a high-tech/high-touch future workplace. In his book *Megatrends,* he predicts a decentralized work force occupied in the "sunrise industries" of tomorrow, as the United States gradually breaks away from the "sunset or smokestack industries" of yesterday and today. Naisbitt calls this period a time of the parentheses—that is, a time of transition from the old industrial-manufacturing society to the new information society. The workers of tomorrow will need more brain power and less brawn power if they are to function effectively in the new work settings. Consequently, there will be a great demand for training and retraining programs to prepare workers for the next phase in the history of work (that is, from farmer to laborer to clerk to technician). This "technician" phase will require a major jump in skill level.

Five Themes

New Age Work Settings. Edward Cornish, editor of *The Futurist,* is a leading advocate of the Green Scenario. In *Careers Tomorrow* Cornish (1983) describes the "strange new fields" that may emerge as New Age work settings.

- *Videodating services.* This service will give rise to occupations that produce commercial videodating tapes of customers, with biographical data and characteristics of desirable dates. A client will be able to review a number of biographies and videotapes before selecting the preferred date. Cornish believes that the rising divorce rate and mobility of society will make this kind of service especially attractive in the future.

- *Phobia fighting.* In this service "phobia therapists" will be employed to help people with phobias overcome their fears.
- *Electric car service station.* Service stations are needed for the 2,000 battery-operated cars now on the road and for the 9 million vehicles that—according to a Department of Energy forecast—will be operating by the year 2000. If the forecast holds true, about 50 percent of the total automobile fleet will be battery operated.
- *Erotic boutiques.* This service will grow as the sexual revolution continues to loosen people's attitudes toward erotic subjects. These shops would offer a variety of erotic wearing apparel, prints, artwork, greeting cards, and the like. Direct sales in people's homes also are forecast.
- *New security devices.* This high-technology field would take advantage of advances in electronics to provide an array of new equipment for protection of domiciles and workplaces. Cornish sees production and sales of security equipment as a major growth area.
- *Brain food stores.* As new breakthroughs occur in determining the effects of nutrition on brain functions, new retail health-food stores will specialize in various items for individuals who wish to improve their intellectual powers. Cornish predicts that there may be jobs for people to service machines dispensing mind-improving drugs in schools and elsewhere.
- *Genetic engineering.* This high-technology field will, according to Cornish, lead to a number of new industries, each of which might eventually employ thousands, possibly millions, of workers. Genetic engineering firms would produce various forms of bacteria, drugs, and chemicals to improve mankind.
- *Truffle nurseries.* This type of nursery would captialize on the public's appetite for this black fungus delicacy. New grafting and germinating procedures may make expanded production of truffles possible. If this technology proves viable commercially, truffle growing may become a separate occupation.

Changing Workplace Relationships. A number of futurist writers are concentrating their vision on the changing nature of the workplace. Hirschhorn (1984), for example, envisions increasingly complex computerized production systems in manufacturing. He also predicts that these systems will give rise to a new type of working relationship between management and workers, who will be required to diagnose a variety of problems generated by error-prone machine systems. Hirschhorn thinks that the exercise of judgment by both workers and management will become increasingly important in tomorrow's workplace and that, in fact, there will be a blurring of lines between management and workers. Craftsmen, machine operators, and engineers will have to become generalists who can deal with unstructured and open-ended problems. The new manufacturing setting will thus demand a developing "culture of learning." Supervisors will function as teachers with teams of workers who are constantly learning on the job. Much of this learning will take the form of trial and error, and there will be an emphasis on learning from past failures.

While Hirschhorn thinks that tomorrow's factories will be highly automated and robotized, he also believes that there must be an emphasis on both social (worker-management interaction) and technical systems in a new era of integrated learning and working environments. This type of interactive setting will enable workers and managers to respond to unique events, opportunities, and failures. In the best of settings, workers will control automated machinery, using innovative control panels and functioning in small teams without close supervision; supervisors will be in charge of multidisciplinary teams; and the size of upper management will be sharply reduced.

The new technologies, in Hirschhorn's view, will not restrain social interaction and reduce everything to a formula. Instead, a humanizing of the workplace will occur in spite of further heavy mechanization. For example, workers and supervisors will frequently team up to solve problems and meet mutually agreed upon goals.

In addition, Hirschhorn thinks that more attention must be paid to such matters as emerging phenomena, tacit knowledge, and interpersonal processes. Finally, if there is to be an appreciation of organizational design choices while highly advanced technologies are being developed, there must be an increasing dependency on informal modes of learning, design, and communication. Hirshhorn's vision seems to have materialized at the new General Motors assembly plant in Fort Wayne, Indiana, where work is done in teams and everyone—not just management—is involved in selection of lighting, tools, and equipment. The word is that there is a changed "culture" in the plant. Thousands of hours have been spent on education to bring about the right mix of people and technology for this new method of production.

Robots in the Workplace. The idea of robots in the workplace has fascinated people for years. James S. Albus (1983, 1984), a frequent contributor to *The Futurist,* is an outspoken supporter of the view that robots will have dramatic and lasting effects on the manufacturing process in the United States. He has predicted that robot production will grow from the current level of 1,500 per year to between 20,000 and 60,000 per year by 1990. That rate would suggest about a million robots in operation by the year 2000. Although the current status of robot development is still quite primitive, Albus envisions robots that will be equipped with a multitude of sensors that will enable them to see, touch, determine force, and measure proximity. These new robots will be able to react to sensory input and adapt to changing or unexpected conditions. Their "memories" will store drawings of parts and plans for assemblies, so that they can perform complex tasks with a minimum of instruction or supervision from humans. They will be able to cut and fit materials, and will know how and where to construct walls, lay pipes, paint, pour concrete, and the like. They will be able to move about freely in buildings, shipyards, and even in natural environments such as fields, forests, air, and water. Lower cost will be one of the benefits of these developments for fabricated structures and manufactured goods.

It will be in factories, according to Albus, that the most significant robotic developments will take place. In the totally automated factory, computer-controlled flexible manufacturing systems can operate overnight and on weekends with little or no human supervision. This type of operation will take over most of the tasks performed by workers, and productivity will be doubled because of round-the-clock machine operations. These automated factories will even be capable of a significant degree of self-reproduction. That is, automated factories will begin making the components for other automated factories, so that each generation of machines will produce machines less costly and more sophisticated than the last. Clearly, this view of future production is the ultimate in high-technology application.

Hunt and Hunt (1983) believe that the number of robots in the United States will range from a minimum of 50,000 to a maximum of 100,000 by 1990. This type of growth implies an average annual growth rate of between 30 and 40 percent over the decade of the 1980s, or roughly a seven- to fourteen-fold increase in the total robot population. Correspondingly, between 32,000 and 64,000 new jobs will be created in four broad areas: robot manufacturing, direct suppliers to robot manufacturing. robot systems engineering, and corporate robot users. The biggest single occupational impact will be in jobs created for robotic technicians, followed by electrical and mechanical engineers. Engineers and technicians will likely account for over half of all jobs created.

The Changing Job Mix. Marvin J. Cetron (1983, 1984), another leading advocate for the high-tech/high-touch scenario, believes that many if not most of the new jobs of the future will be based on computer technology. He is a strong promoter of computer understanding and operation. Here are some of his general forecasts in the changing job mix (1984):

- *A moving labor force.* The sunbelt will continue to grow, but Detroit, South Bend, Battle Creek, Muncie, and other aging areas in the Northeast and Midwest will become industrial ghost towns.

- *A shorter workweek.* By 1990 the average worker will put in thirty-two hours per week and twenty-five hours by the year 2000. A new benchmark of acceptable unemployment of 8.5 percent will stabilize by 1990.
- *Reduced influence of organized labor.* With the phasing out of the big manufacturing industries—such as steel, rubber, auto, and textiles—the influence of labor unions will dwindle.
- *A growing computer industry.* Its rapid rate of growth over the last ten years will continue during the next decade.

Cetron (1983) has described some of the occupations that he thinks will be found in tomorrow's workplace and has given the number of expected openings in these occupations. According to Cetron, the following occupations will become increasingly important in the changing job mix in the 1990s:

- *Energy Technician* (650,000 jobs). Jobs in this area will increase dramatically as new energy sources become marketable.
- *Housing Rehabilitation Technician* (500,000 jobs). Intensifying housing demand will be met by mass production of prefabricated modular housing, using radically new construction techniques and materials.
- *Hazardous Waste Management Technician* (300,000 jobs). Many years and billions of dollars may be required to clean up air, land, and water. New industries will add to the demand with new wastes.
- *Industrial Laser Process Technician* (600,000 jobs). Laser manufacturing equipment and processes, including robotic factories, will replace much of today's machine and foundry tools and equipment.
- *Industrial Robot Production Technician* (800,000 jobs). Extensive use of robots to perform computer-directed "physical" and "mental" functions will displace hundreds of thousands of workers. But new workers will be needed to ensure fail-proof operations of row after row of production robots.
- *Materials Utilization Technician* (400,000 jobs). New materials are being engineered and created to replace metals, synthetics,

and other production substances unsuited for advanced manufacturing technologies.

- *Genetic Engineering Technician* (250,000 jobs). Genetically engineered materials will be used extensively in three general fields: industrial products, pharmaceuticals, and agricultural products. New and modified substances will be produced under laboratory-like conditions in industrial mass-production quantities.
- *Holographic Inspection Specialist* (200,000 jobs). Completely automated factories will use optical fibers for sensing light, temperature, pressure, and dimensions. This information will be transmitted to optical computers, which will compare it with stored holographic, three-dimensional images.
- *Bionic-Medical Technician* (200,000 jobs). Mechanics will be needed to manufacture bionic appendages while other specialists work on highly sophisticated extensions of sensory and mental functions (seeing, hearing, feeling, speaking).
- *Automotive Fuel Cell (Battery) Technician* (250,000 jobs). These technicians will perform tests and services for new fuel cells and batteries used in vehicles and stationary operation, including residences.
- *On-Line Emergency Medical Technician* (400,000 jobs). Needs for paramedics will increase directly with the growth of the population and its aging. In forthcoming megalopolises and high-density residences, emergeny medical treatment will be administered on the spot, aided by televised diagnoses and instruction from remote emergency medical centers.
- *Geriatric Social Worker* (700,000 jobs). The nation's aging population will require more and more mental and social care.
- *Energy Auditor* (180,000 jobs). Auditors will use the latest infrared devices and computer-based energy monitoring to work with architects, product engineers, and marketing staffs in the production, sales, and operation of energy conservation and control systems for housing, industrial plants, and machinery.
- *Nuclear Medicine Technologist* (75,000 jobs). These technologists will work with medicines and serums using radioisotopes. As the isotopes are absorbed in tissues and muscles,

diagnosticians can observe functions of normal and/or damaged tissues and organs and can determine treatment needs and responses to medication, thus reducing the need for surgery.

- *Dialysis Technologist* (30,000 jobs). These technologists will operate new portable dialysis machines and the expected greater number of hospital dialysis machines.
- *Computer Axial Tomography (CAT) Technologist/Technician* (45,000 jobs). Thousands of qualified technicians will be needed to install, maintain, and operate CAT scanning systems and assist in the analysis of these scans.
- *Positron Emission Tomography (PET) Technician/Technologist* (165,000 jobs). PET scanners are used for diagnoses of disorders of the brain. The need for qualified workers in this field will increase with advances in and the growing use of this technology.
- *Computer-Assisted Design (CAD) Technician* (300,000 jobs). The computer can produce more, better, and faster designs than traditional design methods can. It can be used to design modes of transportation, dwellings, or other products and will affect education, employment, and ways of work more than any other single technology.
- *Computer-Assisted Graphics (CAG) Technician* (150,000 jobs). Rapid growth of computer-assisted graphics will affect the education, training, and employment of all graphics technicians as has no other event in graphics history. Demands for artists and technicians will increase tenfold, largely because of an increase in demand for new forms and dimensions of graphics to portray objects, schemes, and scenarios before they are actually produced.
- *Computer-Assisted Manufacturing (CAM) Specialist* (300,000 jobs). CAM systems will permit all the design, development, specification, and logistics data to be pulled out of CAD and CAG data bases and reprogrammed into computer-assisted manufacturing programs, which will then operate most of the production without (or with minimal) human intervention.
- *Computerized Vocational Training (CVT) Technician* (300,000 jobs). Utilizing the demonstration capabilities and versatility

of CAD software in conjunction with computer graphics, educators and trainers will be able to depict any object and any action with a vividness and dynamism that will produce higher learning benefits than any other mode ever employed. Students will be able to assemble or disassemble the most complex mechanisms, construct the most artistic forms, and design dwellings and structures without ever leaving their computer terminals.

Emerging Careers. The notion of emerging or new career fields is a key concept in the Green Scenario. These new fields will not replace current occupations but will offer additional job opportunities. A leading advocate of this point of view is S. Norman Feingold, president of the National Career and Counseling Services in Washington, D.C. In his article "Emerging Careers: Occupations for the Post Industrial Society" (1984), Feingold defines an emerging career as one that has the following characteristics:

- Has become increasingly visible as a separate career area in recent years.
- Has developed from preexisting career areas, such as medical care and personal or business services.
- Has become possible because of advances in technology or actual physical changes in our environment. For example, home computers, solar industries, satellite television, and water pollution equipment are a few of the many areas that have engendered new, emerging careers.
- Shows growth in numbers of people employed or attending emerging education and training programs.
- Requires skills and training.
- Does not appear and then disappear in a very short period of time.

One of the biggest areas of emerging careers is the information industry. Today 55 percent of the workers in the United States are in information industries. More people are involved in information and communication than in mining, agriculture, manufacturing, and personal services combined. Some experts are calling the changes an ''information revolution.'' By the year 2000, 80 percent of the work force will be information workers. Here are some of the emerging career areas in the information industry:

- *Operation of information systems.* Abstractor-indexers process the intellectual content of documents for convenient retrieval. Bibliographical searchers use modern computerized information systems and data bases to identify or retrieve pertinent publications. Information brokers perform specialized information retrieval services for a fee.
- *Management of information systems.* Information center managers supervise facilities that organize knowledge of a specific subject area.
- *Design of information systems.* Application or systems programmers write large-scale computer programs or modify existing programs in order to solve information problems in business, science, education, and other fields.
- *Research and teaching.* Computational linguists analyze work and language structure to determine how the computer can manipulate text for indexing, classification, abstracting, search, and retrieval.

Other emerging careers can be found in the ''ocean industries'' and in the fields of robotics, space, and energy. Out of these broad career fields comes the following list of specific occupations, which—according to Feingold and Miller (1983)— might appear in a future *Dictionary of Occupational Titles:*

Aquaculturist	Child advocate
Artificial intelligence technician	Color consultant
	Community ecologist
Asteroid/lunar miner	Community psychologist
Battery technician	Contract administrator
Biomedical technician	Cryologist technician
Bionic medical technician	Cultural historian
CAD/CAM technician	Cyborg technician

Dance therapist
Dialysis technologist
Divorce mediator
Electronic data-processing
  (EDP) auditor
Electronic mail technician
Energy auditor
Ethicist
Executive rehabilitative
  counselor
Exercise technician
Exotic welder
Family mediator/therapist
Forecaster
Forensic scientist
Fusion engineer
Genetic biochemist
Genetic counselor
Graphoanalyst
Hibernation specialist
Horticulture therapy assistant
House and pet sitter
Housing rehabilitation
  technician
Image consultant
Indoor air quality specialist
Information broker
Issues manager
Laser technician
Massage therapist

Microbial geneticist
Myotherapist
Naprapath
Neutrino astronomer
Nuclear fuel technician
Ocean hotel manager
Ombudsman
Oncology nutritionist
Orthotist
Plant therapist
Pollution botanist
Protein geometrician
Relocation counselor
Retirement counselor
Selenologist (lunar
  astronomer)
Shrimp-trout fish farmer
Shyness consultant
Software club director
Solar engineer
Space botanist
Space mechanic
Sports law specialist
Strategic planner
Telecommunications systems
  designer
Thanatologist
Treasure hunter
Underwater archeologist
Volcanologist

Popular Versions of the Green Scenario

Adrian Paradis, Robert Weinstein, and others have adapted the futurists' writings for career-information-seeking high school and college student audiences. These writers translate the futurists' forecasts into less technical terms and write for wider circulation in books such as *Jobs for the 21st Century* (Weinstein, 1983) and *Planning Your Career of Tomorrow* (Paradis, 1986). According to these popular versions, thousands of jobs will disappear and thousands more will be created to take their place. In this extension of ideas, anything having to do with a computer promises to be lucrative and long lasting. The demand factor, it is stressed, will remain strong for the next decade and beyond. For example, Paradis writes that a majority of present-day manufacturing positions will be wiped out as machines come into our factories.

Weinstein provides vocational guidance information by writing about "the Robotizing of America." He describes a workplace in which many industries will be run entirely by robots. There will be varying levels of robots: unskilled robots, semiskilled robots, and highly skilled supervisory robots. Weinstein also tells his readers that soon each home will have at least one robot. These robots will perform all the household chores—cleaning, cooking, driving the car, and at the end of a long day mixing the evening drinks.

In short, these writers accept much of what is being forecast and pass it on to mainly young readers with few if any conditions or disclaimers. They seem to be saying, "This is definitely how things are going to be. Plan for this particular view of the future. There are no other points of view or possibilities."

Pros and Cons of the Green Scenario

The Green or Go Scenario emphasizes that the United States is moving very rapidly toward a new working future. There will be numerous changes in the kinds of work performed, where it is performed, and when it is performed. The advocates of this scenario see an emerging revolution in the workplace and think that current educational programs are not preparing people for this vastly different world of work. In summary, the supporters of the Green Scenario see a future that is (1) highly technical, (2) highly speculative, and (3) highly imaginative. In essence, the futurist viewpoint holds that:

- Robots and computers will take over much of the workplace.
- Emerging new or unknown occupations will develop and replace old, outdated ones.
- The Information Age will replace the Industrial Age.

A good argument can be made for each of these three major points. The issue for counselors and others in the helping professions and, more important, the students or people with whom these professionals will work is: What is the likelihood that all this is going to take place? It seems clear that rapid changes are occurring in the workplace, but the questions that must be raised are:

- What will be the extent of the change?
- How long will it take to implement?
- Where will the impact be most notable?
- How long will these changes take?
- What will the changes cost?
- Can the changes really be afforded?

Robots and Computers. There is little debate over the progress made in the development of computers and robots. But what impact will they have on the future workplace? That is, although we can produce labor-saving or production-efficient technology, can business, industry, and government *afford* to implement these changes on a cost-effective basis? Many of the forecasts of the futurists are indeed *possible* and *probable,* but are they *economically feasible?* In short, there may be, as Feingold forecasts, ocean hotel managers, selenologists, thanatologists, and volcanologists. The questions the reader must raise are: How many? Who will provide the preparation? Where do they work? When will they be needed? Can we afford to prepare and pay people in these occupations? A person may be well advised to follow a traditional field of preparation while keeping an eye on some of these forecasted growth occupations as future possibilities.

Emerging Occupations. Earlier in this chapter, there were several lists of emerging occupations or new work settings as seen by

Cetron, Feingold, and Cornish. In fact, no one knows how much these occupations are likely to grow. None of them is likely to have as many new openings as *secretary, nurse,* or *auto mechanic.* But the futurists do not seem to want to talk about the big occupations that employ thousands of workers today. Furthermore, these highly specialized emerging occupations may lead to dead-end jobs for overspecialized and overprepared workers. Finally, are emerging occupations just subspecialties of older occupations—not really new and emerging at all? Of course, we should not disregard the emergence of new occupational specialties, but we also should emphasize the broader traditional fields, which also are growing. In short, the emerging occupations will not become major employers of workers overnight, and none or very few of them are major occupational factors now. (See Bureau of Labor Statistics, 1982b, for more details on this point.)

Information Age Versus Industrial Age. A simple chart can make a point better than several paragraphs (see Figure 2). Many people use this chart to show that service-producing employment is continuing to outdistance goods-producing employment. However, goods-producing employment is expected to be at 31.4 million in 1995, *up* 6 percent from the 29.6 million employed in 1984. Therefore, according to the best estimates of the Bureau of Labor Statistics, goods-producing employment not only will not disappear but will have a modest gain. Among goods-producing industries, mining and agriculture are expected to lose workers, and construction and manufacturing are expected to gain them.

The indications are, then, that the United States will move increasingly toward an information/postindustrial era, but predictions of the immediate and total demise of goods-producing industries are premature. Both types of industries will provide opportunities for employment in tomorrow's workplace.

What Should Counselors Do?

Counselors should read and take seriously the forecasts made by people associated with the Green Scenario. There are

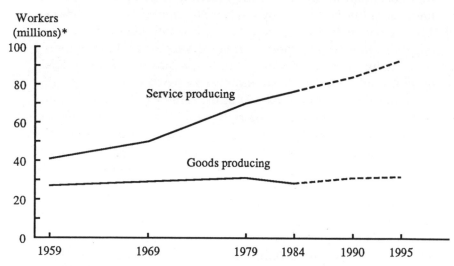

Figure 2. Growth of Goods-Producing and Service-Producing Industries, 1959–1995.

*Includes wage and salary workers, the self-employed, and unpaid family workers.

Source: Bureau of Labor Statistics, 1986b, p. 17.

some bright and able people writing and speaking in this field. Counselors should keep in mind, however, that this is only *one* scenario—not *the only* scenario—and should not be misled by arrogant or loud talk or one-sided written pronouncements about any *one* future rather than several possible futures. There may be a great deal of truth in this scenario, but for the moment, there is no way of knowing how much truth. In any event, there is still going to be a need for:

Teachers	Salespeople
Nurses	Farmers
Engineers	Laborers
Accountants	Fast-food workers
Carpenters	Custodians
Electricians	Cashiers

Most traditional occupations are going to stay around, stay large, and continue to have openings. Counselors will want to watch the trends and forecasts coming forward from the writers connected with the Green Scenario but should remember that it is at best one of many possible futures.

Suggested Readings

Cetron, M. J. *Jobs of The Future: The 500 Best Jobs—Where They'll Be and How to Get Them.* New York: McGraw-Hill, 1984.

Written by one of the main spokespersons for the high-technology future, this book contains chapters on the office of the future, services, health, engineering, communication, factories, and manufacturing.

Cornish, E. (ed.). *Careers Tomorrow: The Outlook for Work in a Changing World.* Bethesda, Md.: World Future Society, 1983.

The best of articles from *The Futurist* by writers such as Amitai Etzioni, Gary Hart, Willis Harman, Lester Brown, and James O'Toole. From robots to implications of smart machines for employment.

Cornish, E. (ed.). *The Computerized Society: Living and Working in an Electronic Age.* Bethesda, Md.: World Future Society, 1985.

Selections from recent issues of *The Futurist,* the official periodical of the World Future Society. Includes articles by James Albus, Fred Best, Marvin Cetron, Norman Feingold, and others.

Didsbury, H. F., Jr. (ed.). *The World of Work: Careers and The Future.* Bethesda, Md.: World Future Society, 1983.

A collection of invited papers for the 1983 WFS special conference on "Working Now and in the Future," held in Washington, D.C., in August 1983. Papers by John Diebold, Arthur Shostak, David Macarov, Robert Theobald, and others.

Feingold, S. N., and Miller, N. R. *Emerging Careers: New Occupations for the Year 2000 and Beyond.* Garrett Park, Md.: Garrett Park Press, 1983.

Feingold and Miller offer forecasts for a wide variety of work settings, such as space, ocean, and energy-related employment.

4

The Yellow
or Caution Scenario:
Evolution, Not Revolution

Advocates of the "Yellow" Scenario envision an *evolution* in the workplace over the next ten to twenty years—*not* a *revolution.* It would be unfair to call this, as some charge, a "status quo" position because it certainly is not. However, there is far more discussion here about replacements of workers than about growth in new jobs. There is also far less discussion of emerging occupations and more emphasis on existing occupations and what is likely to happen to them. Writers who urge a cautious stance rely heavily on government data sources, such as those from the Bureau of Labor Statistics, Small Business Administration, Bureau of the Census, Department of Education, Department of Defense, and other federal agencies. Many of these writers, in fact, are staff members of the Bureau of Labor Statistics.

Finding material on the Yellow Scenario is no problem; wading through it is. Consider only a handful of the well-researched and well-written publications of the Bureau of Labor Statistics: the *Monthly Labor Review* and *Occupational Outlook Quarterly,* followed by the *Occupational Outlook Handbook* and the *Occupational Projections and Training Data*—both published every two years.

Much of the information that the Bureau of Labor Statistics uses comes from state employment commissions such as the Virginia Employment Commission, which maintains a state data research and analysis system. Most states also have Occupation Information Systems (OIS), which collect data from a variety of state educational, governmental, and private sources. Many of the states produce high-quality information about the labor market, and this helps to give the national (Bureau of Labor Statistics) system a solid foundation.

Those who contribute to the Yellow Scenario are not all staff members of the Bureau of Labor Statistics, however. A growing number of respected and able economists and others also see the future in a cautious light. The scenario sketched out in this chapter will give an overview of industrial and occupational projections to the year 2000, a sound rationale based on the solid research of the Bureau of Labor Statistics. Then seven major themes, which stand out in the Bureau of Labor Statistics publications as well as from a number of studies carried out by independent observers, are described; and the pros and cons of the scenario are evaluated.

Overview of the Yellow Scenario

Any edition of the *Occupational Outlook Handbook (OOH)* or summaries in the *Occupational Outlook Quarterly,* put together by the staff of the Bureau of Labor Statistics (BLS), clearly indicate the main position of the Yellow Scenario. The *OOH* is published biennially (the 1988–89 edition is the latest) and brings together the key points representing this scenario. Through a series of charts and tables, the entire picture of the past, present, and future of the work force is laid out. What follows is abstracted from some BLS material projected to the year 2000 to reflect two of the main points related to industries and occupations stressed in this scenario.

Employment by Industry. Employment is projected to rise by 21 million in the 1986–2000 period. The increase—more than 19 percent between 1986 and 2000, or 1.3 percent a year—represents a slowing of employment growth compared to 1972–1986, when it was 2.2 percent a year. This slowing reflects, in large part, slower growth in the labor force; and, in fact, is not quite so dramatic when compared to the more recent 1979–86 period, during which nonagricultural wage and salary jobs grew 1.5 percent a year.

Service-producing industries will account for nearly all the projected growth. A large increase in jobs is projected for both wholesale and retail trade, a continuation of past trends. Almost 4.9 million new wage and salary jobs are expected in retail trade and more than 1.5 million in wholesale trade. The finance, insurance, and real estate industry is projected to add more than 1.6 million jobs—a considerable slowing when compared with the nearly 2.4 million jobs added over the previous fourteen years. The service industries themselves will expand by more than 10 million jobs; health-care services and business services will be important contributors as they continue to produce new services that greatly add to their overall demand and employment growth. Federal government employment is expected to remain stable, but state and local governments are expected to expand by 1.5 million.

Among major groups in the goods-producing industries, the projections show increasing employment only in construction, in which employment will rise 890,000. Because of important gains in productivity, manufacturing employment is projected to decline by more than 800,000 jobs during the 1986–2000 period, even though output is expected to increase 2.3 percent a year. However, many manufacturing industries are projected to grow, some quite rapidly, despite the overall decline. Manufacturing as a whole will still provide more than 15 percent of all wage and salary employment in the year 2000, according to the projections. Employment gains are expected in printing and publishing, drugs and pharmaceutical products, computers, plastic products, and instruments industries. Generally, the manufacturing industries expected to decline in employment have already been declining for years; these include basic steel, leather goods, shoes, tobacco, some of the textile and most of the basic metal-processing industries, and many of the food-processing industries.

Employment by Occupation. The average growth projected for occupations, like that for industries, is 19 percent. Five occupational groups are projected to grow faster than average during the 1986–2000 period: technicians, service workers, professional workers, sales workers, and executive and managerial employees. Only two groups—agriculture, forestry, and fishing workers, on the one hand, and private household workers, on the other— are projected to decline. Three groups are expected to grow more slowly than average: precision production, craft, and repair workers; administrative support workers, including clerical workers; and operators, fabricators, and laborers.

Information is available for 1986 on the level of education attained by workers in the major occupational groups. A comparison of this information with projected employment indicates that the share of jobs in which most workers had completed high school will decline slightly, while the share of jobs in which most workers had less than a high school education will decline more sharply.

Seven Themes

Replacement Needs. Most discussions of future job opportunities focus on the growth of employment in industries and occupations. Since the faster-growing industries and occupations generally offer better opportunities for employment and advancement than slow-growing ones, employment growth is a good gauge of job outlook. Another element in the employment outlook, however, is replacement needs. Replacement openings occur as people leave occupations. Some transfer to other occupations as a step up the career ladder or to change careers. Some stop working, return to school, assume household responsibilities, or retire.

Through the 1990s *most jobs will become available as the result of replacement needs.* Among occupations, however, the number of replacement jobs, and the proportion of total job openings created by replacement needs, will vary significantly. The occupation's size, the earinings and status of workers, length of training required, average age of workers, and proportion of part-time workers determine the number of replacement jobs in an occupation. Occupations with the most replacement openings generally are large, with lower pay and status, lower training requirements, and a high proportion of young and part-time workers. Examples are file clerks, cashiers, construction laborers, and stock handlers. Workers in these occupations who lose their jobs or leave voluntarily often are able to find a similar job quickly. They also have not spent much money or time in training for their jobs, so there is limited incentive to stay in such occupations. Occupations with low training requirements often attract workers with limited attachment to the labor force, such as young people working part time.

The occupations with relatively few replacement openings, in contrast, are ones with high pay and status, lengthy training requirements, and a high proportion of prime-working-age, full-time workers. Architects, dentists, and medical laboratory technicians, for example, generally have spent several years acquiring training that often is not applicable to other occupations. These workers enjoy good pay and high status but would find it difficult to change to other high-paying occupations without extensive retraining.

Occupations with little or no employment growth or slower-than-average growth can still offer many job openings. Bienstock (1981) warns that we have spent a great deal of time in the last twenty-five years looking at new and emerging occupations when these occupations will account for only a small part of the job openings that can be expected in the next decade: "If you are looking for where the jobs are going to be, look at where they are now. Keep an eye on the replacement market" (p. 5).

Occupational Profile. The economy is expected to generate 15.9 million additional jobs between 1986 and 2000. Twenty-seven occupations are expected to account for a considerable portion of this projected job growth (see Table 4, Chapter Two). These occupations are numerically large—all had 300,000 or more workers in 1986. More than half had over a million workers. Occupations that require extensive training are not found to any great extent on the list. Those requiring little formal training are in the majority, with less than one-fourth of the occupations generally requiring a college degree.

Twenty occupations with the highest percentage of growth rates between 1986 and 2000 are shown in Table 3 (Chapter 2). The list is dominated by occupations that are tied to expanding industries and that have been among the fastest growing in the economy for the past decade. Almost half of the twenty occupations on the list are either in the computer or health fields. For some occupations the high growth rates reflect recovery from the 1981–82 recession. Note also that the fastest-growing occupations generally are not found on the list of occupations that will add the most new jobs over the period.

Occupations expected to decline over the period generally are concentrated in industries that are contracting or being severely affected by technological change (Table 5). For example, railroad brake, signal, and switch operators are concentrated in a declining industry, while stenographers are being affected by technological change. Most of these occupations have been losing jobs in recent years. This is not the result of any sudden shift.

A final point about occupational profiles, job growth, and absolute changes in numbers of persons employed. Figure 3 shows clearly that percent change in employment, taken alone, reflects only part of the story. Legal assistants (or paralegals) will have almost a 100 percent change in employment, whereas secretaries will have only a 9.6 percent change in employment. When absolute change in employment is taken into account, however, almost 270,000 *new* secretaries will be needed between 1984 and 1995, whereas only 51,000 legal assistants will be needed. The conclusion is obvious: Consider both percent change in employment and absolute change in employment.

Rapid Growth of Service Industries. Under what it calls its moderate-growth (as opposed to high-growth or low-growth) estimates for the period 1984–1995, the Bureau of Labor Statistics (BLS) predicts that nearly 16 million new jobs will be created. Nine out of ten of these new jobs are expected to be in the service-producing industries—for example, in retail trade, miscellaneous business services, and health services (Bureau of Labor Statistics, 1985). Of these industries retail trade is by far

Table 5. Fastest-Declining Occupations, 1986–2000. (Numbers in thousands.)

Occupation	Employment		Change in Employment, 1986–2000	
	1986	Projected, 2000	Number	Percent
Electrical and electronics assemblers	249	116	133	53.7
Electronic semiconductor processors	29	14	15	51.1
Railroad conductors and yardmasters	29	17	12	40.9
Railroad brake, signal, and switch operators	42	25	17	39.9
Gas and petroleum plant system occupations	31	20	11	34.3
Industrial truck and tractor operators	426	283	143	33.6
Shoe sewing-machine operators and tenders	27	18	9	32.1
Station installers and repairers, telephone	58	40	18	31.8
Chemical equipment controllers, operators, and tenders	73	52	21	29.7
Chemical plant and system operators	33	23	10	29.6
Stenographers	178	128	50	28.2
Farmers	1,182	850	332	28.1
Statistical clerks	71	52	19	26.4
Textile draw-out and winding machine operators and tenders	219	164	55	25.2
Central office and PBX installers and repairers	74	57	17	23.1
Farm workers	940	750	190	20.3
Coil winders, tapers, and finishers	34	28	6	18.5
Central office operators	42	34	8	17.9
Directory assistance operators	32	27	5	17.7
Compositors, typesetters, and arrangers, precision	30	25	5	17.1

Source: Bureau of Labor Statistics, 1988, p. 59.

the largest and is expected to continue its rapid growth. Occupations included in this growth category are sales clerks, waiters, waitresses, cashiers, fast-food preparation workers, store managers, technical sales representatives, sales floor workers, stock clerks, kitchen helpers, short-order cooks, and fuel pump attendants. Most of these occupations are open to people who are reliable, pleasant, and neat and who have basic reading, writing, and arithmetic skills. But turnover is high in these occupations, so that their replacement needs are large. This field is ideal for young workers just starting out or older workers who want varied hours and even part-time employment.

''Miscellaneous business service'' is a catchall phrase that includes management, consulting, and public relations services,

Figure 3. Percent and Absolute Changes in Employment of Secretaries
and Legal Assistants, 1984–1995.

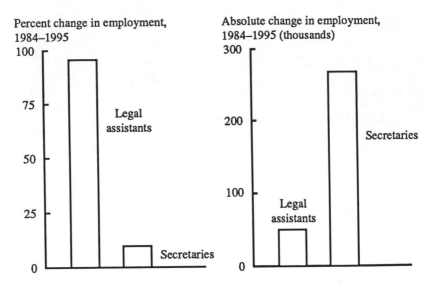

Percent change in employment, 1984–1995

Absolute change in employment, 1984–1995 (thousands)

Source: Bureau of Labor Statistics, 1986b, p. 19.

detective agencies and protective services, research and development laboratories, equipment rental and leasing services, photo-finishing laboratories, commercial testing laboratories, and trading stamp services (to name a few). This area accounted for nearly one new job out of twenty between 1974 and 1984. In the period ending in 1995, these services are projected to grow much faster than the economy as a whole and to provide many new jobs.

The health services area represents about 6.2 million jobs at present and is projected to grow by about 1 million new jobs by 1995. By any standard, though, the health services area of employment is in a transition period. Since 1958 the field has increased employment more than fivefold. The next decade will likely show continued growth, but at a somewhat slower pace. Some of the factors bearing on the exact location and pace of occupational growth in this area are the debate over methods of financing health care, increased efforts at promoting good health, a shift toward more outpatient care, and the amount of money available to provide facilities for the infirm and the aged. In short, growth in this service area is likely, although exactly where the growth will occur is difficult to forecast. Three exceptions stand out: registered nurses are expected to grow by 452,000 by 1995; nurses' aides, orderlies, and attendants by 348,000; and licensed practical nurses by 106,000.

High-Technology Employment: Fast Growth but Few Jobs. The point made about job growth and absolute changes in employment has a direct bearing on employment in high-technology occupations. The Bureau of Labor Statistics staff studied the issue at great length, and Riche (1983) reported the results. The major findings of the investigation were as follows:

- Employment in high-tech industries increased faster than the average for all industries during the 1972–1982 period. In 1982 technology-oriented employment totaled 3.3 million, or about 3.2 percent of total employment.
- Because of their small size, high-technology industries accounted for a relatively small proportion of all new jobs nationwide, although they did provide a significant proportion of new jobs in some states and communities.
- Between 1982 and 1995, employment in high-tech industries is projected to grow 45.3 to 49.3 percent—somewhat faster than the average—and high-tech industries are expected to generate 1.5 to 1.6 million new jobs.
- High-tech industries will continue to account for only a small proportion of new jobs through 1995; scientific and technical workers will account for only 6 percent of all new jobs through 1995.
- Among the occupations that will generate the most new jobs within the high-technology field are electrical and electronics technician, computer systems analyst, electrical engineer, and computer programmer.

Growth in high-technology employment also will vary greatly from state to state and region to region. California has by far the largest number of persons employed in high technology, with New York, Texas, Massachusetts, New Jersey, Florida, Illinois, and Pennsylvania following behind. As a region, New England leads the way in proportion of high-technology employment. The region—with its high-quality educational institutions and ample supply of skilled workers— generally has provided an ideal environment for these industries.

Computers and the Workplace. How extensively are computers used in the workplace? What, exactly, do workers do with computers and how did they learn to do it? In their study of 140 major occupations in industries where computers are used, Goldstein and Fraser (1985a) attempted to answer these questions. They found that workers who use computers fall into three main groups:

1. Occupations requiring extensive computer training—for example, computer programmers and computer systems analysts
2. Occupations in which some workers may need to learn how to program computers—for example, engineers, chemists, mathematicians, accountants, and auditors
3. Occupations requiring only brief training in operating computers—for example, travel agents, secretaries, and typists

In an article in the *Occupational Outlook Quarterly,* Goldstein and Fraser (1985a, p. 29) summarized their findings as follows:

> In summary, about one in eight of all workers now use a computer. Of these, about 5 percent need extensive computer training. Less than 10 percent need to learn programming. All the rest—more than four out of five of all who use computers— are in occupations where using computers means only operating them; these workers learn the necessary skills in a few hours to a few weeks of training, most of which is given on the job or by manufacturers of the equipment.

It may seem paradoxical that a technology many people associate with abstruse mathematics and electronics could have attained such widespread use with relatively little special education and training. But such innovations as the automobile, television, and the telephone have become nearly universal while requiring relatively few highly trained workers—mostly engineers and craft workers—to manufacture, install, and repair them. Computers are becoming prevalent mainly because they have been constantly and ingeniously improved to make them easy to use.

This study by Goldstein and Fraser has done much to put the so-called computer revolution in the workplace in better perspective. According to these researchers, the need for computer training has been vastly overstated. In their view, computer operation skills are simply a part of the broad range of skills needed on any job—not the single most important, as some would advocate. Therefore, they urge young workers not to fear that they will be frozen out of the job market because they have not learned about computers.

Changes in Clerical Work. Despite all the glossy descriptions of the "highly automated office of the future," most advocates of the Yellow Scenario believe that clerical employment will remain strong. In BLS projections, employment for secretaries is expected to grow from 2.8 million to 3 million by 1995. Receptionists and information clerks, switchboard operators, and general office clerks are among the occupations with the largest job growth between now and 1995. Hunt and Hunt (1986), in a study entitled "Clerical Employment and Technological Change: A Review of Recent Trends and Projections," question the forecasts that office-based automation will result in widespread job loss in this field:

In summary, we found no persuasive evidence that there will be a significant decline in clerical jobs in the future. The forecasts of declining clerical employment are based on overoptimistic expectations of technological improvements or exaggerated productivity claims on behalf of existing technology. In our opinion, current office technology offers significant improvements in product quality and modest improvements in productivity. There is as yet no empirical evidence of an office productivity revolution that will displace significant numbers of clerical workers.

On the contrary, we think there are many factors which will contribute to the job growth of clericals in the future. Chief among these is the simple fact that clericals are so diffused in the national economy. Moreover, to the extent that clerical jobs are concentrated in particular industries, it has been in sectors growing faster than average. Therefore, even allowing for negative employment impacts from office automation, it is extremely difficult to believe that the growth of this large, diverse, and diffused major occupational group could be much below the average growth for all occupations for the next decade [p. 285].

So the long-heralded demise of clerical employment is not likely to come about, according to this study by Hunt and Hunt. Since the 1960s forecasters have regularly talked about the expected fall in clerical employment. A look at long-term trends seems to provide convincing evidence that this large field of employment will not only continue but will show some modest growth over the next decade.

Second Thoughts on Work. In the insightful book *Second Thoughts on Work,* Levitan and Johnson (1982b) look very carefully at the pace of the computerization and robotization in the American workplace. They conclude that the pace of change will be moderate (evolutionary) rather than rapid and drastic (revolutionary) because of (1) the cost involved, (2) the questionable need to further automate some processes, (3) the need to maintain a humanizing factor in delivering goods and services, and (4) the natural slowness to adapt to such changes after an initial surge.

Levitan and Johnson do not envision a workless society where machines have supplanted human workers. They do believe, however, that automation has produced and will continue to produce increased benefits and social progress for the labor force through such changes as shorter workweeks, more vacation time, longer training and education periods, and earlier retirement. Further, rising expectations alone will cause Americans to translate production gains into higher standards of living instead of less work.

Reviewing the changes under way in the workplace, Levitan and Johnson (1982b) see three hopeful trends:

1. *The expansion of individual choice in work.* Increases in quality and quantity of education, the availability of low-cost transportation, and other factors will give individuals more control over where they work, when they work, and what they do at work.
2. *The elimination of unpleasant or undesirable work.* As a part of the redesign and reorganization of the workplace, there will be pressures to eliminate certain types of work or provide much better pay and benefits, so that workers in these less desirable jobs will at least be able to "live for their leisure" rather than for their work.
3. *The growth of concern for human potential in the workplace.* The same forces that are pushing for elimination of undesirable jobs will push for worker participation in everything from lighting to tool purchases.

Levitan (1987) warns against "trendy forecasts" (Green Scenario) and points out that the American workplace is very slow to change—partly because of the large capital expenditures necessary to bring about even small changes. In short, Levitan expects gradual, *not* monumental, changes in work over the next decade (1987–1997). Robots will possibly take over a few of the more unpleasant and repetitive tasks, and computers will assume some jobs currently performed by human brains or brawn. But, on the whole, Levitan takes a cautious attitude toward changes in the upcoming decade.

Pros and Cons of the Yellow Scenario

The analysts who—like Levitan—approach the future with caution believe that it will be much like the present, at least in the short term. To be sure, there will be some minor changes over the next decade, but *no dramatic changes* as viewed in the Green and Red Scenarios. This is a strong middle-of-the-road position that advises us to look at the past and present to determine the most likely future shape of occupations. The positive aspects of this scenario follow:

- Changes in the workplace will be evolutionary, not revolutionary.
- Changes in the future will still leave the broad outline of the work force about where it is now.
- Changes in the future workplace will tend to involve replacement of current workers rather than growth or creation of new jobs.
- Changes in the workplace will still leave occupations looking a great deal like present occupations—much more alike than different.
- Changes in the workplace will still leave openings for people from all educational backgrounds (with solid, basic skills)—certainly not for the college graduate only, as some would imply.

Any "middle-of-the-road" position, such as this scenario takes, may err on both sides of its projections. Obviously, if the Green Scenario is more nearly true for the year 2000, then the Yellow Scenario will appear much too conservative and will have missed many of the far-reaching occupational and workplace changes predicted. On the other hand, if (as Chapter Five on the Red Scenario outlines) there is a much more dismal swing toward low-paying, part-time jobs with low benefits, then the Yellow Scenario may seem to have been far too optimistic. Past experience suggests, however, that a middle position is more plausible than an extreme one.

The negative aspects of this relatively cautious scenario to the year 2000 can be summarized as follows:

- Changes projected may be too conservative.
- Changes projected may be too optimistic.

What Should Counselors Do?

The publications of the Bureau of Labor Statistics in the Department of Labor and the Bureau of the Census in the Department of Commerce are well known to counselors in the United States. The *Occupational Outlook Handbook (OOH)* is still by all accounts the most widely used single source of career information. Over forty states also have access to career information delivery systems (CIDS), such as Virginia VIEW, the Oregon Career Information System, and the Maine Occupational Information System. (See the current *OOH* for a listing of the names and addresses of these systems in each state.) Most of these state systems are based, at least in part, on national labor market information coming out of the BLS. In short, there is ample information available on the Yellow Scenario. Certainly, counselors need to get new editions of the *OOH* every two years and have current subscriptions to the *Occupational Outlook Quarterly* for more frequent updates on national trends and projections. In addition, full advantage should be taken of the state career information delivery systems. These systems are normally updated every year, and a variety of user workshops are available to help counselors understand and use the systems.

No one ever knows all there is to know about the information in this or any other scenario, because it is always subject to review, revision, and debate. *This is a dynamic, not a static field.* Today's data are perishable and subject to change without notice. Courses taken a decade ago are out of date. Therefore, counselors must constantly strive to keep up with new reports. Fortunately, there are ample ways to do that. The suggestions given above will provide a start, and here are a few more:

1. Belong to national, state, and local affiliates of the American Association for Counseling and Development (AACD) and its divisions, especially the National Career Development Association (NCDA), and read their publications. Also consider joining the American Vocational Association (AVA) and the American Society for Training and Development (ASTD)—or at least subscribe to their publications.
2. Attend meetings of state and local AACD affiliates, making sure that the topics of "career information" and "changes in the workplace" are frequently discussed.
3. Attend at least one regional or state meeting or conference per year on career information and changes in the workplace.
4. Especially in a local group, arrange for at least an occasional forum on the job opportunities that will be available over the next five to ten years.
5. Subscribe to and read the *Occupational Outlook Quarterly (OOQ)* and other state career information publications. Subscription to the *OOQ* costs only $5 per year.

Suggested Readings

Bureau of Labor Statistics. *Occupational Outlook Handbook, 1988–89.* Washington, D.C.: U.S. Government Printing Office, 1988.

The single most used source of career information. Excellent section on "Tomorrow's Jobs," with detailed listings for 200–300 occupations and shorter listings for several hundred other occupations. The *Monthly Labor Review* publishes more technical data, and the *Occupational Outlook Quarterly* updates general information between issues of the *OOH.*

Goldstein, H., and Fraser, B. *Training for Work in the Computer Age: How Workers Who Use Computers Get Their Training.* Washington, D.C.: National Commission for Employment Policy, 1985.

Detailed study of how 140 occupations, which make up about 50 percent of the work force, use computers and how the workers get their training. Excellent report on the *real use* of computers in the workplace.

Hunt, H. A., and Hunt T. L. *Clerical Employment and Technological Change.* Kalamazoo, Mich.: Upjohn Institute for Employment Research, 1986.

The definitive study on the effects of office-based automation on clerical workers. Trends over the past thirty years are examined. Overall, economic growth accounted for nearly three-fourths of the expansion in clerical jobs over the past decade. Technological change played only a minor role in shaping employment of clerical workers.

Levitan, S. A., and Johnson, C. M. *Second Thoughts on Work.* Kalamazoo, Mich.: Upjohn Institute for Employment Research, 1982.

A revision of Levitan and Johnson's (William) *Work Is Here to Stay, Alas* (1973). The authors examine a wealth of data, both past and present, to gauge the relative strength of contemporary claims regarding the future of work. Contrary to predictions of imminent crisis, the evidence indicates that the pace of change will be gradual rather than swift, evolutionary rather than revolutionary.

5

The Red or Stop Scenario: Unemployment and Underemployment

Counselors and others in the helping professions will recognize much of this chapter from news reports on radio and television and in newspaper stories with headlines like these:

- Tobacco Company Offers Early Retirement
- Bakery Closes After Fifty Years' Service
- Steel Mill Shuts Down
- Textile Plant Halts Operation
- Tire Operation Moves Overseas
- White-Collar Jobs Cut Back
- Oil Company to Slash Work Force
- Electrical Shop Moves South of the Border

These various pieces of news fit together into a larger picture—the "Red" Scenario—depicting tomorrow's workplace as a dismal setting for 10–20 million American workers. In more technical terms, those who adopt this point of view emphasize the following:

- Downscaling of the work force
- Underemployment of the work force
- Long-term unemployment in the work force

- Displacements in the work force
- Labor surpluses in the work force
- Bypassed populations in the work force
- Two-tier pay scales in the work force

Whatever term is used, this scenario portrays a future of low-paying and low-skilled jobs for millions in the work force. Among the advocates of this scenario are organizations such as the American Federation of Labor–Congress of Industrial Organizations, in the reports *The Future of Work* (1983) and *Crossroads for America* (1987); economists such as Barry Blueston and Bennett Harrison, in *The Deindustrialization of America* (1982) and *The Great American Job Machine* (1986); and Eli Ginzberg, in *Good Jobs, Bad Jobs, No Jobs* (1979).

The Red Scenario gives the bad news about both today's and tomorrow's workplace. In fact, some would no doubt argue that in those regions of the United States where persistent high unemployment remains a problem, we can already discern the unfolding of this scenario. This chapter presents the case for the Red Scenario in terms of six major themes: (1) the shift away from manufacturing, (2) the downscaling of jobs, (3) continuing high unemployment, (4) the dwindling middle class, (5) outsourcing workers, and (6) weakening job opportunities for college graduates.

Mainly, we will be looking at the big picture or the megatrends in the nation's (and the world's) economy. The more personal side to this story, which has to do with the effect of ''downscaling'' or ''underemployment'' on individual workers, also has been featured in weekly newsmagazines, in the ''people'' sections of the Sunday papers, and on national and local television. A number of books also chronicle the plight of today's displaced workers—for example, *Brave New Workplace* (Howard, 1985) and *Modern Madness: The Emotional Fallout of Success* (LaBier, 1986).

Howard points to the declining importance of work in people's lives—caused by the changes in the workplace that rob workers of their identity and dignity. Working life can be improved, he believes, through the *repersonalization* of the workplace—an effort by labor and management together to assume social control over technology. Howard thinks that the current situation is quite one-sided: control is in the hands of large corporations, and they have a narrow view of what the worker and workplace should be like. He counters the Red Scenario by asking us to look upon the world of work as a realm of democratic social choice.

If Howard focuses on the plight of workers in the lower and middle wage ranges, LaBier (1986) looks mainly at young, upwardly mobile professionals between 27 and 47 years of age and describes the emotional fallout that has accompanied their success. LaBier sees these young professionals, who are in the middle and upper wage ranges, as being dissatisfied with what work is doing to their lives, and he notes that their unhappiness with their work is manifested in feelings of detachment, boredom, anxiety, depression, and anger. Like Howard, LaBier calls for changes in the workplace in order to create a stronger sense of relationship, understanding, and dedication on the part of both employers and employees.

Six Themes

Shifting Away from Manufacturing. Blueston and Harrison (1982, 1986) have called attention to the widespread, systematic disinvestment in the nation's basic productive capacity—that is, industries losing market share, moving plants to overseas locations, or simply going out of business. These changes have been taking place in the "sunset industries" (or rust belt industries) over the past decade, and advocates of the Red Scenario see no significant changes in the decade(s) ahead. The following illustrations have been collected from newspaper clippings and various sources, such as *Crossroads for America* (American Federation of Labor–Congress of Industrial Organizations, 1987):

The Steel Industry
"There is no free trade in steel," conceded
U.S. Labor Secretary Bill Brock when he was the
U.S. Trade Representative in 1984. The Europeans

in 1977 limited their steel imports to 7.5 percent of their consumption, as part of their program to modernize their steel industries. The Japanese import little or no steel from other nations. As a result of the closing of these markets, imports now have captured 26 percent of the U.S. market. More than 200,000 steel production jobs have been lost since 1979—a drastic cut of 60 percent of American steel jobs. By mid-1986 some of America's largest steelmakers, including LTV Corp. and Wheeling-Pittsburgh, had declared bankruptcy—and others are teetering on the edge.

The Auto Industry

The United States has the largest and, among auto-producing nations, the most open market in the world. Until 1980, when Japan surpassed the U.S., we were also the world's largest motor vehicle producer. Behind high tariff walls and with other forms of targeted assistance, Japanese production grew rapidly from 100,000 in 1955 to 6.2 million in 1972—and more than 12 million vehicles produced in 1985. Half the vehicles produced in Japan are now exported—and half of these are sold in the U.S. Yet with the exception of the U.S., every major auto-producing country has limits on Japanese imports ranging from 2,000 in Italy and 2.5 percent of the domestic market in France to 10 percent of the market in Germany and Britain. Japan is currently "restraining" itself to U.S. sales of 2.3 million cars per year; yet more than half of our massive $50 billion trade deficit with Japan was in motor vehicles and parts. Most analysts believe that, in the absence of major changes in management philosophy and U.S. trade and industrial policy, by 1990 the share of our own auto market supplied by domestic production of U.S.-based companies could fall to only 55 percent (from 75

percent in 1985)—and as low as 50 percent when
the effect of imported parts is factored in. That
could mean the loss of another 500,000 jobs from
the auto and supplier industries—on top of the
400,000 lost since 1978. Meanwhile, fewer than
1,900 U.S.-made cars were sold in Japan in 1985.

The Tire Industry

More than thirty tire plants, employing nearly
1,000 workers each on the average, have been permanently closed down since 1973, for a loss of
30,000 U.S. jobs. Imports now hold 25 percent of
the U.S. market, up from 7–8 percent previously.
In Akron, Ohio, once the "tire capital of the world,"
there is no longer even a single production line for
passenger car tires. The few new U.S. tire plants
built in the last ten years are mostly foreign owned,
and none of their workers enjoys the benefits of
union representation.

The Textile and Apparel Industry

Since 1981, there has been a doubling of U.S.
textile and apparel imports and the loss of 350,000
jobs, more than three-quarters of them held by
women and minorities.

The Coal Industry

In one state—West Virginia—the coal industry has lost an estimated 70,000 jobs in the past
thirty years. It happened this way. Before the technological changes of the 1950s, more than 100,000
people worked in West Virginia's coal mines. By
1978 the number had dropped to 63,000 and to
54,000 in 1982 and 35,000 in 1983. Current estimates are at about 30,000 coal miners, with no
growth in sight. Meanwhile, because of improved
productivity, coal production has soared and employment has dropped.

The Railroad Industry

In 1947	4,000,000 workers
1987	400,000 workers
Job Loss =	3,600,000 workers

As an example of the effects of industrial decline, let's look at one American city—Fort Wayne, Indiana. Following the 1983 closing of the International Harvester plant in Fort Wayne, managers and clerical staff who were eventually able to find other jobs took pay cuts of up to 40 percent; the average factory worker's pay cut was 20 percent. It took these workers an average of nearly forty weeks to find their next job, and the toll on the average working family in Fort Wayne was a loss of $6,159 in family assets. Nearly one-fourth of the blue-collar workers and more than one-third of the clerical workers were never able to find another full-time job. These grim realities also caused profound social and personal problems in Fort Wayne.

Another way of understanding the alternative future painted by the Red Scenario writers is to look at the types of new jobs created in the United States economy. Blueston and Harrison (1986) report the following statistics:

- Between 1973 and 1984, nearly 20 million new jobs were added.
- Between 1981 and 1986 alone, 10 million new jobs were added.
- Since 1981 employment in manufacturing has declined by more than 500,000.
- Since 1981 all of the total net growth in the number of civilian jobs has been in private-sector *service* employment.
- Between 1979 and 1984, the number of workers with earnings of $14,024 or more declined by 1.8 million, while workers earning less than $14,024 increased by 9.9 million.
- Since 1979 nearly 97 percent of net employment gains among white men have been in the low-wage jobs.
- Between 1970 and 1980, white women made employment gains in high- and low-wage jobs, but they made very few gains in middle-wage jobs.

- Minority men and women showed a renewed trend toward low-wage jobs.
- The trend toward low-wage jobs was found in all regions of the country—especially the Middle West, where middle- and high-wage employment declined between 1979 and 1984 by more than a million jobs.

Blueston and Harrison (1986) conclude that the economic restructuring of the 1980s—including the loss of jobs in the manufacturing sector, the continued growth of the service economy, and the reorganization of work toward more part-time schedules—has left in its wake a proliferation of low-wage jobs. In fact, 58 percent of all net new employment between 1979 and 1984 paid annual wages of less than $7,000.

The writers of the report *The Future of Work* (American Federation of Labor–Congress of Industrial Organizations, 1983) see clearly the emergence of a "two-tier work force":

As computers and robots take over more and more functions in the factory and the office, a two-tier work force is developing. In some cases, a few jobs are being upgraded. In many other cases, jobs are being downgraded. (In some production processes, computerization may lead to a narrowing of skill differentials between supervisors and production workers when both need detailed knowledge of a relatively complicated process.)

At the top will be a few executives, scientists and engineers, professionals, and managers, performing high-level, creative, high-paid full-time jobs in a good work environment. And the executives among them will decide whether the work will be done by people or by robots, whether the work will be done in Terre Haute or Taiwan.

At the bottom will be low-paid workers performing relatively simple, low-skill, dull, routine, high-turnover jobs in a poor work environment. These jobs will often be part time and usually lacking job security and opportunities for career

advancement. Too often these jobs are oversuper-
vised and lacking in any control over the pace of
work.

Between these two major tiers will be fewer
and fewer permanent, well-paid, full-time, skilled,
semiskilled, and craft production and maintenance
jobs, which in the past have offered hope and opportunity and upward mobility to workers who start
in low-paid, entry-level jobs. Many middle-management jobs will also be gone [p. 8].

Downscaling of Jobs. What does the shift away from manufacturing mean to millions of workers in the United States? Two
main sources will be utilized to paint this part of the picture:
Good Jobs, Bad Jobs, No Jobs (Ginzberg, 1979) and *Technology and
Structural Unemployment: Reemploying Displaced Adults* (Office of
Technological Assessment, 1986). Ginzberg studied workplace
trends from 1950 to 1976 and concluded that three kinds of conditions were emerging:

1. *Good Jobs*
   - High wages
   - Attractive fringe benefits
   - Regular employment (full time)
   - Positive working conditions
   - Job security
   - Opportunities for promotion
2. *Bad Jobs*
   - Low wages
   - Minimal or no fringe benefits
   - Intermittent or part-time work
   - Poor working conditions
   - Lack of job security
   - Limited opportunities for advancement
3. *No Jobs*
   - High levels of unemployment
   - Large numbers of "discouraged workers"
   - Long-term unemployment
   - 10–20 million *different* people unemployed each year

Over the past twenty-six years, Ginzberg concluded, most of the job growth has been in "bad jobs." These jobs are mainly in service industries, where weekly earnings are below average—either because the industries pay low hourly rates (as in retailing) or because they provide less than full-time work, and often for both reasons. Between 1950 and 1976, about two and a half times as many new jobs (18.2 million versus 7.1 million) were added in industries that provide below-average weekly earnings as were added in industries that provide above-average earnings. More than three out of every five new jobs created were in retail trade or services, where many jobs are part time and wages are traditionally low. (See Table 6.)

Overall, the labor market statistics lend substantial support to the view that the United States economy has developed a *dual labor market*, in which white men have preferred access to the "good jobs" while women and members of minority groups generally get trapped in "bad jobs." In general, Ginzberg does not see significant changes in this long-term trend unless social and economic policies are changed so that a much larger array of "good jobs" will be available—especially for women and minorities.

Another dimension of the downscaling of jobs was reported by the Office of Technological Assessment (1986). This

Table 6. Average 1987 Hourly Wage Rates
in Declining and Expanding Industries.

Declining Industries		*Expanding Industries*	
Metal Mining	$13.00	Finance, insurance, real estate	$ 8.76
Leather manufacturing	6.06	Retail trade	6.12
Textile manufacturing	7.18	Services, all fields	8.47
Tobacco manufacturing	13.81	Wholesale trade	9.61
Tires and tubes	14.03	Hotel and lodgings	6.12
Steel manufacturing	13.84	Food service	4.41
Petroleum and coal products refining	15.72	Business services (guards, custodial, computer service)	8.71
Lumber	8.40	Health services	8.70
Railroads	14.26	Telephone	13.21

Source: Bureau of Labor Statistics data, 1988e, pp. 82–97.

report focused on the displaced worker—a person who had held a job for at least three years and was laid off because automation, changing trade conditions, offshore production, and changing consumption patterns had led to plant closings or relocations, abolition of positions on a shift, or slack work. Between January 1979 and January 1984, 11.5 million workers lost their jobs for just such reasons. Of those 11.5 million workers, 5.1 million had had their jobs for at least three years and were considered displaced workers. For the most part, these displaced workers had to learn new skills, relocate, or look for other permanent work.

By January 1984, 1.3 million of the 5.1 million displaced workers were still unemployed; some 500,000 had been unemployed for more than twenty-seven weeks. About 730,000 people had left the labor force (meaning that they were not looking for work), some by choice but many out of discouragement or by retiring earlier than they might have wished. During the entire five-year period, nearly one-fourth of the 5.1 million displaced workers were without work for more than a year. Many of the 3.1 million workers who were reemployed had experienced real difficulties finding new jobs. During the five years, nearly one-third of those who found jobs and who reported their earnings had taken pay cuts of 20 percent or more, and over one-tenth of former full-time workers had taken part-time work.

Displaced workers are typically white males of prime working age with a steady work history in a blue-collar job in the Midwest or Northeast. However, many other groups are represented. One-third of displaced workers are women; 12 percent are black; 18 percent are over 55. Forty percent of the full-time work force is female, 11 percent is black, and 12 percent is over 55. Even though women are actually underrepresented in the population of displaced workers, and black people are represented in proportion to their share of the work force, these groups fared significantly worse than white men in regaining employment after being displaced.

Less skilled and less educated workers are more likely to be displaced and are also more likely to have trouble finding new jobs. Among the 5.1 million workers displaced from 1979 to 1984, the most overrepresented occupational group by far was machine operators, assemblers, and repairers, who comprised 22 percent of the displaced workers but only about 7.5 percent of the work force. Less likely to be displaced and more likely to find replacement jobs were professionals; executive, administrative, and managerial workers; technicians; salespeople; and service workers.

The occupational group most at risk (machine operators, assemblers, and repairers) is concentrated in manufacturing, and, indeed, manufacturing workers experienced job losses far out of proportion to their numbers. Nearly half of the displaced workers were from manufacturing. The largest job losses occurred in nonelectrical machinery, automobiles, primary metals, and textiles and apparel. Together, these four sectors accounted for nearly 21 percent of all displaced workers, although they employ only about 6 percent of the work force.

Geographically, the hardest hit was the Great Lakes region—Michigan, Ohio, Indiana, Illinois, and Wisconsin. This region accounted for 24 percent of the displaced but only about 18 percent of the work force. The Middle Atlantic area (New York, New Jersey, and Pennsylvania) and the East South Central region (Mississippi, Alabama, Tennessee, and Kentucky) also had more than their share of displaced workers as reported by an MDC (1986) report, *Shadows in the Sunbelt*. Since these regions also are centers of manufacturing, this regional concentration is not surprising.

Displaced homemakers are another part of the larger displaced worker picture. These are women whose principal occupation has been homemaking and who have lost their main source of financial support because of becoming divorced, widowed, or separated; or they are married but their husbands are unable or unwilling to support them. Estimates of the number of displaced homemakers range from more than 2 million to about 4 million. Displaced homemakers share problems of finding good jobs with other displaced workers, but the barriers they face are often greater because they lack job experience or because their existing skills are not transferable to new "good jobs," so that they may need retraining or education in order to find steady, well-paid work. In short, the portrayal of the 5.1 million displaced workers in the labor force gives solid support to those who advocate the Red Scenario.

Continuing High Unemployment. The Red Scenario writers point to the continuing high unemployment rate (see Table 7 and Figure 4) as solid evidence to support their position. The unemployment "lows" are getting higher every ten years, and the "highs" also are getting higher every decade; and no changes in this trend are forecast. The long-term (forty-year) forecasts show the "highs" continuing to move up each decade.

The Council on International and Public Affairs has released a series of reports entitled *The Underbelly of the U.S. Economy: Joblessness and Pauperization of Work in America* (Morehouse and Dembo, 1984–1988). In these reports the "jobless rate" takes into account "all those who want a full-time job but cannot find one." By this definition, the official figures put out by the Bureau of Labor Statistics do not reflect what is really taking place in the labor market, because (1) part-time workers who want full-time work are included in the Bureau of Labor Statistics full-time employed rate, (2) discouraged workers who have not tried to find work in the preceding four weeks are not included in the BLS unemployment figures, and (3) civilians who are not in the labor force and cannot find jobs also are not included in the BLS unemployment rate. (See Table 8 for some comparison figures in late 1985.)

Table 7. Unemployment Rates, 1950s–1980s.

1950s	Low	2.9 (1953)
	High	6.8 (1958)
1960s	Low	3.5 (1969)
	High	6.7 (1961)
1970s	Low	4.9 (1970 and 1973)
	High	8.5 (1975)
1980s	Low	5.3 (1988)
	High	10.4 (1983)

Source: Bureau of Labor Statistics, 1988b p. 489; 1988d p. 8.

Figure 4. Unemployment Rates, 1950–1983.

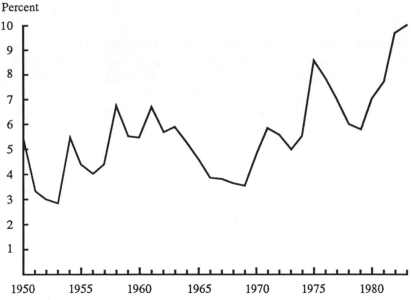

Source: Bureau of Labor Statistics, 1988b p. 489; 1988d p. 8.

Dwindling of the Middle Class. According to Kuttner (1983), in his controversial article on "The Declining Middle," most of the current jobs are in high- or low-paying portions of the new service economy, and the middle-income jobs have dwindled. Between 1958 and 1968, he points out, service industries added 4 million jobs, and state and local government added another 3.5 million. In contrast, manufacturing, which pays on average about three times the minimum wage, lost 3–4 million jobs in the early 1980s. High-paying (middle-class) construction and production work taken together account for about one job in eight today, compared with one in four in 1950. The wage curve once looked like the normal curve of distribution: a few high- and low-paying jobs at both ends and most middle-income jobs in the middle. Now, there is not much of a middle left.

Neal Rosenthal, chief of the Occupational Outlook section of the Bureau of Labor Statistics, takes the opposite point

Table 8. Comparison of BLS Civilian Unemployment Rate with Jobless Rate. (Numbers are in thousands.)

	1977	1978	1979	1980	1981	1982	1983	1984	1985	1986	1987
BLS civilian labor force	99,009.	102,251.	104,962.	106,940.	108,670.	110,204.	111,550.	113,544.	115,461.	117,834.	119,865.
BLS civilian employment	92,017.	96,048.	98,824.	99,303.	100,397.	99,526.	100,834.	105,005.	107,150.	109,597.	112,440.
BLS unemployed	6,991.	6,202.	6,137.	7,637.	8,273.	10,717.	10,717.	8,539.	8,312.	8,237.	7,425.
BLS unemployment rate	7.1%	6.1%	5.8%	7.1%	7.6%	9.7%	9.6%	7.5%	7.2%	7.0%	6.2%
Part-time employment	21,204.	21,441.	22,918.	22,930.	26,012.	25,439.	24,895.	24,427.	24,682.	25,226.	28,007.
Discouraged workers	1,026.	863.	771.	993.	1,103.	1,568.	1,641.	1,283.	1,204.	1,121.	1,026.
Civilians not in the labor force who want jobs	5,775.	5,446.	5,427.	5,675.	5,835.	6,559.	6,503.	6,070.	5,933.	5,825.	5,714.
Jobless persons	14,048.	12,981.	12,907.	14,877.	15,878.	19,546.	19,725.	16,791.	16,320.	16,154.	18,542.
Jobless rate	14.4%	12.9%	12.5%	14.4%	14.9%	17.9%	17.8%	15.0%	14.3%	13.9%	15.8%

Source: Morehouse and Dembo, 1988, p. 4. Based on U.S. Department of Labor, Bureau of Labor Statistics, *Employment and Earnings*, various issues, 1978–1988.

of view. Rosenthal (1985), using Bureau of Labor Statistics data, shows that top-, middle-, and lower-wage occupations have gained roughly the same wage increases in the 1973–1982 time period. He also argues that, even though there has been declining employment in "smokestack" or "sunset" goods-producing industries, the overall earnings for those who are left are not significantly different. Finally, industries as a whole pay their production workers (the largest group of employees in these industries) a strong middle-class wage. According to Rosenthal, the declines in wages between 1960 and the middle 1970s have not persisted. The trends in the last decade are toward a balanced three-tier (not two) wage range in the work force. The controversy goes on. Is the middle class dwindling?

Creation of a Large Contingent Work Force. According to Pollock and Berstein (1986), "contingent workers" (sometimes called "dispensable," "expendable," "disposable," or "leased" employees) could make up as much as 25 percent of the work force. Some of these workers are just plain part-time workers who, in many cases, would rather work full time. Since 1983, for example, the number of airline part-timers has more than doubled to 49,000 or about 12 percent of all workers in the industry. In retailing, part-timers make up an estimated one-third of the entire retail employee work force. Bureau of Labor Statistics figures show that the average wage for part-time workers is $4.17 per hour, whereas the average wage for full-time workers is $7.05. Moreover, about 70 percent of part-timers have no employer-provided retirement plan, and 42 percent have no health insurance coverage.

Pollock and Berstein cite as an example a pipe fitter with ten years' seniority who is laid off from his job at a Gary, Indiana, steel mill. He was making $13 an hour and receiving ample fringe benefits. Later, he was hired back through a subcontract at $5 per hour and no benefits. Such "subcontract workers" make up an estimated 7.5 percent of the steelmakers' work force, up from 3 percent in the mid-1970s. This entire process is referred to as turning core workers (regular full-time workers) into contingent ones.

All this movement toward something other than full-time jobs has greatly expanded the activity of the temporary help agencies, such as Kelly Services and Manpower Temporary Services. Between 1970 and 1986, the number of people employed by all temporary help firms grew by more than 400 percent, from 184,000 to 760,000. Often a company may dismiss a worker who is then hired by a temporary help agency, or the company may contract for a new worker through the same temporary help agency. In either case the producing company pays the temporary help agency for wages and benefits but can control the worker's time on the job, depending on needs of the marketplace. Thus, a company can control costs and the size of its work force by maintaining only a small core of regular full-time workers.

This practice is now the subject of union-management negotiations in the auto and steel industries, and the U.S. Senate is expected to take a look at the practice in hearings originally scheduled for 1988. If companies continue to create large contingent work forces, the long-time economic outlook for millions of workers without permanent full-time employment will be dismal.

Weakening Job Opportunities for College Graduates. In a study of U.S. Bureau of the Census data over three decades (1960s through 1980s) Rumberger (1983) found that labor market opportunities for college graduates declined from the 1960s to the 1970s and 1980s, at least in terms of the types of jobs secured. But comparisons with earlier periods reveal that the 1960s were atypical; graduates in that period enjoyed better opportunities than graduates either before or after.

Between 1960 and 1980, the educational attainments of the United States labor force grew phenomenally. The number of persons with four or more years of college increased 200 percent. By 1980 almost one out of five workers had completed a college degree, and more than one out of four young workers had acquired that much education. Employment in professional, high-level occupations also grew rapidly during this period, but it could not keep pace with the growth in educational attainment. (See Table 9.)

Table 9. Employment by Occupational Categories and Education of
Inexperienced Workers, 1960, 1970, 1980.

	1960	1970	1980
Proportion with high-level jobs:			
Less than high school	3.2	2.6	2.1
High school graduates	6.7	6.4	6.8
College 1–3 years	23.7	18.8	17.5
College 4 years	67.9	73.9	60.5
College 5+ years	74.7	80.5	76.0
Proportion of four-year college graduates with:			
Professional jobs	66.3	70.0	47.5
Managerial jobs	4.8	5.9	14.4
Sales jobs	9.9	6.2	7.8
Clerical jobs	12.5	10.6	15.1
Other jobs	6.5	7.3	15.2

Note: Sample consists of all employed workers, 16 years old and over,
except those working without pay, with five years of experience or less (Experience = Age – Years of schooling – 6).
Source: Rumberger, 1983, p. 30; citing data from U.S. Bureau of the
Census.

Even before the rapid expansion of higher education, not
all college graduates were assured of high-level jobs; one-third
were employed outside professional and managerial occupations
in 1960. During the 1960s, despite their growing numbers,
young college graduates increased their chances of finding high-
level jobs. The decade was a golden era for college graduates.
But during the 1970s opportunities deteriorated. By 1980 the
situation for new college graduates was similar to the situation
in 1960. The rise and fall in opportunities was especially pro-
nounced among women, who were much more dependent than
men on changing opportunities in the teaching profession.

The outlook for the 1980s and 1990s also appears bleak,
according to Rumberger (1983). Educational attainments of the
work force will continue to increase, largely because older, less
educated workers will be replaced by younger, more educated
workers. Employment growth will not produce widespread opportunities in high-level, high-technology fields, contrary to conventional beliefs. In fact, employment growth in professional
and managerial occupations will be smaller than in either the

1960s or the 1970s. College graduates may continue to hold a competitive advantage in the labor market and have a low unemployment rate, but an increasing number will be forced to accept jobs not commensurate with their level of training.

Pros and Cons of the Red Scenario

The writers whose ideas have been reviewed in this chapter see a relatively bleak occupational outlook for the 1990s and beyond. Much of this unhappy forecast comes about because of significant national and international forces, such as:

- Continuing problems in the United States import-export balance
- Flood of imports in basic United States industries, such as steel, auto, textiles, rubber, and electronics
- Shifting world market for United States products
- Eroding of the United States industrial base

These factors and the six themes presented in this chapter lead to the following conclusions about the Red or Stop scenario:

1. The future looks grim for some 10–20 million workers in the United States. They can expect to be unemployed or underemployed for extended periods of time over the next decade or so. Many will never regain the earnings level they once had.
2. Most (but by no means all) of the new jobs being created are low-skilled, low-paying jobs in the private service sector of the economy, often available to workers on less than a full-time, regular employee basis.
3. The future looks grim for a growing underclass of workers whose jobs are being deskilled, downshifted, or downgraded into what some call a dual or two-tier work force.

The AFL-CIO (1983) calls this a labor surplus economy with too few jobs and too many workers. Clearly, a major challenge for tomorrow's workplace will be to provide job opportunities for a larger portion of the work force over the next ten to twenty years than have been provided for the past ten to twenty years. Strong innovative thinking will be needed to deal with a labor surplus economy. Whatever the case, there are some pros and cons to this scenario. Not everyone agrees on all the points raised. Here are some of the more controversial ones:

1. This scenario is too negative and pessimistic and focuses too much attention on certain current problems.
2. This scenario presents just one side of the changing world of work—the downhill picture.
3. This scenario is too political in its point of view and presents only a narrow perspective—not the larger, brighter side of the issue.
4. This scenario makes things like trimming down bloated middle-management positions look bad when they are really good, since they enable companies to deal with overstaffing problems.
5. This scenario makes working less than full time (with full benefits and wages) sound bad, whereas many people want to work part time or as temporary workers.

What Should Counselors Do?

Like the other two scenarios described in Part Three, this one has some strong and compelling evidence to support it. For example, the number of workers employed by temporary help firms in the period 1970–1986 grew by more than 400 percent, from 184,000 to 760,000, with no end in sight. Counselors should keep up not only with the Green Scenario's predictions of bright futures and plenty of high-tech occupations but also with the less optimistic forecasts of the Yellow and Red Scenarios. Some have labeled the Red Scenario the bleak underside of high tech.

The impact of the Red Scenario differs widely from place to place around the country. Here are some specific action suggestions:

1. To get a feel for the extent of its impact in your locale and state, invite state employment commission representatives

to speak to counselor groups about the jobless rate versus the unemployment rate.

2. Try to determine from area union and management officials the extent to which contingency workers are being used in your region.

3. Invite some young workers to appear before counselor groups to talk about their jobs. Find out whether they most nearly represent the type of person described in Howard's *Brave New Workplace* or LaBier's *Modern Madness*.

4. Have someone review reports of state and regional economic development forecasts and studies by the state extension service on this subject.

5. Get the local newspaper to carry a series of articles on the topic or arrange a series of local forums on the three scenarios.

6. Plan a local counselors' meeting with representatives of some of the temporary help outfits, such as Kelly Services, Manpower Temporary Services, or Norrell Services, to become informed about their current activities.

7. Invite a panel of workers 30–50 years of age who have recently lost their jobs (because of plant closings or layoffs) to speak informally to a group of counselors about the effects of the job loss on their personal lives.

Because it is "bad news," there is a tendency not to want to read or hear too much about this scenario. It is strongly suggested here that finding out all there is to know about *all three* scenarios is an important ongoing objective. Reading a book or going to a meeting will not do it. This is a matter for continuously updated information. Changing economic, social, and political conditions create a climate whereby there is a constant need to be well informed on current conditions as well as medium- and long-range forecasts—from a variety of points of view.

Suggested Readings

American Federation of Labor–Congress of Industrial Organizations. *The Future of Work.* Washington, D.C.: AFL-CIO, 1983.

Report by the Committee on the Evolution of Work proclaims that the United States is a labor-surplus society with persistent shortages of jobs (4–6 million) for able and willing workers. The result of a labor surplus is excessively and persistently high unemployment, which creates an underclass and threatens the stability of the nation's economic, social, and political institutions.

Blueston, B., and Harrison, B. *The Deindustrialization of America: Plant Closings, Community Abandonment, and the Dismantling of Basic Industry.* New York: Basic Books, 1982.

The one book to read to get a sense of the depth of the feeling behind the Red Scenario. The authors detail the decline of the American manufacturing system with a careful analysis of the facts over the past twenty-five years. They see the results of this deindustrialization as shuttered factories, displaced workers, and a newly emerging group of ghost towns.

Ginzberg, E. *Good Jobs, Bad Jobs, No Jobs.* Cambridge, Mass.: Harvard University Press, 1979.

The author takes a long look at the post–World War II economy from 1950 to 1973 and does not like what he sees— namely, a dual labor market where there are a few really good jobs and plenty of bad jobs with low pay, poor benefits, and no job security. The current alternative to these two choices is *no jobs.* Ginzberg outlines his sometimes unorthodox solutions and calls for policy changes that are needed to create millions of *good jobs.*

Howard, R. *Brave New Workplace,* New York: Viking Penguin, 1985.

A serious look at some of the early implications of the postindustrial workplace. Howard sees inequities and increasing social conflicts in corporate America. He feels that corporations are using new technologies to expand managerial control at the expense of worker satisfaction, autonomy, and even efficiency. He calls for a repersonalization of the workplace.

Morehouse, W. and Dembo, D. *The Underbelly of the U.S. Economy: Joblessness and Pauperization of Work in America.* Special Reports 1–7. New York: Council on International and Public Affairs, 1984–1988.

    A series of quarterly reports by the staff of the Council on International and Public Affairs, based in New York. The reports look at changing patterns of work and show how they are affected by changes in technology in the United States, other industrialized societies, and the Third World.

Rumberger, R. W. *The Job Market for College Graduates, 1960–1990.* Palo Alto, Calif.: Institute for Research on Educational Finance and Government, Stanford University, 1983.

    This study of college graduates takes a look at Bureau of the Census data since 1960 to determine where the graduates are working. The results show the 1960s and early 1970s as unusually bright periods for employment of college graduates. In the 1950s and the 1980s, a more normal situation—more competition for jobs—prevailed.

PART THREE

Wild Cards in the Changing Workplace: New Career Possibilities

This part of the book examines three relatively unknown aspects of tomorrow's workplace—entrepreneurship, small business, and work at home—which are here referred to as ''wild cards in the work game.'' While there is no shortage of opinions about the current status and future impact of these three options, there are few hard facts about the scope of any of them. No one really knows how many people, here and now, are actually engaged in these three areas. As a result, it is impossible to determine how entrepreneurship, small business, and work at home might expand or contract in the future.

Nevertheless, indications from various sources suggest that these three areas of employment do offer great promise. An increasing number of economists—and even some politicians— see these three options as the areas of growth and excitement in the United States over the next several decades. Here, then, may be the new directions for the work force of the year 2000. Some of these new jobs will come under the heading of ''high technology,'' but high tech will not be the only, or even perhaps the major, influence on future job opportunities relating to the three wild cards in the work game.

In general, entrepreneurship, small business, and work at home are not emphasized in traditional counseling or teaching at any educational level or in any setting. When there is a Career Day, large employers in the area are invited in to talk about large-scale employment. For Job Placement Days, representatives from the nearby electrical manufacturing plant, the big textile company, or the automotive parts industry are invited to meet with students and discuss possible work opportunities. Although large companies undoubtedly will continue to hire replacement workers, the trend is clearly toward jobs in the three areas covered in this part of the book. Counselors, teachers, and others in the helping professions will need to consider what is out there in new and emerging areas of work as well as keeping an eye on the traditional places of employment. It is not an either/or situation! Tomorrow's workers will find a growing number of opportunities in the area of the three wild cards, as well as with conventional employers. Here is a thumbnail sketch of the contents of Part Three:

Chapter Six, on entrepreneurship, explores the type of business enterprise that is truly innovative in the sense that it creates a genuinely new product and even changes the habits and values of consumers. This spirit of enterprise has promoted creativity and delivery of all kinds of job opportunities in just about every aspect of the American work setting, manufacturing, and service alike. The chapter discusses the special attractiveness of entrepreneurship to women and minorities and describes seven especially noteworthy entrepreneurial businesses.

Chapter Seven, on the growth of small business, presents a profile of small businesses nationwide and gives particular attention to a major source of small business opportunity, namely, franchising. Again, seven examples of successful small businesses, including three franchises, are provided. Advice is given to counselors on how they can become better informed about what is happening in this growing sector of employment.

Chapter Eight explores the growing work-at-home trend. It describes various types of self-employment at home (traditional occupations, such as music teacher and free-lance photographer; direct sales; crafts, including cottage industries; and miscellaneous jobs such as house sitting or operating a bed-and-breakfast establishment). Once again, seven examples of successful work-at-home people are presented, and some suggestions on how counselors can relate to what is happening on the "home front" are given.

Counselors should also take note that there is some overlap in the occupations discussed in these three chapters. It is certainly possible for an entrepreneur to operate a small business or sole proprietorship and to work at home. But the point of these chapters is to emphasize the importance of these three areas in creating new types of job opportunities for enterprising and adventurous individuals.

6

Lures of Entrepreneurship

This chapter sketches out for counselors and others some of the promising opportunities available due to the lure of entrepreneurship. For the most part the topic of entrepreneurship only grabs an occasional headline or minimal space in a professional journal, but it is one of the cutting edges of a changing world of work and leisure. This chapter draws together some of the many parts of this puzzle.

One of the "in" words of the 1980s is *entrepreneurship*. The term is tossed around so much and is so loosely defined that almost any businessperson can be termed an entrepreneur. There are plenty of books and magazines on the subject. Probably the most notable magazine is *Venture,* which concentrates its news and features on entrepreneurial business owners and investors. The magazines *Black Enterprise* and *Entrepreneur* also focus attention on entrepreneurial activities. An association consisting of college students and faculty—called the Association of Collegiate Entrepreneurs (ACE for short)—also is promoting the topic. This association publishes a newsletter, holds a national convention, and issues an annual list of the "top 100 young entrepreneurs" (30 years old or younger). The 1987 list included the following names:

- Brett Davis, 28, Troy Nichols Mortgage, a lender in Dallas; 1986 revenues $1.1 billion
- Michael Dell, 22, PC's Limited, mail-order computer components, Austin, Texas; $75 million

- Debbi Fields, 30, Mrs. Field's Cookies, Park City, Utah; $70 million
- Stephen King, 30, Pizza Huts of Cincinnati Inc.; $44.5 million
- Jay Adoni, 28, Admos Shoe Corp., shoe manufacturer in Brooklyn, New York; $35 million
- David Copperfield, 30, David Copperfield's Disappearing, Inc., magician and magic supplies, Los Angeles; $30 million
- James Calano, 29, CareerTrack, Inc., seminar presenters, Boulder, Colorado; $26 million
- Kevin Curran, 27, and Doug Macrae, 28, General Computer, hardware manufacturer and software publisher, Cambridge, Massachusetts; $26 million
- Keith McClusky, 27, McClusky Chevrolet, a dealership in Cincinnati; $20 million

But it might be asked why the subject of entrepreneurship rates a separate chapter in this book. Very simply, the recent expansion of job opportunities in the United States is, in large part, the direct result of entrepreneurial activity. Moreover, recognition and encouragement of this type of activity are bound to produce a ripple effect: As a new venture expands and becomes successful, it is very likely to hire more employees and thereby contribute to even faster job growth. So entrepreneurship is important both for its own sake and as a potential stimulator of job creation and development.

Definitions of entrepreneurship are plentiful. There is an *Encyclopedia of Entrepreneurship* (Kent, Sexton, and Vesper, 1982), and an ample number of scholarly papers and texts are available on the subject. After reviewing some 250 years of definitions of entrepreneurship, Long (1983) came up with three essential elements: (1) uncertainty and risk, (2) complementary managerial competence, and (3) creative opportunism. According to Long, these terms have been interwoven in various permutations in just about all the historical or classical definitions of entrepreneurship. Herbert and Link (1982) also introduce the terms *innovation* and *adjustment to disequilibria* as necessary to any definition of this activity. After noting that entrepreneurial ventures do not have to involve high risks, provided that people know what they are doing and use good judgment, Drucker (1985) points out that such activities (1) need to be systematic, (2) need to be managed, and (3) need to be based on *purposeful* innovation.

Ray Kroc, who at age 52 started McDonald's in 1955, is a classic example of the entrepreneur. Kroc became fascinated by the efficiency and the fine food at a drive-in restaurant operated by the McDonald brothers in San Bernardino, California. He decided to learn their system and bought the rights to use their name and to franchise their operation. Because it combined value to the customer with a standardized product, a simple process, and tools to deliver the product, McDonald's was virtually an overnight success. It has since become a multi-billion-dollar industry that has changed the eating-out habits of Americans.

In contrast, a brother and sister who open a new sporting goods store in a shopping mall are simply gambling on the continuing popularity of certain recreational activities. They are not creating new consumer demand or stimulating new sources of satisfaction. Therefore, the sporting goods store is simply a small business; it is not an entrepreneurial enterprise.

The term *entrepreneur* is not tied to size or growth or individual or corporate undertaking. For example, the General Electric Company, an old-line major manufacturing company, frequently starts entrepreneurial ventures. One such venture, G. E. Credit, has created an entirely new look in commercial credit and broken the banks' longstanding lock on commercial loans. Large firms that try to keep this spirit of innovation alive have sometimes called it *intrapreneurship,* because it occurs within the company and enables the company to keep some of its highly creative and innovative people, who might otherwise leave to work in smaller entrepreneurship firms.

This chapter will now turn to some of the reasons for the surge of interest in entrepreneurship and why this area may be of special interest to women and minorities. It will then give seven examples of ongoing entrepreneurial businesses and make some suggestions as to what counselors and others in the helping professions can do to become better informed about the subject.

Entrepreneurial Era

In line with the widely held belief that various economic and social phenomena move in cycles, there are a number of writers who think that the United States and many countries abroad are entering a period of intense entrepreneurial activity. Drucker (1985), for example, contends that the United States is about to begin a significantly new period of development—a period during which we will have an "entrepreneurial economy" in an "entrepreneurial society." He calls for an overhaul of our various systems to create this new society. Our educational system, for example, must begin to promote the teaching of entrepreneurial values, concepts, principles, and examples from kindergarten through college. Our political system should provide tax incentives to start new ventures, should encourage the formation of innovative groups, and should reward outstanding leadership in entrepreneurial activities.

Once the framework for such a new system has been established, there can be a normal, steady, and continuous flow of new entrepreneurial starts. There will be some failures along the way, of course, but this kind of system would create flexible and self-renewing practices and would motivate individuals to work hard for the success of their enterprises. Drucker thinks that, for the most part, these enterprises should be decentralized, autonomous, and small-scale operational units in both public and private settings.

Drucker also argues that high-tech enterprises represent only *one* aspect of innovation and entrepreneurship. An important one to be sure, but not the major one, as the great bulk of innovations are in other areas. Between 1970 and 1985, he points out, high-technology firms created about 6 million jobs (approximately the same number that were lost by employees in declining manufacturing and other industries). In that same period, 35 million other jobs were created in new enterprises that were not high tech at all; most were at best middle tech or low tech or even no tech!

Botkin, Dimancescu, and Stata (1984) believe, as Drucker does, that the United States is on the verge of a new wave of social-economic development. They think that we should focus on the *innovators,* that is, on those individuals who are providing the creative ideas that will fuel this new wave of opportunity. They urge us to embrace and encourage the innovative process, and they call for a new spirit of participation in such innovative activities as the creation of new products and services; the development of new production processes and management styles for various work settings; and, most important, the opening up of new jobs in new ventures. The authors note, in addition, that this spirit of innovation can be applied to older industries as a way of revitalizing them.

Botkin, Dimancescu, and Stata see the United States as a country that delivers on new ideas rather than simply talking about them. To them, it is this "can-do" spirit that should be fostered as we turn our attention to the innovative process. We must teach young people about this process, recognize its many different forms, and place proper value on its outcomes. This in turn requires a correct mix of innovative practices in the public (nonprofit) and private sectors, in concert with or separate from the educational community.

An example of this innovative process in operation can be observed at Interknitting Ltd. of Cobleskill, New York. The plant opened ten years ago with ten employees in an abandoned textile mill. The work force has grown to 240 employees, and the plant operates twenty-four hours a day. Owner Bruno Hofmann has been successful in the tough textile market because he has developed a modern operation that goes for a specialized market—designer fabrics. The heart of the operation is a research and development staff of six design specialists with eight knitting machines working on new product design. In this setting innovative risks are taken, and everybody works hard. Success for the past decade in this plant shows how the application of the innovative, entrepreneurial model works.

Growing Opportunities for Women and Minorities

Entrepreneurship offers special opportunities for women and minorities because they can build their own firms and not have to fight their way up through an entrenched corporate or bureaucratic structure. Or, at least, they can work in a smaller and less structured setting that offers entrepreneurial opportunities.

A recent report in *USA Today* indicated that $18 billion had been generated in 1982 by firms in which Asian-Americans and American Indians were the principal owners ("Asian, Native Americans . . . , 1986). Most of these businesses are small because that is the typical enterprise in the community-oriented background of these minority individuals. Owners of the businesses say that they work hard and put in long hours so that they can eventually pass the business along to the next generation in the family. This generation-to-generation concern seems especially strong in Asian-Americans; therefore, entrepreneurial activity is a way to pass on the financial heritage of the family. According to the report, only one-fifth of the firms hired outside help. Most of these firms were in food services (such as restaurants or bars), retail sales, health services, and automotive services (auto dealerships and service stations). A small but growing number were in computer-related businesses.

The magazine *Black Enterprise* has been a showcase for models of promising black-owned businesses. In the June issue each year, the magazine features the top 100 black businesses. The magazine also carries a host of articles on where to get help in launching a new venture. For example, one recent article described the Minority Business Development Agency (MBDA), which in 1985 provided assistance to 9,000 individuals, mostly black. Some of the profiles in *Black Enterprise* are of successful businesses owned by blacks. For instance, in 1985 Raymond N. Johnson's Interstate Landscaping Company made $60 million, and the J. E. Ethridge Construction Company made $20.7 million. There are also models of successful young business types. For example, Kenneth Carter, age 15, is chief executive officer of K. C. Catering Service, which he began when he was 13 years old. He has a staff of ten but does most of the food shopping himself. He clears at least $600 per event and in 1985 grossed $10,000.

A recent book, *America's New Women Entrepreneurs* (Harrison, 1986), provides women in business with helpful information on the tactics and techniques of achieving success. In doing this, it features thirty-two women who have made it to the top in their business or profession and who, according to Harrison, have two characteristics in common:

1. Commitment. Each of them was driven to go far beyond the 9-to-5 job concept, and each realized that the road to success would mean long hours and hard work.
2. Self-Confidence. All these women strongly believed that they could make a contribution. In the early stages of an entrepreneurial journey, this may mean acting more confidently than one actually feels. With a series of successes, however, true confidence will follow.

In addition, all of them put their energies into being innovative and creative, that is, into finding the new and novel edge in a business or profession. They also had a genuine love for the line of work they were in and tried to contribute to its advancement, as opposed to being in the work simply for the sake of money. Finally, they were willing to take risks and were not afraid of failure, recognizing that vital lessons can be learned from a setback. What is all-important here is the courage to take the initial risks. That is the difference between able people and entrepreneurs—being willing to take the *risks!*

Some of the women whose insights appear in this book are:

- Mary Kay Ash, chairman, Mary Kay Cosmetics
- Dale Hanson Bourk, president, Publishing Directions
- Mary C. Crowley, president, Home Interiors & Gifts, Inc.
- Donna Epp, president, Creative Fabric Design, Inc.
- Marge Schott, president and owner, Cincinnati Reds
- Lynette Spano Vives, president, Software Control International

For women who merely want to have some independence and freedom through entrepreneurship, magazines such as *Working Woman* and *Working Mother* feature articles about entrepreneurial opportunities on a smaller scale. Similarly, a book entitled *Entrepreneurial Mothers* (Gillis, 1984) provides background on successful models, and suggestions on how to get ideas, how to put those ideas into practice, and how to balance the delicate relationship between work and family. Gillis calls these emerging opportunities "microbusinesses"—smaller, more personal firms that put more emphasis on initiative and creativity and can result in better products and services. This type of business may start out in the home, with just the woman working part time and also handling her homemaking duties. In time, the woman may decide to rent outside work space and to hire part-time or full-time employees as the business expands. These microbusinesses are for the most part service oriented, but they can be product focused as well. They are built on well-grounded and familiar skills of the women, with as little start-up capital as possible.

This type of microbusiness—growing out of the innovation, creativity, and risk taking on the part of the entrepreneurial mothers—can provide thousands of job opportunities. For example, a woman who enjoys growing and arranging flowers may begin to attract the attention of friends and neighbors. She may be asked to choose and arrange flowers for their parties and then for church socials, receptions, and weddings. As the social occasions become larger and larger, she gradually adds part-time and then full-time help. Eventually, each member of her family assumes a role in the expanding microbusiness. In this type of positive environment, the self-esteem of everyone connected with the enterprise should get a boost.

Entrepreneurs—Lucky Seven

What follows are brief descriptions of seven entrepreneurial firms, selected from a file containing dozens of examples. In each instance an individual has taken a fairly original idea and created a market for a particular item or service.

1. Replacements Ltd. Bob Page owns about 500,000 pieces of china and crystal. His Greensboro, North Carolina, company was started in 1981 and specializes in replacing china and crystal. The annual sales run around $5 million from the 15,000 patterns in stock. Page, age 42, turned a hobby of flea market fancying into an *Inc.* magazine top 500 company in six

years. The firm employs sixty-three people handling eleven
phone-order lines, packing, and filling orders. Page works six
days a week and rarely leaves before 7 P.M. On Sundays he
usually rides around to flea markets in the area, looking for
bargains and hard-to-find items and visiting with friends in the
business. He still enjoys what he is doing and likes the hands-
on part of the business so much that he has hired an office
manager to take care of the daily routine. With all that china
and crystal, he still eats out most of the time.

2. Guest Supply, Inc. John J. Todd and Ray Romano
incorporated Guest Supply in 1979 with $6,666 in the bank.
It had $11.7 million in revenues in 1984 and is expecting a poten-
tial market of $400 to $450 million in the not-too-distant future.
The company sells customized packages of personal-care products (such as soap, shampoo, and lotions) to several hotel chains,
including Hilton, Westin, Sheraton, and Holiday Inns. At first,
the two men assembled the packages on John Todd's dining
room table. Members of both the Todd and the Romano families
pitched in to help. No one received any pay. But with nearly
$800,000 in income for the company in 1984, they do not have
to work for nothing anymore.

3. The Necessary Trading Company. New Castle, Virginia,
is a town of fewer than 1,000 people, but on the main street
it can boast of a successful entrepreneurship. Bill Wolf is president of the Necessary Trading Company (NTC). He started
the company in 1982 in an effort to provide a complete line of
products and services for successful biological agriculture—from
large commercial and family farms to the backyard gardener
and orchardist. NTC sells farm and garden supplies through
an attractive mail-order catalog. It offers a range of products
that can preserve and improve the biotic potential of the natural
soil. The company employs twenty-five people and is one of
the largest employers in this sparsely populated mountainous
area of Virginia. Annual sales were expected to top $1 million
in 1987.

4. Spee Dee Oil Change and Tune Up. Gary Copp is
the 32-year-old president of Spee Dee Oil Change and Tune
Up, a New Orleans–based company that expects to have 1,800

franchise outlets by 1990. He noticed that people who bought gasoline at self-service pumps were not taking time to have their cars properly serviced. So he dreamed up a quick (nine-minute) oil-change method. In 1986 there were sixteen Spee Dee locations in and around New Orleans. Sales increased by a whopping 2,158 percent by the end of 1986, ranking Spee Dee eighty-fourth on the *Inc.* 500 list of America's fastest-growing private companies. Sales went from $110,000 in 1980 to $3.75 million in 1985. Franchising is next for this entrepreneur. He provides prospective franchises with a five-week training program. He says that the three keys to successful franchising are quality, standardization, and simplification.

5. *On Sat.* The magazine for some 300,000 backyard satellite dish owners is *On Sat.* Douglas G. Brown and Chris Schultheiss are partners in the business, which grossed $14 million and netted $3 million in 1985. The publishing business is housed in an old sewing thread mill, which has been refurbished as a state-of-the-art printing and graphics plant. The former mill was built in 1905 in Brown's hometown of Shelby, North Carolina. In addition to *On Sat,* Brown and Schultheiss publish *Satellite Retailer,* a magazine; *Satellite Times,* a biweekly newspaper; and *STV,* a monthly consumer magazine for home satellite owners. The publishing operation was recently expanded to ninety people. These small-town entrepreneurs see new applications for satellite and video technology every day.

6. BACOVA Guild, Ltd. The sole employer in BACOVA, Virginia is BACOVA Guild, Ltd. BACOVA—which takes its name from BAth COunty, VirginiA—is a sleepy village of forty-five cottages tucked away in the Allegheny Mountains, formerly a "company town" for a wooden barrel stove operation in the 1920s. The company, founded in 1975, sells products that are embellished with original wildlife designs created by Grace Gilmore. The designs appear on fancy mailboxes, waste paper baskets, thermometers, and doormats. The company's products are now carried by major retailers such as J. C. Penney, Sears, Roebuck, Kmart, and Target Stores. In addition, the distinctive products are advertised in more than a hundred mail-order catalogs, such as the L. L. Bean, Abercrombie and Fitch, Eddie Bauer, and Orvis catalogs.

The company enjoyed only modest artistic success until 1983, when two young tennis pros—Pat Haynes and Ben Johns—at the nearby Homestead resort in Hot Springs, Virginia, took over the company ownership. Since then, the BACOVA Guild has been on a steady upward swing, with $4 million in sales in 1985, $10 million in 1986, and $19 million in 1987, and earned a place on the *Inc.* magazine list of fastest-growing private companies. The company is expected to top the $40 million mark in five years. Not bad for a firm with only 250 full-time-equivalent employees.

7. GLIE Farms, Inc. Curiously, the nations largest indoor herb farm is located in the middle of New York City—the South Bronx. GLIE Farms started out in 1979 growing mushrooms, herbs, and flowers that were distributed locally. By 1985 the farm was serving more than 300 restaurants and markets and grossing $1.2 million in sales. Now the entrepreneurial venture has expanded to an ultra-modern greenhouse complex, which during an average week handles more than 2,000 pounds of herbs that are harvested, cleaned, packed, and shipped to more than 800 restaurants and markets nationwide.

The business is staffed mainly by previously unemployed men and women who were at first paid through a federally funded gardening program. The farm now employs sixty-three people under the direction of Gary Waldron, a former IBM executive who started the project while on a one-year leave of absence from his company. When his year was up, he decided that he would rather develop an entrepreneurial adventure than work for a corporate giant. He has been with the community-oriented business ever since and believes that it has been successful because the employees have a deep personal investment in it. In a small business, such as this, everyone's job is important. And when employees see that there is a certain humaneness in management and in the way that people interact with each other, their jobs become more than just jobs. They feel that they are part of the company and can spring ideas on the boss.

These seven illustrations are meant to show the difference between entrepreneurial activity and other small businesses or work-at-home ventures. An accountant, for example, may work at home, but this does not make him an entrepreneur. A family that opens a franchise ice cream shop in a new shopping center will probably not bring to its venture the innovative spirit found in Replacements, Ltd. To refer once again to Long's (1983) definition of entrepreneurship, all seven of our examples are characterized by (1) uncertainty and risk, (2) complementary managerial competencies, and (3) creative opportunism. In addition, each one started small but was able to grow and prosper.

It should be emphasized that these seven are merely *examples* of a much larger cadre of successful entrepreneurial enterprises. Every city has its share, and every issue of *Entrepreneur, Venture, Inc.,* and *Black Enterprise* magazines has numerous reports on similar firms.

What Should Counselors Do?

This section will present five positive steps that counselors can take to achieve a better understanding of entrepreneurship and to improve their ability to impart information about entrepreneurial opportunities to others. For many counselors entrepreneurship is a new and different topic. Many have worked in public and private agencies and institutions where entrepreneurship was not understood, much less encouraged or allowed to flourish. Therefore, building a base of understanding is really a first step. From there, other directions can be taken—such as promoting educational programs, providing visibility to entrepreneurship, encouraging informal contacts and associations, or just being a source of more information if that is what is needed by some aspiring genius.

Be Knowledgeable on the Subject. This chapter has set forth some basic ideas about, and principles of, entrepreneurship, but the subject goes far beyond these few pages. The next step might be to consult the suggested readings at the end of this chapter. This is not an exhaustive list by any means, but the books annotated there will themselves contain further suggestions for reading.

How else can you become better informed about entrepreneurship? First, read local, regional, and national newspapers for coverage of the subject. In 1985, for example, *USA Today* ran a five-part series on entrepreneurs who had achieved notable success. Second, watch for programs on entrepreneurship sponsored by local or state chambers of commerce. Third, be on the lookout for good television or radio programs on the subject. Fourth, take credit and noncredit courses (including seminars and workshops offered by local schools, community colleges, four-year institutions, or other educational groups). Finally, together with other counselors in your area, visit some local entrepreneurs. Try this for several afternoons a month and see what you come up with.

Promote Educational Programs. The six-volume *National Survey of Entrepreneurial Education* (see Vesper, 1985) is a comprehensive resource for those interested in promoting educational programs. Each volume contains detailed course descriptions, sample syllabi, and examples of program announcements, at two- and four-year colleges and universities, high schools, and selected business assistance agencies. In addition, Stewart and Boyd (1986) have an excellent article on the values of entrepreneurial education.

Franslow and Compton (1982) at Iowa State University have developed a course in entrepreneurship for senior high schools. Their book includes fifteen sample lesson plans, vocabulary lists, good references, and other useful course materials. Vivien K. Ely (1983) has written a first-class *Teacher's Guide for Entrepreneurship Education.* This book includes guidelines for planning instructional programs, selecting resources, and planning units. It also contains twenty pages of very useful references.

Provide Visibility. Here are some ways to make people aware of entrepreneurs and entrepreneurship:

- *Models.* Let the people with whom you work see and hear what entrepreneurs are like. Set up an Entrepreneur-of-the-Month program, where you bring in local examples of successful people. If you work in an educational setting, try to find some alumni who are successful entrepreneurs and ask them to return to the campus to speak about their experiences. Otherwise, arrange for class or Career Day speakers or stories in local newsletters.

- *Bulletin Boards.* Clip out stories from local, regional, and national newspapers and magazines that fit your theme.
- *Rewards for Success.* Nothing seems to work like rewarding success and making it visible. Establish a program to reward local entrepreneurs, and be willing to spend considerable time seeking out these people. Maybe you can get a local club such as Rotary, Lions, or the Jaycees to help you in funding these people and recognizing them for their success.

Bring Together Creative Geniuses. There seems to be some magic in the air when creative people get together. At any rate, this is what happens when members of the Association of Collegiate Entrepreneurs assemble. Headquartered at Wichita State University in Kansas, the group has campus chapters all over the country, and their purpose is to provide a meeting place for innovators.

An illustration may be in order here. James Madison University (JMU) in Harrisonburg, Virginia, has a chapter of the Association of Collegiate Entrepreneurs. Established in 1984, the chapter had two members. There are now seventy-five members, representing over two dozen academic majors. The chapter has had representation at the ACE national meetings for the past three years. In 1986–87 the group developed several new products. For example, the "Duke Dogs," created by JMU senior Jeff Harper, are replicas of the school's mascot. Harper sold forty-three dozen of these dogs on a recent Parents' Weekend and expects to sell at least $35,000 worth by the end of the school year. The local ACE chapter will receive a percentage of the profits for its help. This kind of creative mix that comes through a local ACE chapter or something like it has proven to be a fertile ground for the creative enterprise.

Be a Source of Assistance. If a person walked up to you tomorrow and asked "Where could I go to study entrepreneurship in a college?" what would you say? Not sure? Well, here is a beginning list:

Associations

American Entrepreneurs Association, 2311 Pontius Avenue, Los Angeles, Calif. 90064. AEA publishes more than two hundred "How to Start a Business" manuals (about $40 each). For $24.50, you can join the AEA; write for more information.

American Women's Economic Development Corporation (AWED), 1270 Avenue of the Americas, New York, N.Y. 10020. AWED offers long-term training and assistance to women who own their own business or who would like to start one. Programs range from hourly counseling sessions to an eighteen-month training program. Fees range from $25 for the one-and-a-half-to-two-hour counseling session to $350 for the eighteen-month program.

American Women Entrepreneurs, 60 East Forty-Second Street, New York, N.Y. 10165. Entitles members to medical benefits, a members-only hotline, and special travel rates.

Catalyst, 14 East Sixtieth Street, New York, N.Y. 10021. A nationwide organization for women with careers, which is beginning to step into the area of entrepreneurship for women. Publishes listings of career counseling centers across the country. Write for additional information and listings of its career opportunities series.

National Association of Black Women Entrepreneurs (NABWE), 220 Woodward Towers, Detroit, Mich. 48226. NABWE sponsors monthly workshops, has established several regional and national networks, and publishes a monthly newsletter. Membership in NABWE is $60 per year for women who own a business, $40 per year for women who do not yet own a business, and $100 per year for corporate membership.

Women's Referral Service, Inc., Corporate Office, P. O. Box 3093, Van Nuys, Calif. 91407. A nationwide resource network offering information and technical assistance to entrepreneurial women.

Periodicals

> *Black Enterprise,* Earl G. Graves Publishing Company, Inc., 295 Madison Avenue, New York, N.Y. 10017. Subscription price: $15 per year.
>
> *Entrepreneur* magazine, 2311 Pointius Ave., Los Angeles, Calif. 90064. Subscription price: $17.95 per year.
>
> *Inc.* magazine, 38 Commercial Wharf, Boston, Mass. 02110. Subscription price: $18 per year.
>
> *Venture* magazine, Inc., 35 West Forty-Fifth Street, New York, N.Y. 10036. Subscription price: $18 per year.

Resources

> U.S. Department of Commerce, Office of Publications and Public Affairs, Main Commerce Building, Washington, D.C. 20230. Write requesting the address of the district office closest to you and a publications list.
>
> Bureau of the Census, Federal Office Buildings 3 and 4, Suitland, Md. 20233. Write for a publications list. There is a wealth of materials on geographical population and industry trends, including the *Census of Business,* which provides information on retail, wholesale, and service industries; the *Statistical Abstract of the United States;* and the *Country and City Data Book,* which contains statistics on income, employment, housing, and population. Characteristics are listed for every state, county, and city.
>
> Internal Revenue Service, Taxpayer Service Division, 111 Constitution Avenue, N.W., Washington, D.C. 20224. Write for a publications list. The IRS offers materials covering everything you could possibly want to know about starting a business.
>
> Chambers of Commerce. Many local chambers of commerce furnish economic statistics on their communities, offer technical and professional support, and will help businesses locate sites for factories and stores within their towns. To contact your local chamber, write the

National Chamber of Commerce, 1615 H Street, N.W., Washington, D.C. 20006. Also ask for sources of state information and state industrial directories.

Trade Associations. Trade associations are membership organizations specializing in a particular line of business. They are often excellent sources of information and assistance. For a complete list of associations, consult *National Trade and Professional Associations of the United States and Canada and Labor Unions* and the *Encyclopedia of Associations,* vol. 1, both available in your local library.

Educational Institutions. Colleges and universities are becoming more responsive to the special needs of women regarding business management and financial skills. Small business development centers (SBDCs) are located in some state universities. These centers serve as one-stop sources of business information and educational materials. They operate similarly to the agriculture extension service.

Suggested Readings

Botkin, J., Dimancescu, D., and Stata, R. *The Innovators: Rediscovering America's Creative Energy.* New York: Harper & Row, 1984.

The authors believe that America is on the verge of a major new surge of economic development, propelled by "the innovators." These people will make new products, create new production processes, and thereby create new jobs.

Drucker, P. F. *Innovation and Entrepreneurship: Principles and Practices.* New York: Harper & Row, 1985.

The best book in the current batch of books on the subject. Drucker thinks that the United States is entering a new era of entrepreneurial economy, which will lead to an entrepreneurial society. He believes that entrepreneurship is a process that can be taught, and he points up the differences between real entrepreneurs and other small business or work-at-home people.

Gilder, G. *The Spirit of Enterprise*. New York: Simon & Schuster, 1984.

The author finds evidence of a new spirit in the United States, namely, the spirit of enterprise. He finds this spirit embodied in those people who are up before dawn and busy long after dark. In contrast, there are the "entitled children"—those who want and expect everything to be given to them. In Gilder's view, the future belongs to hardworking people who are animated by the spirit of enterprise.

Harrison, P. (ed.). *America's New Women Entrepreneurs*. Washington, D.C. Acropolis Books, 1986.

A set of personal reflections by thirty-two of the top women entrepreneurs in the country. These women explain how they rose to the top of the company structure and how they managed to stay there.

Kinstone, B. *The Student Entrepreneur's Guide*. Berkeley, Calif.: Ten Speed Press, 1981.

This how-to-do-it book, written when Kinstone was a senior at Stanford University, made him a folk hero to young college students. Kinstone draws on his own experience and that of other young entrepreneurs to raise and answer tough questions about the business world for students.

7

Small Business:
Where the Action Is

The late British economist E. F. Schumacher captured the imagination of a great many people with his two books in the 1970s, *Small Is Beautiful* (1973) and *Good Work* (1979). In both books his central thesis was that small-scale technologies and small economic units serve social (including quality-of-life) functions as well as economic purposes. Small, according to Schumacher, is beautiful and in most cases economically feasible and efficient. Nonetheless, the United States has generally preferred bigness: big business, Big Ten, big industry, big cars, big everything. "Bigness" has been carefully chronicled in the magazines of this genre—such as *Forbes, Nation's Business, Fortune,* and *Business Week.* Many of these periodicals even brought out lists of the top 100 or 500 "big businesses." Now times are changing. The top ten businesses in *Ward's Business Directory* for 1986 lost 215,400 jobs. Sears, Roebuck (down by 50,000 jobs), Kmart (down 45,000 jobs), and General Electric (down 36,000 jobs) led the downward job slide. Contrast these job losses in "big business" with the annual Dun & Bradstreet reports on new business starts for 1985 and 1986:

Business Starts	New Jobs Created
251,597 in 1986	1.2 million
249,770 in 1985	1.3 million

Most of these new starts in 1985 and 1986 were in small businesses with an average of 4.85 employees in 1986 and 5.37 employees in 1985. The changing world of work and leisure is reported not in the list of magazines above but in *Black Enterprise, Entrepreneur, Inc., Solo, Success, Venture, Working Woman,* and other similar new periodicals. These attractive publications are the symbols of the emerging workplace.

David Birch (1987) thinks that the Dun & Bradstreet figures are too low. In 1985, according to his figures, 700,000 new companies were formed, compared to 90,000 start-ups in 1950 and 200,000 in 1965. In addition, 400,000 new partnerships were formed in 1985, and there were 300,000 newly self-employed people. In other words, 1.4 million new enterprises were created in 1985. These 1.4 million new enterprises, he thinks, created approximately 1.4 million new jobs in the private sector of the United States economy. This growth in small business contrasts with the picture of the entire *Fortune* 500 companies alone, which employed *2.2 million fewer* people at the end of 1985 than they did at the start of 1980. In short, the bigger companies are getting smaller rather than continuing to grow, whereas small business is growing at a rapid and expanding pace.

It is clear, then, that a true wild card in tomorrow's workplace will be this growth in small businesses. The story is so big that a short chapter such as this cannot really do justice to it. Unfortunately, too, the sources of information about small businesses are often in conflict and fail to report comparable data. A further complication is that the growth in small businesses has been quite uneven over regions and industries.

In 1985 Congress appointed a commission—composed of education, industry, business, government, and labor leaders— to study the potential of small business in the United States. The commission's report, issued in February 1986, said that the nation should establish a goal of creating 10 million new jobs through small business (National Commission on Jobs and Small Business, 1986). One of the commission's main recommendations was that a partnership of leaders from all walks of life be formed to encourage capital-formation institutions— pension funds, insurance companies, and banks—to become much more responsive to the start-up needs of small businesses. The commission's report, moreover, highlighted the following points to call attention to the role of small business in the United States:

- Businesses with fewer than 100 employees account for 34 percent of all private, nonfarm employment. Those with fewer than 500 employ 48 percent of that force.
- Small firms produce 38 percent of our gross national product.
- In 1986 the Department of Commerce estimated that small firms had generated 50 percent of all major innovations in the past thirty years.
- The number of women-owned businesses has been increasing three times as fast as the number of businesses owned by men. The number of self-employed blacks and Hispanics has increased substantially in the last ten years.

This chapter reports on the scope and breadth of small business in the United States and then looks at the expanding area of franchising around the country. It also describes another "lucky seven" small businesses. Although there is no commonly held definition of what constitutes a small business (definitions range from "businesses with fewer than 100 employees" to "fewer than 250" to "fewer than 500"), in this chapter "small business" will be defined as any business, public (stock available for sale to the public) or private (individual or family owned), with 500 or fewer employees.

Rapid Expansion

The best single source of information about the scope of small business is *The State of Small Business: A Report of the President* (Small Business Administration, 1986). This is a fact-filled book put together by the federal government's agency in charge of small businesses. Here is a summary of the report (pp. xiii–xviii):

The number of new businesses continues to increase: there are now over 15 million small businesses in the United States. Measures of business starts and closings fluctuated in 1985. Business incorporations increased by over 5 percent, while business starts increased more than 16 percent. Business failures—businesses that closed with a loss to a creditor—increased by 9.6 percent and bankruptcies rose 11.5 percent, reflecting past high rates of growth and the economic slowdown in 1985.

Employment in the U.S. economy reached a record high in 1985, with nearly 110 million Americans on the job. Employment growth in small business–dominated industries, at 5.1 percent, far outpaced that of large business–dominated industries, at .7 percent. Growth was strongest in construction, services, and retail trade, three industries in which small businesses predominate. Manufacturing and mining, both dominated by large businesses, showed only a small employment gain and an employment loss respectively.

The number of women entrepreneurs continues to grow. From 1977 to 1983, the number of women-owned businesses increased annually by 9.4 percent, well above the 4.3 percent increase in men-owned businesses. One reason for this growth is women's greater participation in the work force. Expanded work experience has given more women the training and skills they need to operate a successful business. Other factors may include dissatisfaction with working in large corporations, the aging of the population, and technological innovation, particularly the introduction of affordable microcomputers and telecommunications that give women more flexibility to work at home.

Small business makes substantial contributions to job creation and retention. Small firms generated most of the net new jobs during the economic downturns from 1979 to 1983 and continued to be the major employer of younger and older workers, women, and veterans. These jobs were created in both traditional and nontraditional small business industries.

The economic climate was healthy for small firms in 1985, and industries dominated by small firms outperformed the economy in its third consecutive year of growth and expansion. Small firms continue to be major contributors of new jobs, as well as prolific and efficient producers of innovative products, services, and industrial processes.

Small business owners represent a broad cross section of the American populace, and they are the major employers of the young, the elderly, women, and veterans. In all phases of the business cyle, small firms have demonstrated their capacity to create employment, and their inventive capabilities make substantial contributions to economic growth.

Fastest-Growing Small Industries

	Percent Change in Employment
Total, small business–dominated industries	5.1
Radio, TV, and music stores	15.4
Computer and data-processing services	14.2
Credit reporting and collection	13.7
Sanitary services	11.5
Masonry, stonework, and plastering	11.3
Carpentry and flooring	11.2
Engineering and architectural services	10.0
Real estate agents and managers	9.9
Mailing, reproduction, and stenographic services	9.2
Nonresidential building construction	9.2

State and Regional Conditions. Eight of the nine Small Business Administration (SBA) Regions had some growth in new business in 1985. Some regions far outstretched the others. For example, the nine New England states almost doubled the new business starts in the next closest region—East South Central, 18.5 percent growth versus 7.4 percent growth. The Middle Atlantic, South Atlantic, and East North Central regions all added new business incorporations at a rate faster than the national average of 5.3 percent increase from 1984 to 1985. The top twelve states in new business incorporation in 1985 were:

1. Connecticut (up 38%)
2. New Hampshire (up 28.6%)
3. Maryland (up 27.4%)
4. South Carolina (up 24.5%)
5. Louisiana (up 22.2%)
6. Oklahoma (up 17.1%)
7. Maine (up 16.3%)
8. Tennessee (up 12.8%)
9. Michigan (up 12.3%)
10. Pennsylvania (up 11.7%)
11. Massachusetts (up 11.6%)
12. New Jersey (up 10.2%)

The ranking by percentages distorts the rest of the story somewhat. The larger states also showed significant gains in new business, even though the percent gain was not as large as in some of the smaller states:

State	1984	1985	
New York	68,626	72,083	up 5.0%
California	60,952	61,160	up 0.3%
Florida	66,999	71,649	up 6.9%

In New York City alone, 48.7 percent of all the new private-sector jobs from March 1983 to March 1985 were created in small businesses with fewer than 100 employees.

Small Business by Industry. Just as there are wide state and regional differences in the growth of small business, there are wide differences in the types of industries in which small business thrives. An analysis of small business by industry, undertaken by the National Federation of Independent Business (1981), showed that nearly 60 percent of the firms were in the retail and service sectors (see Figure 5). That same conclusion was reached by *Inc.* magazine in its 1987 listing of the 100 fastest-growing small, publicly held companies. For the first time in

Figure 5. Small Business by Industry.

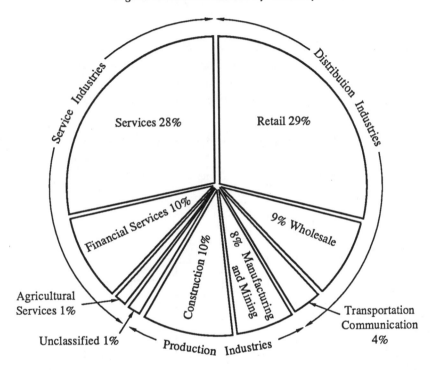

the nine years that *Inc.* had been compiling the list, manufacturing firms were not in the majority. Instead, 55 service companies dominated the 100 fast-track firms. On the leading edge were long-distance telephone companies, broadcasters, medical research firms, and computer-related businesses. The names on *Inc.*'s top 100 companies between 1982 and 1986 had an average sales increase of 3,594 percent, and the average payroll jumped from 46 workers to 786 workers. These top 100 firms are quite efficient, with the average sales per employee increasing from $80,681 in 1982 to $158,273 in 1986. They are also more productive by 50–60 percent over the large firms, according to most estimates. In contrast, the *Fortune* 500 members staggered through 1986 with a total sales drop of 4.6 percent and 600,000 fewer employees.

Ages of Those Who Start a Small Business. People of all ages start businesses. As noted in Figure 6, developed by the National Federation of Independent Business (1981), most people start their business between the ages of 25 and 40.

Figure 6. Ages of People Starting Businesses.

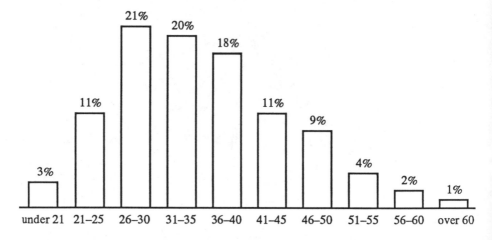

Source: © 1981 the NFIB Foundation, formerly called the National Federation of Independent Business Research and Education Foundation. Reprinted with permission from poster entitled "Small Business in America," 1981.

An example from the top of the *Inc.* 100 list is the Catalyst Energy Development Corporation. The president of the company is John Kuhns, age 37. He once worked as a professional sculptor before he founded Catalyst in 1982. Its sales the first year were $107,000. In 1986 sales were $227 million, up from

$36.5 million the previous year. That represents a growth rate of 212,338 percent in four years. The company is a leader in the field of producing alternative sources of energy, such as burning garbage and harnessing power from falling water. Catalyst was the first independent power producer to put its stock up for public sale. Recent growth has come mainly through a series of corporate takeovers. The company now has assets valued at around $1 billion.

Franchising

What do McDonald's, Texaco, H & R Block, Holiday Inn, Coca-Cola, and 7-Eleven have in common? They are all franchisers. Like many other companies, they use franchising extensively as a means of expansion and growth. In 1983 more than 5 million people were employed in franchise outlets, or about one of every twenty workers. Franchise industry sales rose from $261.7 billion in 1977 to $556.2 billion in 1986 to an estimated $600 billion in 1987.

Restaurants, along with some retailers and service franchises, have performed best among major franchisers. The combined sales of all three groups rose from 6.3 percent to 14.5 percent in 1986. Retail sales by franchise establishments make up 33 percent of all retail sales. According to the best estimates, over 2,000 companies offer franchising opportunities to others. They expect their revenues to grow between 5 and 10 percent a year and the number of outlets to grow by about 7 percent. Clearly, franchising is a major source of small business opportunity. In addition, those who purchase franchises have a much better chance of succeeding than those who go into business alone. The failure rate for the average franchiser is somewhere in the 2–6 percent range. But what is franchising and where are the best opportunities?

Nature of Franchising. Franchising offers a way for established companies to expand their operations and increase their profits without assuming much additional risk. In exchange for helping people establish a business, a company gains access to the financial resources of these small business owners and therefore can expand into more localities than it could on its own. As more outlets are created, the company profits from increased royalties as well as from increased sales of goods and services to the small business operator.

A franchise contract is a legal agreement between a company, known as the franchiser, and an individual or group, known as the franchisee. Basically, the franchiser sells the right to use the company's trademark, trade name, and even the format of the business to the franchisee in exchange for an initial fee and royalty payments (usually a set proportion of sales). Two types of franchise systems exist in the United States: product or trade-name franchising and business-format franchising.

Product or trade-name franchising refers to a distribution system in which the franchisee is licensed to sell items manufactured by the franchiser. Some examples of this type of franchise are gasoline service stations, automotive dealers, and soft-drink bottlers. This is the predominant form of franchising in the United States, accounting for over $312 billion in sales in 1983.

Business-format franchising is broader in scope than product or trade-name franchising and usually includes a business format in addition to a product line or trade name. This format typically includes a marketing plan or strategy, a well-defined operating plan, and quality control. Business-format franchising accounts for most of the growth in franchising since 1970 and is the most familiar type to consumers. These franchises accounted for over $110 billion in sales in 1983. Sales volume as well as the number of firms and employees grew rapidly over the last ten-year period. This type of franchising includes restaurants; nonfood retailers, such as hardware stores; convenience stores; personal services, such as hair salons; and business aids and services, such as personnel agencies and tax preparation services.

The success of business-format franchising has given rise in recent years to conversion franchising—that is, an independent company converting to a franchise operation. For example, a local real estate brokerage firm may decide to affiliate with a national company, such as Century 21, in order to break into a wider market or to maintain its competitive position.

Advantages of Franchising. The appeal of franchising is that it enables people without previous business experience—a major source of small business failures—to become their own boss. By having access to the managerial and financial resources of a large organization, individuals can reduce many of the risks associated with establishing a new business. And these risks are considerable. The Small Business Administration estimates that two of every three new businesses fail within five years. In contrast, the International Trade Administration estimates that only two or three of every hundred business-format franchises are terminated each year.

Franchising is a relatively safe way to become self-employed, because, in the first place, franchises generally offer a proven business format, a way of selling goods and services that is likely to succeed in any area. Most franchisers also offer extensive training programs and also may help the newcomer select a site to ensure maximum traffic, plan the store's design, and negotiate a lease. Some franchisers even assist in arranging financing for the venture.

The franchiser continues to provide services to franchisees throughout the life of the franchise contract. Ongoing services vary among franchises, but typically include centralized purchasing to obtain quantity discounts and lower prices, quality control to ensure customers' satisfaction, market research to help meet customer preferences, advertising and promotion to expand the customer base, and refresher courses on various aspects of the venture. These services help the owner develop a clientele more quickly than an independent firm would.

Which Franchisers Are Doing Well? Service-oriented franchises have replaced fast food as the most attractive opportunities in the field today. Among the ones that were doing best in 1987 were:

• Home services (maid services, carpet or upholstery cleaning, home remodeling). This category was expected to have sales of $4.9 billion in 1987. Maid services alone in that year were expected to grow in revenues by 20 percent, according to a Commerce Department survey.

- Business and professional services (accounting, payroll, employee benefits consulting firms). As large companies continue to restructure, merge, and slim down their work forces, more of them are contracting for these kinds of services.
- Recreation and entertainment businesses (including racquetball, restaurants with video games or pool tables, recreational vehicle rentals, and even miniature golf). Mike McDermott, editor of *Franchise* magazine, expected sales in these areas to grow by 40 percent in 1987.

Franchising's Best. *Venture* and *Entrepreneur* publish lists of the best bets in franchising. *Venture,* in its February 1987 issue, lists 50 of the newest franchise companies (those that began selling franchises in 1985 or later) that have opened the most establishments. *Entrepreneur* lists 500 companies as the ''best'' franchises—using a formula that includes start-up costs, number of establishments open, years in business, and growth rate. (See Tables 10 and 11.)

Of the more than 2,000 franchise opportunities, everything from A to Z is available. Automobile franchises make the most money, but there is an incredible array of other options that might interest potential small business owners or workers. Here are some examples: Four Seasons Greenhouses (over 200 franchises), Deck the Walls (over 250 stores nationwide), Duds 'n Suds (a laundering and beer franchise), Caribbean Clear (swimming pool purifiers), Perma Cream (bathroom resurfacing), Steamatic (total cleaning service), Celluland (cellular phone franchises), Decora Closets (expert closet design), and Lindal Cedar Homes (custom log and cedar homes).

For More Information. For those who want to learn about what is involved in becoming a franchiser, these two publications from the International Franchise Association (IFA) can help: *Franchising: The How-To Book,* by Lloyd Tarbutton ($14.95 paper-

Table 10. Sample of Companies Included in *Venture*'s List of
50 "Best" Franchises.

Company/Business	No. of Franchises
Novus Windshield Repair/auto services	
Minneapolis	525
Friendship Inns/hotel, motel	
North Bergen, N.J.	106
Allison's Place/retail clothing	
Los Angeles	74
T. J. Cinnamon's Gourmet Bakeries/specialty foods	
Kansas City	70
Americlean Mobile Power Wash/building maintenance	
Gettysburg, Pa.	67
Express Services/temporary employees	
Oklahoma City	65
The Box Shoppe/packaging and shipping	
Indianapolis	57
Penguin's Place Frozen Yogurt/specialty foods	
Thousand Oaks, Calif.	45
Snelling Temporaries/temporary employees	
Sarasota, Fla.	43
Optimum Health Systems, Inc./health services	
Cincinnati	41

Source: Adapted from Roth, D. M., p. 38.

Table 11. Sample of Companies Included in *Entrepreneur*'s List of
500 "Best" Franchises.

Company/Business	No. of Franchises
Domino's Pizza/pizza	2,262
Pizza Hut/pizza	2,597
Wendy's Hamburgers/fast foods	2,319
Hardee's/fast foods	1,755
McDonald's/fast foods	6,921
Budget Rent-A-Car/auto, truck leasing	3,200
Dairy Queen/Brazier/soft-serve ice cream	4,888
7-Eleven/convenience stores	2,895
Service Master/carpet, upholstery cleaning	3,365
Jazzercise/fitness centers	3,319

Source: Adapted from "Eighth Annual Franchise 500," 1987, pp. 98–183.

back plus $2.50 postage), and the booklet *How to Be a Franchiser,* by Robert E. Kushell and Carl E. Zwisler III ($5 to nonmembers of IFA). Write to the IFA at 1350 New York Ave., N.W., Suite 900, Washington, D.C. 20005. Despite their titles, these are not self-help books, but they highlight the problems that franchisers will eventually have to resolve with professional help.

New editions of the *Franchise Opportunities Handbook* and *Franchising in the Economy* will be available shortly in paperback. Write to the Superintendent of Documents, Washington, D.C. 20402, or call (202) 783-3238.

The Lucky Seven

Included here are three businesses that began small and grew to the point where they could venture into the franchise arena. They were successful in a very small start and appear to be headed for even greater success as they spread out into franchising. The four other examples are taken from a section on "Small Business" that appears frequently in *USA Today.* These four illustrate the geographical spread (from Maine to California) as well as the conceptual spread (from harps and hot stoves to photo collections to a unique restaurant). There are thousands upon thousands of cases just as rich and as interesting as these. They are in every small town, suburban region, or big city. The number of small business success stories is truly legion.

1. Peter Burns is a 27-year-old franchiser who owns Island Moped. There are twenty-two shops scattered from Bar Harbor, Maine, to Sanibel Island, Florida. He came up with the idea of the business as a class project when he was a student at the University of Virginia in 1977. He started out on Nantucket Island, Massachusetts, by spending $5,000 to purchase fifteen inexpensive motorized bicycles. The idea caught on, and he grossed nearly $50,000 in the first thirteen weeks. He expected to sell franchises for $35,000 each and reach $2 million in sales in 1984.

2. Art dealer Donald Austin is the 52-year-old president of Austin Galleries, Inc. He wants to sell forty franchises for

Austin Galleries by 1991 with $30 million in sales from originals and prints. He is betting that there will be a continuation of the current upscale interest in good art to support his gallery expansion project.

3. I Can't Believe It's Yogurt had nine stores in Dallas, Texas, in 1982. The franchise chain expected to have 175 stores selling its frozen yogurt by the end of 1987, with $11 million in revenues. The operation is run by brother and sister Bill and June Brice, who were students at Southern Methodist University working part time in a frozen yogurt store in 1977. They are taking advantage of the current interest in anything that professes to have a health food orientation and fits into the dieting mode. Their franchises now sell for $20,000 and require $130,000 in start-up capital.

4. "They didn't play blues when they lost their jobs," Sebastopol, California. When the company that employs you suddenly closes, it doesn't necessarily signal the end of your career. For Chris and Teresa Caswell, it was a beginning. In 1977, after the harp-making shop where they were working closed, they spent $2,000 setting up their own shop. Since then, they have sold more than 600 reproductions of ancient Celtic-style harps and harp-making kits at prices from $369 to $2,200. To keep sales coming in, Caswell Harps advertises to a mailing list of about 500 musicians and music schools. Annual sales: about $75,000 and climbing. "The harp is coming back," says Chris Caswell. It's used in classical music and is becoming popular in New Age jazz—and even has been used on a Michael Jackson album. Among the customers: Gail Butler Levant, who composed the theme music for television's *Remington Steele*.

5. "Wis. couple make hay in the photo business," Osceola, Wisconsin. Who says you can't live where you work? Rohn and Jeri Engh live and work on a 120-acre farm and run a company that does business around the globe. PhotoSource International supplies photographs to publishers of books, magazines, and newspapers. Rohn was a free-lance photographer and Jeri a free-lance journalist when they started the business in a barn with $125 in 1976. They found clients by purchasing mailing lists from other photo suppliers and started publishing a news-

letter. Now, through a network of photographers, PhotoSource has access to 7 million pictures. The company sells copies to such clients as Time-Life Books for prices starting at $100. As the business has grown into a $200,000-a-year enterprise, the Enghs have kept the atmosphere casual—business attire is mostly blue jeans. The office still is in the barn, where computers sit on desks below a hayloft. "Sometimes our employees have to ski to work, but they don't mind," Rohn says. "Sometimes a farm animal wanders in while we are working, but I don't think they mind, either."

6. Graffiti Removal, Los Angeles, California. If the first market you target isn't right, try another. That's what brothers Tim Sullivan, 40, and Michael Sullivan, 35, did when they saw the writing on the wall. The Sullivans, who operated a janitorial service until 1976, worked in a neighborhood that had a persistent problem with graffiti. So they bought a $1,500 paint-spraying machine and formed Graffiti Removal. The brothers found few takers among small business owners, so they approached local governments and won contracts with fifteen Southern California cities to clean public and private walls. Typical price: $120 for sandblasting and painting a wall six feet high and twenty-five feet long. Usually, one cleaning does it; the Sullivans say the graffiti rarely reappears. The company has grown to ten employees, and the brothers have decided one marketing campaign was enough: City officials from as far away as Chicago are seeking them out.

7. "She cooks up unique business that's hot," Thorndike, Maine. In an age of microwave ovens, Bea Bryant saw her niche in the kitchens of the past. At Bryant Stove Works, the focus is on restoring antique wood-burning cookstoves to blazing glory. Bryant collected the old wood burners as a hobby until 1972, when she decided to sell a few of her duplicates to finance her children's college education. She borrowed $20,000 from a bank and went into business with her husband, Joe. As word spread—and Bryant took out an ad in the *Old-House Journal*—the business took a different turn. Most people who responded to the ad told Bryant they already had stoves but needed them fixed up. Now, customers across the USA and Canada ship their stoves, which can weigh as much as 550

pounds, to rural Maine for a $600 to $1,000 cleaning-and-repair job. From California, the shipping alone can cost $250. Why do people bother with the old wood burner? Bryant says one reason is that the stoves are made well and require restoration only once in a person's lifetime. A growing interest in owning old houses and furnishing them authentically contributes to her business, too. Revenues last year [1986]: more than $500,000.

Drive down any street in America and you will find clusters of businesses just like these seven. There is a new craft shop over on the corner, and a new microbrewery a few doors away. Someone else has just tried her wings by opening a muffin shop. Wherever you turn, you will find examples as rich as the ones used here. To come up with other ideas, keep an eye on newspapers and magazines. *Inc.* and *Franchising* are full of information about small businesses. Perhaps Schumacher was right—there is Good Work, and it is becoming increasingly clear that Small Is Beautiful.

What Should Counselors Do?

For many years now, large companies have dominated the business world and held the public's attention. All that one hears about are the companies that make up the Dow Jones Industrials or Standard & Poor's 500—it really seems to be a case of the bigger, the better. For example, in many locations the Career Day program on campuses traditionally brings in the area's largest employers—even though they may not be hiring or are hiring only replacements. On the college campus, the main effort is to get the big companies—such as IBM, General Motors, General Electric, Rockwell International, and Exxon—to interview in the placement center. But recent trends suggest that big companies are reducing their work force:

- United Airlines lays off 1,016 employees
- New GM layoffs bring total to 35,000
- Unisys plans to trim 2,400 more jobs for a total of 12,000 cut off
- Mellon Bank to cut up to 3,000 jobs by the end of 1987

If these trends continue, it will be increasingly difficult to attract the traditional interviewer to a campus visit.

So, what to do? This section offers a few ideas on how counselors can relate to the growing job market in small business. This shift will not be an easy one for most counselors. First of all, it tears away at some longstanding traditions of where the jobs are. Second, it is hard to find and relate to these smaller companies because they have trimmed-down staffs and are more concerned with producing goods and services than with building "corporate relations" with counselors. Third, it is difficult to maintain contact with small companies because they usually are more fluid than large ones. They move, they change phone numbers, they shift personnel around. Nevertheless, counselors should try to establish and maintain these contacts if they are to help students enter the new world of the *Inc.* top 100.

Read and Report. The list of basic sources of information at the end of this section and the list of suggested readings at the end of this chapter should enable you to make a start in learning more about small business. There are usually plenty of similar books in the economics/business sections of area booksellers. If not, you may want to encourage bookstores and libraries to set up separate shelves and to order more books on the topic. You may even have to give a hand by providing a starter list. Be sure that local newsstands stock some of the newer magazines on the topic. *Inc.* magazine, for instance, is a bright, colorful, well-written, and dynamic periodical. Just having it on the shelf should attract some curious browsers. You might want to set up eye-catching bulletin boards containing information about small businesses. In addition, you and your counseling co-workers may want to start a systemic reading and discussion program on the emerging area of small business. To share the knowledge you gain from this program, you might start a column on "New Books on Small Business" or "New Developments in Small Business," to be run in local or state counseling journals or newsletters. On a more modest scale, you might devote a session or a portion of a professional counselors' meeting to brief reviews of new books or new developments in the small business area.

Visit and Confer. The best way to find out what is going on in small business in your vicinity is to go out and make some visits. Maybe the local chamber of commerce or a civic club such as Rotary or Lions can get you started. Both should know about a new office supply store that is expanding or a new manufacturer of slip rings. Such visits, perhaps undertaken once or twice a month, will help you build a new network of friends in small business and will give you a sense of the working atmosphere in these firms. You might want to invite some of these small business owners to speak—for instance, on the subject "The Promise of Small Business"—at an upcoming local, regional, or state counselors' association meeting.

Debate and Discuss. To raise the level of visibility of small companies, you might arrange a series of debates or forums on the topic of "Big Business Versus Small Business." This could be a year-long continuing dialogue on emerging trends in both places of employment and the advantages and disadvantages of working in either setting. Both management and nonmanagement people could take part in the discussions. Everybody could benefit by knowing more about both workplaces. Another way to provide visibility for the emerging small employees would be to have a series of "brown bag lunches" or breakfasts and invite various franchisers to talk and answer questions about the pros and cons of franchising. They could discuss how to obtain start-up financing, how to choose a location, how to find good employees, and so on.

Explore Advantages to Women and Minorities. As mentioned in Chapter Six, women and minorities are turning to small business to avoid the crowded corridors of big business, with its "old boy networks" and traditional discrimination. Special advantages to women and minorities need to be explored with representatives of both groups and made visible first of all to counselors and then to the people with whom counselors work. Bring some of these new small business people into your work setting to share some of their experiences. Or maybe schedule a forum on "Women and Minorities in Small Business." Do whatever it takes to make the opportunities visible.

Learn Where to Find Basic Information. One of the hallmarks of good counselors is being a source of accurate, up-to-date career information. Counselors cannot be expected to know everything, but they can be expected to know how to find out answers to a wide range of inquiries. Knowing the resources in the fast-growing area of small business is a big job because of the rapid expansion in the field. For starters, the Small Business Administration's national, state, and regional offices are basic resources. In addition, many two-year and four-year colleges and universities have established small business centers to help people explore the possibility of starting a new venture or to help small business owners resolve problems that they are encountering. The Cooperative Extension Service in land-grant universities may also be a source to check out for small business support, at least to find out whether it is promoting any "Small Business Expos" or "Franchising Days" or similar activities. Finally, information should be secured about SCORE—Service Corps of Retired Executives—an organization partially funded by the SBA and staffed by volunteers who have agreed to render free service to small business people. For almost twenty-three years, people have turned to SCORE's 12,000 retired business people in 400 chapters. SCORE's mission is to strengthen small companies as they get started, grow, falter, or prosper. The group worked with 154,000 firms in 1986 and held 13,000 workshops. SCORE volunteers will help with writing business plans, preparing loan applications, and establishing good management procedures.

Some other resources follow.

U.S. Small Business Administration
1441 L St., N.W.   8:30 A.M. to 5 P.M. EDT
Washington, D.C. 20416   Phone: (800) 368-5855
A long list of pamphlets and books available on request.

International Franchise Association
1350 New York Ave., N.W. (Suite 900)
Washington, D.C. 20005
The place to turn to for franchising information.

National Federation of Independent Business
P.O. Box 7515
San Mateo, Calif. 94402
The Research and Educational Foundation has helpful information.

USA Today. The largest-circulating newspaper in the country is a constant source of information about all phases of small business. There are frequent columns on interesting case studies of promising small business venture. Franchising information is featured in two- to four-page special sections containing lists of opportunities.

Inc.
Inc. Publishing Corp.   Subscription order:
38 Commercial Wharf   Box 2538
Boston, Mass. 02109   Boulder, Colo. 80321
Features in this magazine include "Insider," which contains advice from experts; "Washington" political news; "Spotlight," which highlights specific businesses; and "Investments." Recent articles have reported on entrepreneurship in Europe and an annual executive compensation survey. Lists top 100 small businesses each year and also publishes an annual *Guide to Small Business Success.*

Nation's Business
Chamber of Commerce of the U.S.
1615 H Street, N.W.
Washington, D.C. 20062
Features in this magazine include a small business report and a guest column. Recent comments in the guest column were on entrepreneurship. Recent articles were on entrepreneurial couples and on franchising.

American Journal of Small Business
University of Baltimore Educational Foundation
Charles at Mount Royal, Baltimore, Md. 21201
A feature of this magazine is a review of recent publications for

the small business owner, such as *Back to Basics Management*. Recent articles include "Small Business Exporting" and "The Most Critical Problem for the Fledgling Small Business: Getting Sales."

Suggested Readings

Birch D. *Job Creation in America: How Our Smallest Companies Put the Most People to Work.* New York: Free Press, 1987.

David Birch is president of Cognetics in Cambridge, Massachusetts. This book, based on seven years of research by Cognetics, reports that small firms with fewer than twenty employees create ninety-eight percent of all net new jobs. This "Innovation Revolution" helped create 9 million new jobs, mostly in small business, in the 1980s.

Feingold, S. N., and Perlman, L. G. *Making It On Your Own.* Washington, D.C.: Acropolis Books, 1985.

For the person who has the "itch" to start a small business, this may be just the book to get him or her going. It contains a list of 397 businesses that the authors think have the greatest potential for the future. It also provides encouraging tips—especially for women, young adults, persons with disabilities, minorities, and retirees—and contains some information on such topics as partnerships and business planning. Finally, it lists numerous sources of further information.

Goldstein, A. *Starting on a Shoestring.* New York: Ronald Press, 1984.

The author, an attorney, discusses and dismisses six commonly held myths about the difficulties of getting started. The book contains illustrations of successful small businesses that have followed the author's advice.

Schumacher, E. F. *Small Is Beautiful: Economics as If People Mattered.* New York: Harper & Row, 1973.

The late British economist Schumacher writes from the heart, but he also brings to bear wide and varied experience in making the case for a scaled-down economy. From his point of view, a small business is free, efficient, creative, enjoyable, and enduring. Schumacher is also the author of a good companion book, simply titled *Good Work* (1979). Both books build a rationale for a philosophical, moral, and economic change to a smaller-sized workplace where people are important.

Small Business Administration. *The State of Small Business: A Report of the President.* Washington, D.C.: Small Business Administration, 1986.

Probably the most comprehensive book available on small business. There are extensive charts, tables, graphs, and lists, along with strong summaries of the essential facts. Especially good overview material in a very readable format. Chapters on veterans, women, and minority-owned businesses as well as self-employment. Excellent background resources for presentations on the scope of small business in the United States.

Solomon, S. *Small Business USA.* New York: Crown Publishers, 1985.

Not a how-to-do-it book, this volume instead makes the point that small business ventures are absolutely vital in rebuilding the American economy and extending free-market values. Indeed, the author argues that the emergence of a "small business economy" is even more important now than in the past. Included are many good illustrations of all kinds of successful small business people.

8

The Work-at-Home Trend

In 1985 there were 7.8 million self-employed persons in non-agricultural industries in the United States. A major portion of those counted as self-employed are working at home. Many others who work at home are not counted because they are not self-employed. They work for someone else and therefore are counted as employees, or they are simply not counted at all. Because no one really knows the exact number of work-at-home people, this area is sometimes labeled the "invisible work force" and sometimes the "underground economy," which does not want to be counted, especially by the Internal Revenue Service. At any rate, in a wide variety of occupations, the self-employed represent a growing segment of the work force. They go by many names, such as cottage industries workers, electronic cottage workers, flexiplace workers, home workers, independent location workers, remote workers, telecommuters, teleworkers, or worksteaders.

By definition, the work-at-home person is someone who simply is working out of a residence—which could be an apartment, a room, a house, or a farm. Farmers, of course, for many years made up a large segment of those who worked at home. But as the number of farmers gradually declined, their place in the statistics was taken by the "production pieceworkers" of the early 1900s. Eventually, the "sweat shop" conditions under which many of these people had to work led to state and federal legislation banning such labor. The number of at-home workers declined until the early 1970s, but since 1970 the number of work-at-home persons has been steadily on the increase. That increase and what those people do for a living is the subject of this chapter, which describes the scope of this less than visible segment of the work force, the types of work done at home, and several successful work-at-home individuals. A short profile of some of the available support groups will be given, and some suggestions on what counselors can do to assist people to become more knowledgeable about work-at-home options will follow.

Scope of Work at Home

There are two types of work-at-home situations: (1) the person essentially is self-employed (for instance, as a music teacher, an artist, a professional or trade worker, or a salesperson); (2) the person works for someone else (for instance, as an insurance salesperson, a data-entry worker, or a newspaper columnist) and telecommutes from home. A great many of the above-mentioned 7.8 million self-employed are in the first category of work-at-home people, but not all self-employed people work from their homes. These people have the option to work at home or not. Often, as they become better established and their practice or business expands, they move their office out of their homes.

The other large segment of the at-home workers, the telecommuters, have some type of hookup with their employers via computer tie-ins. This fast-growing group is expected to reach 10 million by 1990. Among the well-known national companies that have work-at-home programs are American Express, Bank of America, Control Data Corporation, International Business Machines, Metropolitan Life Insurance Company, Pacific Bell, United Airlines, Walgreen Company, Weyerhaeuser Company, and Xerox.

Because telecommuters mostly work for other people— not for themselves—they are not likely to be counted in the self-employed group. Estimates vary widely on how many workers are counted in their number. One estimate is 25 million people, or roughly 25 percent of the work force; another is 10–15 million telecommuters. Both seem much too high. Jack Niles,

a University of Southern California researcher who is credited
with coining the term *telecommuters,* estimates their number as
between 20,000 and 30,000 in 1984. Niles's figures are probably
closer to reality.

In the larger picture of *all* those working at home, the numbers get even higher (some also might say wilder). Atkinson
(1985) relates the following estimates on the low side: 2 million
people with home-based businesses (reported by the U.S. Bureau
of the Census); 5 million home businesses in 1983 (estimated
by the Small Business Administration); 10 million businesses at
home (according to AT&T researchers); 10 million businesses
listing home address as a principal place of employment in 1984
(reported by the U.S. Chamber of Commerce). The best estimate probably is in the 5–10 million range. As to the future,
some people believe that a full one-third of the work force will
eventually carry out some portion of its work at home. It is certain that a growing number of people want to stay at home and
work and that a growing number of opportunities are available
to those people. Consequently, the current trend in the rapidly
increasing numbers of at-home workers is unlikely to slacken
in the near future—although two factors may limit the increase
somewhat: local zoning laws may not permit certain types of
work in specified areas, and national or state labor regulations
may prohibit certain types of production or piecework from being
done at home. Many unions are fighting the work-at-home
movement, especially in "piecework production."

Advantages and Disadvantages
of Working at Home?

There are probably as many answers to that question as
there are people who work at home. But William Atkinson, in
his book *Working at Home: Is It for You?* (1985), has surveyed
the research in the field and come up with the following major
points:

Major Benefits of Self-Employment
Opportunity to set up your own system
Freedom to make your own decisions

No need to make compromises

Freedom from company and co-worker "games" and internal politics

Freedom to begin work when you wish

Freedom to set your own hours and work schedule

Freedom from meetings, unreliable co-workers, and so on

Security of knowing you will succeed or fail based on your own merits, not on someone else's successes or failures

Freedom from a boss you don't like to work for

Major Drawbacks of Self-Employment

Necessity to set up your own system

Necessity to make your own decisions

No co-workers or bosses to rely on

Necessity to rely on yourself solely

Necessity to be self-disciplined and self-motivated

Lack of guaranteed paycheck, company benefits, and so on

No one to "pass the buck" to

Major Benefits of Working at Home

Ease

Freedom to live where you wish

No commuting hassles

No time spent getting "dressed" for work

Additional productivity because of fewer interruptions

No expense for wardrobe, commute, parking, meals, and so on

Reduced auto and home insurance costs

Solitude

Opportunity to spend more time with family

Limited need to send children to day-care centers

Major Drawbacks of Working at Home

"Fuzzy" line between work and personal life

Need to locate separate, private space for working

Potential for becoming involuntary workaholic

Business interruptions evenings and weekends

Lower productivity if unable to get motivated

Interruptions from neighbors, friends, and family
Loneliness
Family squabbles caused by "close quarters"
Feeling unprofessional

In essence, it is a personal choice. What may be an attraction to one person is a drawback to someone else. Some people, because of physical mobility problems, may have little choice except to stay at home to work. Work at home certainly is not for everyone, but it is clearly a choice that people should be aware of and may want to explore for possible opportunities that fit into their personal life-styles and expectations for their future workplace.

Types of Self-Employment at Home

There are roughly four major categories of the self-employed who work at home: (1) traditional, (2) direct sales, (3) crafts (including real cottage industries), and (4) other miscellaneous opportunities.

Traditional. The current run of television shows presents a number of characters who work at home. For example, the top-rated *Bill Cosby Show* depicts a physician working out of a basement office in the family residence. *My Sister Sam* is about an advertising business operating out of an attractive apartment. The *Designing Women* are four interior decorators who work at home in a southern colonial house in Atlanta. These are fairly traditional types of work-at-home occupations. Here are twenty other examples, from *A* to *V*:

Accountant	Nursery (child care)
Artist	Photographer
Beautician	Real estate agent
Cook	Tailor
Dentist	Typist-secretary
Editor	Taxidermist
Farmer	Tax preparer

Insurance agent	Teacher (music, art, and so on)
Lawyer	Upholsterer
Musician	Veterinarian

Direct Sales. Almost everybody probably can name the top five direct sales companies: Avon Products, Amway, Fuller Brush, Mary Kay Cosmetics, and Tupperware. Beyond these five, there are a great many smaller companies—selling everything from ladies' lingerie to designer fabrics. The Direct Selling Association estimates that home sales amounted to more than $8 billion in 1985. A few people make more than $30,000–$50,000 each year from such sales, and a great many people make $10,000–$20,000. If one wants to sell and also wants to stay at home, this area of direct sales of consumer products is an attractive alternative because there is little capital outlay and results come from hard work. According to recent estimates, more than 2 million people are involved in direct sales.

Crafts, Including Cottage Industries. There may be as many as 30,000 people who work full time at producing everything from aprons to zithers. They sell their wares at craft fairs and shopping malls (there are about 6,000–8,000 such shows per year) and at flea markets (there are about 4,000 such markets each year). Some of these markets are open all year; others only on weekends and during peak vacation periods.

Craft work may be the single largest grouping of the several work-at-home types. Some estimates are that 40–50 percent of all those involved in work at home are engaged in some type of craft activity—both part time and full time. The activities are rather well known, but here are twenty-five examples:

Antique refinisher	Macrame worker
Apron maker	Musical instrument maker
Artist	Needlepoint (or cross stitch
Basket maker	or candlewick) embroiderer
Calligrapher	Potter
Candlemaker	Quilter
Ceramicist	Seamstress/tailor

Chair caner	Silkscreen artist
Doll maker	Stained glass maker
Dry flower arranger	Welder
Furniture maker	Wood-carver
Jeweler	Wreath Maker
Leather crafter	Zither maker

The scope of craft work is almost unlimited. For the more talented, there is teaching, writing (instructional articles and books), retail and wholesale selling of related craft materials, or packaging kits with instructions for the do-it-yourselfer. The very talented may even create innovative equipment, materials, and supplies. In short, craft work can be a satisfying leisure activity, or a "moonlighting" source of income, or a full-time venture that involves creating, showing, selling, displaying, writing, or teaching.

There has also been a renewed interest in the "original cottage industries." These were the home labors of the 1700s and 1800s, especially in Europe. The workers were members of local guilds and cooperatives. They were skilled men and women who sold their goods at local fairs and markets as well as local shops or guild outlets. This work all but disappeared at the end of the nineteenth century but now is flourishing in a 1980s revival, especially in Great Britain. This revival is chronicled in a fascinating book by Britisher Marjorie Filbee called *Cottage Industries* (1982). Some of the traditional crafts which she reports on, in both their earlier and later forms, are:

Lace making	Ropes and nets
Spinning and weaving	Country pottery making
Hand knitting	Furniture making
Smocking	Woodcarving
Printed textiles	Metalworking
Beehives, bonnets, and baskets	Leatherwork

There is emerging evidence that these traditional cottage crafts are enjoying a revival in the United States as well as Britain.

Miscellaneous Work At Home. There is an almost infinite number of work-at-home possibilities that are not confined to the categories of traditional, direct sales, and crafts. In this miscellaneous group, the possibilities are limited only by one's imagination, creativity, time, money, talent, location, and risk-taking ability. The following list can only suggest their scope:

> Lodging services (for instance, a bed-and-breakfast business in an older home)
>
> Food services (for instance, a weekend catering business, a dinner-only service in a restaurant, a home bakery, or a candymaking operation)
>
> Personal services (taking care of houses, yards, pets, plants; escorting people; or providing shopping services)
>
> Cleaning services (a residential or commercial cleaning business on a contract basis)
>
> Consulting services (for instance, offering advice on art collecting, weddings, investments, insurance, and taxes for individuals and organizations)
>
> Travel services (planning trips for others or arranging guided tours of museums, national parks, and even foreign countries)

Needless to say, this is just a small sample of the hundreds of possibilities for work-at-home businesses. But two elements are essential in all cases: First, the individual must have the skill to produce a product or service that others want to purchase. Second, he or she must make sure that there is a market for that product or service. It takes a careful match of these two elements to make a work-at-home venture succeed.

The Lucky Seven

Work-at-home people are to be found in every small town, suburb, and big city in the land. Specialized magazines and newsletters in the field carry numerous case studies in just about every issue. Entrepreneurs, owners of small businesses, and work-at-home people are all around us. We tend to think that most people work for large employers—the IBMs and Exxons of the world—when in fact the number of people who work in smaller settings has been steadily increasing for many years. There is a need to make this latter group more visible to the individuals in our society who are making career decisions. Very often, they do not even know that the option of becoming an entrepreneur or small business owner is open to them.

The following illustrations are about work-at-home people from New York to Florida and out to Missouri and Minnesota. Four of them involve couples who work in projects together. This is frequently the case in work-at-home situations—the whole family joins in.

1. Custom Meats and Custom Catering, Blacksburg, Virginia. Larry and Charlotte Linkous are neighbors of mine here in the small town of Blacksburg. Larry worked as a butcher at a local market for a number of years. When the market went out of business, he decided to take his customers with him and opened Custom Meats fourteen years ago. Customers kept asking why he did not open a catering business and cook up those great meats; so Custom Catering came into being nine years ago. Both businesses are doing well. Larry and Charlotte enjoy meeting the public and like running their home-based businesses. Their sons, Noah and Taylor, help in the business when they are not tied up with schoolwork.

2. Show-Me Bar-B-Q Sauce, Columbia, Missouri. Harry H. Berrier is a 65-year-old retired professor of veterinary medicine at the University of Missouri, Columbia. He has turned a hobby into a $128,000-a-year home business that is still growing. Dr. Berrier makes his tangy sauce in the basement of his Columbia home with the help of his wife and various students on a part-time basis. Once made, Show-Me Bar-B-Q Sauce is shipped all over the United States and abroad. The "Show-Me" label derives, of course, from the Missouri State motto, which was actually his third choice for a name. The first two had already been trademarked in 1975, when he got around to serious barbecue business. He and his attorney were surprised to learn that "Show Me" had not been used—so he got possession of it for his product.

Dr. Berrier has never spent a penny on advertising. He depends solely on word-of-mouth advertising. The quality of the product is beginning to yield higher and higher dividends, with grocery stores and food chains wanting to place larger and larger orders. The product evolved over the past twenty-five years because Dr. Berrier is an unabashed barbecue fanatic. He began mixing various ingredients till he got just the right sweet/sour/smoky taste. He used to make the mix in his kitchen until the chore got too big. Now he mixes twenty-eight gallons at a time in his basement.

3. Hollow Motel, Barre, Vermont. Peg and Bill Whitehouse live in a rent-free home on the grounds of their attractive Hollow Motel in Barre, Vermont. Ten years ago Bill worked as an executive in Greenwich, Connecticut. When his company had a cutback in staff and his job was eliminated, he and Peg bought the twenty-six-room roadside inn. Now they have a renovated pool and an 80 percent occupancy rate. The operation brings in $400,000 a year. They work hard for what they have—taking turns on the desk, cleaning rooms, cutting the lawn, and performing all the maintenance chores. The Whitehouses looked at thirty-eight inns before settling on the Hollow Motel. The place was in good structural shape and well located to attract tourist and business travelers. They are happy with their work-at-home situation. (*Source:* Manley, 1987.)

4. Button Mania, Berkley, Minnesota. Rickie Knowles began making buttons as a hobby in 1982, to get arm muscles back in shape after surgery. "Little did I know how much exercise this would give," she says. In 1984, with the encouragement of her husband, Rickie began to produce custom-designed buttons in earnest, doing buttons for the Detroit Tigers and many stock designs for holiday and special occasions. "My husband helps me in the evenings, and when we get real busy, my youngest daughter jumps in too," Rickie says. "Another daughter, who works full time and has two small children, is the greatest partner I could ask for." While concentrating on a mail-order business, this family business has expanded to include rubber stamps of its exclusive designs. The newest is "Muffin," a Teddy bear. (*Source:* Brabec, 1986a.)

5. Berger Lawn Service, Miami, Florida. Kathy and Scott Berger jointly operate a lawn-care service from their home, in a suburb of Miami. Kathy also has a direct sales toy business. In addition, she has organized Mothers-in-Business, a support group for women who are both in business and mothers; the organization now has about forty members. Kathy and Scott were married in 1980 and about six months later got their first lawn job. At the time, Scott was employed by Eastern Airlines. He worked night shifts for several years while the lawn-care service was getting established—as many work-at-home people do. Gradually, as his separate business grew, he cut back on his hours at the airline. Now he has two full-time employees and is more selective about the types of new lawn jobs he takes on. Kathy handles the inside business of billing and setting up accounts for the lawn service. She has also been successful selling toys, with as many as two or three demonstration parties a week in her busy season from September to December. The Mothers-in-Business group meets once a month to hear speakers and discuss the concerns of the members. (*Source:* Groller, 1985.)

6. Santa Claus Suit & Equipment Company, Albian, New York. Tailoring your business to meet the needs of the holiday season is wise, no matter what your line of work. Elizabeth Babcock, 72, has made her living following that reasoning for the past twenty years. She sews suits for Santa Claus. Her home-based enterprise, the Santa Claus Suit & Equipment Company, fills orders for about 200 custom-made suits a year. She supplies Kris Kringles to stores around the country, from Macy's in New York City to the Emporium in San Francisco. "Neither store has bought one this year, but that's not unusual," Babcock said. "The suits are handmade and very durable." She also repairs suits at the rate of about 200 a year—and sends Santa's hair out for curling. Babcock's suits are patterned after a 1937 design, trimmed in French rabbit fur, and carry price tags of $210 to $400. Her busiest seasons are summer and fall, but she works year-round cutting material and employs three other women who sew for the big elf in their homes. Like any other business owner, Babcock knows she has competition, but stakes her claim to fame: "I'm only one of Santa's many helpers, but

I'm one of a few who's doing this by hand." (*Source: USA Today*, Dec. 22, 1987, p. B-7.)

7. Auto Part Assembly, Guthrie Center, Iowa. Farmers Jack and Beverly Stringer were having a hard time of it until they were offered an opportunity to become rural home industry workers. Each week they put together about 5,400 end-link assemblies, a small automobile suspension part that connects the anti-sway torsion bar to the chassis on General Motors cars. Since August of 1986, about thirty families in Guthrie County have assembled the part as "remote subcontractors" for the Shakeproof company of Elgin, Illinois. Rural America has become the scene of an increasing number of work-at-home projects, as distressed farm families and small-town folks look for ways to survive and stay where they are. The Stringers work in a converted chicken brooding house. The building has a heater and an air conditioner as well as a Citizens Band radio to keep Beverly in touch with Jack when he is out working in the fields. Each week the Stringers and other work-at-home people in the area drive to Guthrie Center to collect and deliver their contracted kits. They like the flexibility of their work, which provides some much-needed cash income and allows them to maintain a cherished way of life. (*Source:* Worthington, 1987.)

Where to Find Support

If you are working with someone who is exploring the possibility of starting a work-at-home venture, you are in luck. There are ample resources to select from. Besides the six recommended sources at the end of this chapter, dozens of paperback "how-to" books are available at almost any good bookstore. If you are in an isolated area, write for a catalog from the New Career Center, 6003 North 51st Street, Suite 105, Boulder, Colorado 80301. For six top national sources to pass along to the people with whom you work, the following are suggested:

1. Center for Home-Based Businesses, Business Assistance Center, Truman College, 1145 West Wilson Avenue, Chicago, Ill. 60640; (312) 989-6112. Leslie W. MacDonald, direc-

tor. A clearinghouse of information on homebased business issues provides assistance to homebased business people by mail, phone, or in person. The center also sponsors craft shows and presents workshops on starting and operating mail-order, day-care, and other businesses in the home.

2. National Alliance of Homebased Businesswomen, P.O. Box 306, Midland Park, N.J. 07432; (201) 423-9131. Marie MacBride, staff administrator. Holds annual meetings featuring management seminars and publishes a newsletter, *Alliance.* About 10 percent of the 1,400 members are men, which may lead to a name change for this organization.

3. National Association for the Cottage Industry, P.O. Box 14850, Chicago, Ill. 60614; (312) 472-8116. Coralee Smith Kern, director. Conducts regional conferences featuring management seminars specifically for homebased business owners. The association also publishes a newsletter, *Mind Your Own Business at Home.* Has more than 2,500 members.

4. *National House Business Report,* published quarterly by Barbara Brabec, P.O. Box 2137, Naperville, Ill. 60566.

5. *Worksteader News,* a monthly newsletter published by Lynie Arden, 2396 Coolidge Way, Rancho Cordova, Calif. 95670.

6. U.S. Small Business Administration, 1441 L Street, N.W., Washington, D.C. 20416; (202) 653-6555. Provides training, counseling, and financial assistance to the small business sector. Publishes a free booklet, *Home Businesses,* which includes an extensive bibliography.

There are some growing resources at the state level as well. For example, nearly 700 people attended the all-Iowa Homebased Business Conference in March 1986 in Des Moines. Governor Branstad told the group that Iowa's homebased businesses are a vital part of the state's economic future. He said that special help is available to Iowans in eleven Small Business Development Centers and through many community colleges. He also suggested the state's business loan program and a venture capital fund as sources of start-up financing. An estimated 15,000–20,000 Iowans already operate homebased businesses. The conference was intended as a stimulus to further homebased enterprises.

New York City was the location of a February 1987 conference on "The New Era of Homework: Directions and Responsibilities," sponsored by the City University of New York, (CUNY) and the U.S. Dept. of Health and Human Services. The meeting was chaired by Kathleen Christensen, who is director of CUNY's National Project on Homebased Work. In addition, many states are following suit by developing active programs under the auspices of the Cooperative Extension Service. In Virginia the Extension Service has organized a seminar entitled "Starting a Homebased Business," which provides information and inspiration to aspiring work-at-home enthusiasts. The seminars cover a wide range of topics on business aspects of working at home as well as the pros and cons of following the road back home. The Virginia Cooperative Extension Service, under the leadership of Ann M. Lastovica, plans to expand its help to potential work-at-home people through 1991. Check with your state's cooperative extension service to see whether similar assistance is available in your area, and be on the lookout for regional, state, and local conferences on the subject.

What Should Counselors Do?

Most counselors are not accustomed to looking around for work-at-home people. Most of us who have been concerned with career development through the life span have looked to the larger employers for trends, information, and potential jobs for those with whom we work. But even though persons working at home (unless they are expanding a homebased business) may not hire someone we refer, they can serve as models for other people to emulate. If current forecasts are correct, up to 25 percent of the work force may be working at home by the year 1995 or 2000. Even if these estimates are not accurate, there are strong indications that homebased workers are a significant and growing sector of the work force—a sector that most counselors do not know much about. The following suggestions may help counselors begin to learn more about the work-at-home trend as part of tomorrow's workplace.

Get Informed About the Subject. Use the six books at the end
of this chapter as a beginning. Then read articles and books
written by work-at-home people. These are firsthand accounts,
which candidly share the disappointments as well as the joys
and satisfaction of working at home. Most of the newsletters
noted earlier in this chapter are edited by dedicated homebased
business people who really believe in what they are doing. In
addition to first-person advice, these newsletters contain some
solid business and financial tips as well as organizational suggestions.

After building a personal base of understanding in this
area, you might try to secure the best of these resources for your
career resource center. A small investment of $50–$100 should
be sufficient for this purpose. If funds are not available, the agency
librarian might help by acquiring some of your suggested titles
and setting up a special shelf. The same thing also may work
with a friendly newsstand or local bookstore manager, who may
be willing to consider your invitation to set up a special section
on "work at home." Finally, a reading list of books, articles,
brochures, and local and state resources would assist the people who want to do some career exploration on their own.

Find Out About Local Resources. The best type of career information is that which is received firsthand. Therefore, you and
the people you work with should try to get some firsthand information about work-at-home situations in your area. But how
do you do that? These people do not have public relations staffs,
advertising staffs, or fancy offices. But they do have satisfied
customers who like their products or services. Ask around. Start
with a piano tuner who almost always works out of his or her
house. Find some people who are in direct sales. Get the word
out that you are interested in buying some toys at a home demonstration party or in learning more about household products from
Amway. Or find out whether there are some small bed-and-
breakfast places nearby; nearly 3,000 were estimated to be in
business in 1986. Ask the operators of a homebased catering
service to prepare a meal for your local professional counselors'
meeting and to speak to the group about work-at-home pros
and cons.

If you work in a school setting, try to set up a recognition program for the "Homebased Business of the Month." Set up some contest rules and have students nominate different work-at-home people for the award. After selecting the monthly winners, feature them around the school during their month. A certificate could be awarded each month. At the end of the school year, you and the rest of the school will know much more about work-at-home people than you did before.

Sponsor Local and Regional Meetings. Small work-at-home businesses often are not very visible. Some owners prefer this, while others would like to be better known but do not have money to spend on advertising. The counselor's job is not to provide free publicity but simply to help others become aware of what work-at-home opportunities and options are available in the community. How to do that? One way would be to team up with the local chamber of commerce to sponsor a one-day conference or seminar on work-at-home businesses in your town. Find some successful people and feature them as speakers. Have panel discussions on the advantages and disadvantages of working at home. This same type of format could be used at local and state meetings of the American Association for Counseling and Development. A series of meetings on "The Three Wild Cards in the Work Game" or a one-day preconvention forum would be useful.

Get Area Media to Help. Most local media are always looking for new ideas. They have a lot of time on the air or space in print to fill every day, so they usually welcome suggestions. Explain that you are interested in letting the community know more about people who work at home. Ask them to run a week-long or month-long series on homebased businesses. Arrange for the segments to be videotaped, so that they can be used for later replay in your job setting.

The Sunday papers are always looking for good feature stories that have human-interest appeal. What could be more interesting than a series of features on persons with disabilities who work at home? The editor of your local or regional magazine—most areas now have such publications—also might consider running a regular feature (for say a year) on work-at-home businesses. You could clip the item in each issue and make an attractive bulletin board.

Suggested Readings

Arden, L. *The Work-at-Home Sourcebook: How to Find "At Home" Work That's Right for You.* Boulder, Colo.: Live Oak Publications, 1987.

Mainly a long list (sources) of companies from Maine to California that hire workers at home. An excellent source for the person who wants to work at home but does not necessarily want to be self-employed. Separate listings of employers by occupation and by state/region. The author has worked at home for the past twenty years and is the editor and publisher of *The Worksteader News,* a monthly newsletter.

Atkinson, W. *Working at Home: Is It for You?* Homewood, Ill.: Dow Jones–Irwin, 1985.

Probably the most comprehensive book on this subject. The book provides good background information and current estimates on the numbers who are self-employed or otherwise employed but working at home.

Behr, M., and Lazar, W. (eds.). *Women Working Home: The Homebased Business Guide and Directory.* Edison, N.J.: Women Working Home Press, 1981.

A collection of articles by nineteen different contributors. A good book but somewhat unevenly written. The editors are also involved with the National Alliance of Homebased Businesswomen and publish a newsletter.

Brabec, B. *Homemade Money.* White Hall, Va.: Betterway Publications, 1986.

The author, one of the foremost authorities on the topic of home business, gives expert advice on getting started, selecting the right business, planning for profits, diversifying, and enlarging. She publishes a quarterly newsletter—*National Home Business Report.* Next to Atkinson's, the best book around.

Feldman, B. *Homebased Businesses.* Los Angeles: Till Press, 1983.

Dr. Feldman teaches at Los Angeles Valley College and has other books in the career area. This book is much more counselor oriented than the others noted and really helps the reader understand the pros and cons of working at home. Includes a list of homebased opportunities worth exploring. The author also has a bimonthly newsletter, *Homebased News,* and offers to put the reader on a mailing list for future seminars.

Filbee, M. *Cottage Industries.* North Pomfret, Vt.: David & Charles, 1982.

The author is British and writes about the fascinating history and folklore of the cottage industries of the 1700s and 1800s. She also describes the current resurgence of these industries in Britain and elsewhere. Good background for the person who wants to know more about the real country crafts.

Career Counseling
for Work and Leisure

This final part of the book examines, in some detail, the relation between work and leisure in an individual's career. In doing so, it focuses on how people can best prepare for a variety of alternative futures through a combination of work and leisure options. It is proposed here that an individual's career development, over his or her life span, results from a continuing interaction of work and leisure activities which should together provide a measure of life satisfaction. Since we cannot know exactly what the work force or workplace of the future will look like, both young and older people should be encouraged to find out about things they really like to do (usually the best clue to that is what they do for leisure) and then see whether those things could lead to satisfaction in a work setting. If not, the various leisure activities may serve as an additional or compensating source of satisfaction.

After nearly twenty-five years of writing and thinking about this subject, I have become convinced that preparing for leisure is just as important as preparing for work—sometimes, indeed, they turn out to be the same thing. Therefore, as one plans for a career, one should bring leisure into full partnership with work in the following fashion: Career = Work + Leisure (C = W + L). The next three chapters bring this concept out in more detail.

Chapter Nine, ''Enhancing Options for Both Leisure and Work,'' is an overview chapter. It establishes the definitions and looks briefly at some of the main components in the future of both work and leisure. There follows a discussion of the inter-relations of work and leisure and a look at some unresolved issues. After describing various work and leisure options, including the new volunteerism, the chapter concludes with some suggestions on how counselors can bring about changes in institutions to better support the work-leisure connection.

Chapter Ten, ''Helping People Put Their Leisure to Work,'' is really the heart of Part Four. It goes from theory (Chapter Nine) to practice. The chapter first issues a challenge— why not encourage people to do what they enjoy?—and then discusses the pros and cons of this approach. It lists occupations and jobs that directly relate to a variety of leisure activities and also provides twenty illustrations of people from various age groups who have actually taken the leap to put their leisure to work. The chapter closes with suggestions on how counselors can invite their clients to take a serious look at this option.

Chapter Eleven, ''Work and Leisure Counseling: A Life-Span Approach,'' describes a six-stage approach to work and leisure development over the life span, emphasizing the crucial differences and similarities in each epoch. A case is then made for a broad-based approach to career counseling, as opposed to leisure counseling or work counseling alone (CC = LC + WC). Finally, there is a discussion of seven principles that will lead to a unified career counseling approach over the life span.

9

Enhancing Options
for Both Leisure and Work

In 1984, for the first time in the sequence of three National Vocational Guidance Association (now the National Career Development Association) decennial volumes, the topic of leisure was elevated to the status of a chapter. Certain obvious changes in America and other Western industrial nations suggested that the topic of leisure deserved that level of attention. Those changes have a direct bearing on tomorrow's workplace:

- Shorter Workdays and Workweeks
- Longer and More Frequent Vacations
- Earlier and Better Financial Retirement for Many
- Greater Availability and Acceptability of Leisure Options
- Higher Levels of Interest in Leisure
- More Unemployment and Underemployment

The thesis of this chapter is that work and leisure are part of one's career and both merit attention by career counseling professionals. There are many signs that leisure is being taken seriously:

- The National Career Development Association (NCDA) has created a Commission on Leisure and Career Development.
- The agenda of NCDA's 75th Anniversary Conference included an invited paper on work and leisure.

- An increasing number of articles on leisure have appeared over the last decade in the *Career Development Quarterly,* the *Journal of Counseling and Development,* the *Journal of Career Development,* the *School Counselor,* and other professional counseling periodicals.
- Some new books, as well as occasional convention programs, are focusing on leisure counseling.
- Publications such as *Leisure Sciences,* the *Journal of Leisure Research,* and the ''Leisure Today'' section of the *Journal of Health, Physical Education and Recreation* report regularly on the topic.

Many writers in the leisure field have established international reputations. (For American examples see de Grazia, 1962; Kelly, 1982b; Kaplan, 1975; Neulinger, 1981; Murphy, 1981. For European examples see Parker, 1971; Roberts, 1981; Dumazedier, 1967; Veblen, 1899; Anderson, 1974; Pieper, 1952.) One can develop a good background on the subject by studying the writings of these authors. Another ten or so professionals in counseling, cited in the reference section of this book, are also building a foundation for a more compatible relationship between work and leisure.

This chapter presents some working definitions of important terms, establishes a framework for the interrelationship of work and leisure, considers some unresolved issues related to leisure, outlines some work and leisure options, and reviews the new volunteerism. It also suggests ways that counselors can assist in bringing about needed institutional responses to the changing role and concept of leisure.

Definitions of Terms

The terms *work* and *leisure* have a great deal of personal meaning for people. Academic definitions can be stated here, but average people already hold a rather firm idea of what both terms mean: ''Work is what you get paid for, and leisure is what you do not get paid for.'' Several years ago a group of elementary school youngsters defined leisure for me as:

Free time or play time
When there ain't nothing to do
When school is out
When studying is done
When I get to do what I want to do
When the family does things together

Adults might define leisure in similar terms, including elements such as "free time," "free choice," and "family activities."

For purposes of this chapter, definitions of work, leisure, career, and career development are adapted from a report by Sears (1982), which was reviewed by a panel of career guidance experts, the then NVGA (now NCDA) board of directors, and *Vocational Guidance Quarterly* editorial reviewers.

> *Work.* A conscious effort (one that does not have either coping or relaxation as its primary purpose) aimed at producing benefits for oneself and/or for oneself and others.
>
> *Leisure.* Relatively self-determined activities and experiences that are available due to having discretionary income, time, and social behaviors; the activity may be physical, social, intellectual, volunteer, creative, or some combination of all five.
>
> *Career.* The totality of work (and leisure) that one does in a lifetime.
>
> *Career Development.* The total constellation of psychological, sociological, educational, physical, economic, and chance factors that combine to shape the career of any given individual over the life span.

In Sears's definitions, the word *leisure* does not appear in the definition of *career*. But it is absolutely essential to my notion of a career: Career = Work + Leisure (C = W + L). I first suggested this formula nearly twenty-five years ago (McDaniels, 1965). The linking together of work and leisure to form the basis for a career over one's life span combines all three terms in a holistic framework. Obviously, other roles can be incorporated into the career concept. Super (1984) includes nine roles in his life career rainbow: child, student, worker, leisurite, citizen, spouse, parent, homemaker, pensioner. He makes a strong case for this broader concept, but in this book the focus is on C = W + L. Through this linkage, leisure can be placed in its proper perspective as an important component of career development. Counselors and teachers will begin to recognize the importance of leisure in elementary school, middle/junior high school, and senior high school. Counselors and other adult service providers can help individuals deal with both work and leisure in one relationship—a career.

The Work = Leisure Connection

Much has been written and said recently about the changing nature of work. Parts Two and Three of this book focus on three possible scenarios for the future of work and three possible wild cards in the work game. A significant national conference was held in Washington, D.C., under the auspices of the World Future Society in August 1983 on the topic ''Working Now and in the Future'' and drew a national gathering. ''Counselors Make America Work'' was the theme of the American Personnel and Guidance Association's 1983 convention. Computerization and robotization of the workplace appear to be influencing almost every corner of American life. Concurrently, leisure is assuming increased importance for the average person. In the light of changes in the nature of work, there is a growing need to draw leisure into the career development/counseling concept.

Reports on the Status of Work. O'Toole (1981) insists that management must perceive employees differently in the next decade. Flexible and sensitive policies will be needed to increase workers' satisfaction and productivity. Rosow (1980) also stresses the need for openness on the part of employers. According to Rosow, greater employee satisfaction and company productivity will be achieved through a wide variety of alternative work patterns designed to improve the work environment. Some examples are flexitime, shared time, part time, four-day weeks, and worker participation in decision making. Nollen (1982) addresses a similar theme. He notes that a large number of workers (more than 12 percent of the labor force in 1982) already have flexible work schedules and that such schedules generally result in high productivity, better job satisfaction, and increased leisure for workers.

Many of the current and anticipated changes in the workplace are coming about because the workers themselves are changing. Two of the leading exponents of the new worker are Daniel Yankelovich and Bernard Lefkowitz (1982b), who have described a basic change in the ethos and philosophy of the American worker. As a result of the social movements of the 1960s and 1970s, a new breed of worker has emerged. These "nontraditionalist" workers are under 35 years of age and make up approximately 44 percent of the labor force—a growing minority. Other workers, labeled "traditionalist," are over 35 years of age and constitute a shrinking majority of 56 percent. The nontraditionalists may enjoy their work, but they are more interested in leisure as a major source of life satisfaction. Yankelovich and Lefkowitz (1982a) believe that, during the next decade or so, attempts will be made to balance the rising expectations of nontraditional employees against the economic, social, and political realities of the workplace.

Stern and Best (1977) have called for increased options for employees who want more than the usual cycle of education-work-retirement (leisure). They found that many workers want more leisure and in more useful time periods—not just an hour a day here and there but extended vacation periods for renewal and self-fulfillment. For many workers, this leisure is more important than additional income and shorter workdays or workweeks. As early as 1973, Best predicted that employees, as they move toward basic security and affluence, will give up additional material goods in favor of nonmaterial goals in order to achieve a more comfortable balance and integration of work and leisure. In a somewhat different vein, Schumacher (1977), the late British economist, advocated more meaningful jobs in smaller employment settings, where an individual or small groups of people use their talents and energies to produce goods and services needed by the population for a decent existence. Also, Fain (1980) has reported a trend toward a steady increase in self-employment in America, especially in the 16–44 age category with a median income of $20,000. In the 1970s the number of self-employed grew by 1.1 to 1.3 million, with another 1.5 million partially self-employed while holding down another job.

Will job dissatisfaction drive people to seek life satisfaction through leisure? A case can be made for both sides of this question. A number of studies show that job satisfaction is holding steady. For example, Chelte, Wright, and Tausky (1982) reviewed all major studies on this subject undertaken in the period 1959–1979. They concluded that there was no significant decline in overall job satisfaction during that period. All the major survey researchers found a generally stable pattern over this period. These results were supported by a study of 7,000 American and Japanese workers (Kalleberg and others, 1983). The researchers found that 81 percent of the American workers were satisfied with their work, as compared with 53 percent of the Japanese. American workers were more willing to work harder (68 percent versus 44 percent of Japanese workers) and were twice as willing to accept the goals and values of the employers. The authors admitted that they were "surprised" that American workers were so much better satisfied with their work and willing to work even harder. These and other results suggest that there may not be gross job dissatisfaction; however, some 20–30 percent of the American labor force may seek satisfaction through alternatives such as leisure. In a labor force of 110 million, a formidable number of workers may turn to leisure for fulfillment and satisfaction.

These selected probes into the future of work can be summarized as follows:

1. More changes can be expected in both workers and the workplace in the next decade.
2. More and more people are seeking a balance of work and leisure in their careers.

3. More varied patterns of work will permit larger amounts of leisure.
4. More people are seeking life satisfaction through self-employment.
5. Extended periods of leisure are desired by many employees, often at the cost of pay increases.

Reports on the Status of Leisure. There are many reports on the status of work; there are far fewer reports on leisure. Few national, comprehensive reports on leisure are noted in the professional journals. Probably the best continuing coverage of the expansion of leisure activities over the past decade has been in *U.S. News & World Report.* The staff of this weekly newsmagazine have done a real service in bringing together bits and pieces of information on leisure and blending them together into a total picture. The most recent update appeared in the August 10, 1981, issue ("Our Endless Pursuit of Happiness," 1981). This report estimated that Americans would spend $244 billion on leisure in 1981, a 321 percent increase in sixteen years. Leisure expenditures were $77 billion more than on defense, and leisure spending accounted for one out of every eight consumer dollars. (See Table 12.) Foreign visitors spent another $12 billion on leisure in this country in 1980. Estimates included expenditures of $2.2 billion on camping, hunting, and fishing. The report also estimated that 55 million people exercise regularly, almost twice the number in 1961. The number of best-selling workout books and videos is noteworthy in this regard.

Earlier articles in *U.S. News & World Report* stressed the steady increase in dollars spent on leisure and in the number of participants and spectators. These reports do not include volunteer or educational self-improvement activities, which are also considered leisure activities.

Two studies by the New York–based Research & Forecasts group provide further insight into the scale of leisure in America. The first, *Where Does the Time Go? The United Media Enterprises Report on Leisure in America* (1982), is probably the most comprehensive study on leisure conducted in recent years. Over

Table 12. Americans Participating in Leisure Activities.

Spectators		Participants	
Event	Numbers (in millions)	Activity	Numbers (in millions)
Automobile racing	51.0	Swimming	105.4
Thoroughbred racing	50.1	Bicycling	69.8
Major-league baseball	43.7	Camping	60.3
College football	35.5	Fishing	59.3
College basketball	30.7	Bowling	43.3
Harness racing	27.4	Boating	37.9
Greyhound racing	20.8	Jogging/running	35.7
NFL football	13.4	Tennis	32.3
Minor-league baseball	12.6	Pool/billiards	31.9
NHL hockey	11.5	Softball	28.5
Soccer	11.4	Table tennis	26.9
NBA basketball	10.7	Roller skating	25.4

Spending (in millions)

TVs, radios, records, musical instruments	$21,612
Wheel goods, durable toys, sports equipment, boats, pleasure aircraft	15,446
Nondurable toys, sports supplies	14,017
Magazines, newspapers, sheet music	8,881
Books, maps	6,962
Admissions to amusements, theater, opera	6,424
Golf, bowling, sightseeing, other fees	6,150
Flowers, seeds, potted plants	4,500
Radio, television repair	3,658
Clubs, fraternal organizations	2,295
Parimutuel net receipts	1,898
Other	14,581

Source: "Our Endless Pursuit of Happiness," 1981, p. 62–63. Copyright, Aug. 10, 1981, U.S. News & World Report.

1,000 people were interviewed in a carefully drawn nationwide sample. Some of the highlights of this report are:

- Reading a newspaper and watching television head the list of leisure activities Americans choose to participate in every day.
- Children in families in which both parents are employed outside the home get more daily attention than children in traditional families, in which only the father is employed.
- Fathers in dual-career families spend much more of their

leisure time in child-rearing activities than fathers in traditional families.

- Television is not a disruptive force in American families; it actually may help bind families together.
- While watching television takes up more of our free time than any other leisure-time pursuit, six out of ten Americans say they do not pay close attention to television programs and often do other things while the television set is on.
- Parents who watch a lot of television daily are as likely as parents who watch little television to participate in activities with their children, interact with their spouses, and participate in community affairs.
- Half of all couples in the United States watch television together every day or almost every day. About 35 percent watch together at least once a week.
- The top objective of Americans during their leisure hours is to spend time with their families. Eight out of ten Americans (79 percent) report that spending time with their families is the most important use of their leisure time, followed by seeking companionship (68 percent), relaxing (67 percent), learning new things (60 percent), thinking and reflecting (57 percent), and keeping informed about local, national, and international events (52 percent).
- Nearly half of all Americans (46 percent) say that they participate in community volunteer activities. Dual-career parents and the parents of older children are the most active volunteers.
- Americans with few responsibilities to other family members have the greatest amount of leisure time. On a weekly basis, senior citizens have the greatest amount of leisure time (43 hours), followed by teenagers (41 hours), single adults (38 hours), childless couples (37 hours), parents with adult children (31 hours), single parents (25 hours), parents in families where only the father is employed (24 hours), and dual-career parents (23 hours).

The second Research & Forecasts study, *The Miller Lite Report on American Attitudes Toward Sports* (1983), reports the result of a random sample through 1,139 national telephone calls. The main finding was that 96.3 percent of the sample relate to sports in an active or passive way at least once a month. Of those in the sample, 42 percent participated in some form of sports activity on a daily basis, with swimming being the most popular. Other activities included jogging, running, tennis, bicycling, bowling, and calisthenics. People gave the following reasons for participation: to improve health, enjoyment, release of tension, and improved mental attitude. Finally, three out of four American parents reported that they sometimes or frequently engage in some kind of athletic activity with their children, and 81 percent reported that they frequently watch their children compete.

Implications of Reports on Work and Leisure. The three major series of reports on leisure can be summarized as follows:

1. Leisure is a major American enterprise, growing rapidly every year in magnitude and importance.
2. The family is a major focus of leisure activities.
3. Television viewing, spectator sports, and participant sports take up a great deal of Americans' time.
4. The American public is seriously involved in volunteer activities.
5. American workers view leisure as a necessity, not a luxury. They want more of it.

Viewed collectively, the findings on work and leisure suggest major changes in both aspects of one's career over the next decade. Leisure time and activities have been growing at a fast pace. Changes in Americans' attitudes toward work and leisure will have a significant impact on career development. More and more people are seeking increased satisfaction from their careers. They are seeking satisfaction in work if they can find it there; if not, through leisure; under the best of conditions, through both. They may look for ways to turn their leisure into work in a small business, an entrepreneurial opportunity, or a home-based employment setting. Individuals entering the labor force, employees looking for new directions in their lives, and employees nearing retirement are seeking a balance between work and leisure in their careers. Until now, career counseling has not been of much assistance because leisure has not been related to work. In the future, career counselors will need to consider a leisure-work combination in order to assist individuals faced with tomorrow's workplace.

Unresolved Issues

If all the present and future trends continue, a number of unresolved issues will remain. Presently, the shifts in the marketplace and the workplace are evolving into significant societal trends. National policy directives and solid research and development activity are not addressing the changes. Few universities have ongoing research programs investigating work or leisure. Occasionally an association such as the World Future Society, the Association for Higher Education, or the National Career Development Association will publish a book, but such groups do not promote sustained research and development activities. The Work-in-America Institute, the Upjohn Institute for Employment Research, and the Center for Research in Vocational Technical Education at Ohio State University are notable exceptions and have an ongoing interest in work.

Only a few centers for the study of leisure exist. The best known of these is the Leisure Behavior Research Laboratory at the University of Illinois, Champagne-Urbana, which is producing highly significant studies by both faculty and graduate students.

The groups that study work seem to show little interest in leisure, and the leisure centers show no visible interest in work. Therefore, the unresolved issues in the work-leisure connection go mainly unattended in a never-never land of mutually exclusive areas of interest. Perhaps career development professionals who have no proprietary interest in either topic can best resolve the issues noted below.

Do We Live in a Work or a Leisure Society? A host of studies have appeared in the *Monthly Labor Review* attempting to answer this question. Moore and Hedges (1971) traced the history of

the work-leisure trends over the past century, finding a reduction in the workweek from the mid-1800s until the 1940s.
Since then, the workweek has remained around thirty-five to
thirty-nine hours. The downward trend clearly seems to have
leveled off. Hedges and Taylor (1980) report the following
findings:

- A number of workers still work more than forty hours a week.
- There has been a slight increase in the percent of the labor
  force employed on a five-day/forty-hour schedule.
- The four-day/forty-hour option has not been largely adopted—
  except in very special situations where energy conservation
  was a concern or difficult transportation problems existed.
- Employees would rather obtain more and longer periods of
  paid leave than a shorter workday or workweek.
- Five percent of all collective bargaining agreements in recent
  years have included provisions for extended paid leaves—
  sabbaticals.

These findings indicate that—although increases are occurring in holidays, paid vacations, and retirement benefits, and
although many people have more money to spend on leisure—
there is no move toward a leisure, nonwork society.

Is Leisure a Dirty Word? Put another way, leisure gets no respect!
Some people in the career education movement avoid the use
of the word *leisure* and substitute the term *nonwork*. Yet, clearly,
most people explore vocational interests through leisure activities. The vocational education literature is almost void of any
mention of the term *leisure*. Nevertheless, millions of people each
year use skills learned in vocational education classes for such
leisure pursuits as cooking, photography, home repair, animal
growing, sewing, planting flower gardens, furniture refinishing,
and on and on—the list is almost endless.

The conventional wisdom is that leisure is not supposed
to lead to any other activity. Leisure is thought of as an abstrac-
tion—an end in itself. It is not a matter of serious concern or
study at the university or at the elementary/secondary school
level. To be sure, a number of colleges and universities have

renamed their recreation program "Leisure Studies," but their interest is mainly in traditional recreational activities rather than the intellectual, creative, social, or volunteer aspects of leisure. A few sociologists, such as John Kelly at the University of Illinois; psychologists, such as John Neulinger at New York University; and economists, such as John Owen at Wayne State University, have evidenced solid and sustained interest in a more broadly defined leisure as it is used here. But on the whole, leisure is regarded as "play," "free time," "laziness," "idleness," and is not recognized as a complex, $244-billion-a-year industry that affects the lives of every man, woman, and child in the United States. Leisure clearly seems to be an abused and misunderstood term. It gets limited respect.

Do Schools Prepare Students for Leisure? About seventy years ago, one of the cardinal principles of education was formulated as "Worthy Use of Leisure Time." This principle has not been carefully observed in our nation's schools. Notable exceptions are art, music, dance, drama, physical activities (for all students), and crafts, which are respected for contributing to student development. But a balanced leisure program is often the first thing to be axed in budget cuts in school divisions across the country. At best, a mediocre job has been done in preparing youth for the "Worthy Use of Leisure Time."

Clearer standards must be set for career guidance, including leisure counseling. As it has turned out, seventy years with a vague cardinal principle have not accomplished much. Goals and objectives need to be established and monitored. Mundy and Odum (1979) have set specific goals for leisure education. The National Recreation and Park Association (1981) has also conducted an active program, Leisure Education Advancement Project (LEAP for short), which attempts to implement a good plan of well-developed goals and objectives. But intervention by career development professionals may be necessary to implement leisure education in the schools. Mundy and Odum suggest an alliance with career education to make both programs stronger. In order to combine leisure education with career education, the broader definition of career (career equals work plus leisure) must be accepted.

Can Leisure Satisfaction Replace Job Satisfaction? If the high level of job satisfaction—80 percent as reported by Kalleberg and his colleagues (1983)—holds true on a national scale, there is still a substantial percentage of workers who are dissatisfied; therefore, of 110 million people in the work force, approximately 22 million workers are unhappy with their jobs—a large enough number to merit considerable attention in attempting to find suitable life/leisure satisfaction. Further, with an unemployment rate that has ranged between 5 and 10 percent, another 10 million workers do not have any job with which to be satisfied or dissatisfied. So a combination of unemployed and unhappy workers may reach 30–35 million. Could more adequate leisure programs help make their lot more attractive? Could, as Schumacher and others suggest, some of those with a high level of leisure skills put these satisfying activities to work in self-employment or small business settings? In effect, by putting their leisure to work, a significant number of Americans can become employed *and* satisfied.

While there is no documented body of knowledge regarding the impact of leisure on career satisfaction, there are some indicators that leisure can be highly satisfying. Both studies by Research & Forecasts (1982, 1983) suggest a high degree of leisure satisfaction. Kelly (1982b) has advocated leisure as the central source of intrinsic satisfaction, as opposed to the extrinsic satisfaction from a product or service rendered. In his view, one's leisure identity grows and expands throughout the life span to accommodate changing family, social, and economic situations. Yankelovich and Lefkowitz (1982a) report that people are seeking life satisfaction in activities that do not depend heavily on the acquisition of goods and services. They agree with Kelly that, for a growing number of Americans, satisfactions will emerge through self-fulfillment, self-actualization, and self-expression—mainly in leisure activities.

Lefkowitz (1979), in a study of 100 people who had left their jobs for various reasons, found that many of them were reasonably satisfied with their "breaktime." These people were seeking relief from the daily pressures, personal well-being, variety, and additional time to devote to family and friends. For the most part, they found what they wanted while on their breaktime. They stayed out of work for two years or more before 60 percent of them returned to some type of regular employment. Forty percent continued to live off the underground or hidden economy and still had not returned to work when this study was completed.

In short, some people can be satisfied with leisure even on a full-time basis. This finding was supported by studies conducted by Tinsley and associates at Southern Illinois University. Tinsley and Teaff (1983) described a group of 1,649 adults, 55 to 75 years of age, highly satisfied with the psychological benefits of their leisure. Some of the satisfactions mentioned were "companionship," "compensation," "security," "service," and "intellectual esthetics." The issue is still unresolved, but there are strong indications that leisure satisfaction could replace or complement job satisfaction for some people.

Which Way Leisure Counseling? Until the past several years most of the writing in the field of leisure counseling was done by people in the field of recreation/leisure services. They seemed to know the leisure area quite well but had limited credentials in counseling. An emerging specialty, leisure counseling, now seems to be attracting the interest of a few counselors and psychologists (see Edwards, 1980; Loesch and Wheeler, 1982; Overs, Taylor, and Adkins, 1977; Tinsley and Tinsley, 1982). The fall 1981 issue of the *Counseling Psychologist* was devoted entirely to the topic of leisure counseling. Many of the recent developments in this new field were summarized by Peevy (1981) in "Leisure Counseling: A Life Cycle Approach." Peevy defines leisure counseling over the life cycle as "that approach through which a person professionally prepared in leisure aspects of counseling attempts to help a counselee to accomplish the developmental tasks of each life stage through the selection and use of appropriate leisure activities" (p. 134).

At present it is difficult to predict exactly which way leisure counseling will go—to recreation or counseling professionals, or perhaps in part to both. Bloland and Edwards (1981) speculate that leisure counseling will be a short-lived specialty, since it will soon be taken in by and considered part of the larger arena of career counseling. If the formula advanced earlier in this chapter, C = W + L, could be expanded to mean Career Counseling = Leisure Counseling + Work Counseling (CC = LC + WC), the direction would be clear. Some counselees may seek help in either leisure or work or both. A skilled career counselor of the future should be able to provide assistance in both areas separately or in a combined holistic approach. Unless the leaders in the field of career counseling are more open to leisure counseling than they have been in the past, however, there may be no place for the specialty to go except to leisure/recreation professionals. Individuals need a holistic, not a compartmentalized, approach in order to find satisfaction in the changing world of work and leisure in the 1990s and beyond.

The New Volunteerism

Volunteerism is a fundamental part of the basic concept of leisure fostered in this book. It provides a constructive opportunity for individuals throughout the life span to be active participants in the W + L = C formula. Hayes and McDaniels (1980) have spelled out a plan for making volunteering through leisure a developmental process throughout the life span.

There seems to be little question that volunteering is on an upswing in the United States. Estimates vary on the number and percent of people involved. Gallup polls show a 13 percent increase in volunteerism (from 27 to 40 percent) between 1977 and 1987 for those 18 years of age and older. That works out to roughly 50 million volunteers in 1987. De Combray (1987) estimates the number of volunteers aged 14 and older as 89 million. These volunteers averaged at least three and a half hours of volunteer activity per week. If they had been paid, the bill would have been $110 billion. According to Gallup's worldwide polling efforts, the United States leads the world in numbers of volunteers. The United Kingdom at best has about 24 percent of adults participating in volunteer activities.

In 1985, according to de Combray, 52 percent of young people aged 14 to 17 were contributing time and energy worth an estimated $9 billion; 43 percent of those aged 65–74, and

25 percent of those aged 75 and older gave some part of their time as volunteers. One well-known group, the Retired Senior Volunteer Program (RSVP), assigned 350,000 seniors to 67 million service hours in 1985, for an estimated cash value of $238 million. Of course, many American notables, including former President Jimmy Carter (who volunteers in the Habitats for Humanity program of building low-income housing in big cities), help to make volunteering very visible.

The current surge of interest has caused *Newsweek* (Feb. 8, 1988) to carry a major story on "The New Volunteerism." According to *Newsweek,* volunteer work has become "trendy" among a growing number of baby boomers, who want to make a social commitment, as opposed to their past concern with networking and materialism. Moreover, a number of corporations are encouraging employees to take part in community service activity. For example, Xerox, IBM, and Wells Fargo Bank are providing "social service leaves"—the corporate equivalent of the sabbatical granted to college professors. Older programs also appear to be getting more support. Membership in the Literacy Volunteers of America, for example, has grown by 42 percent over the past year or so, and there is a waiting list for the twenty-four-hour training program in New York City.

Volunteering can be a major source of long-term satisfaction. When budgets are tight, there is an increased need for volunteers to step forward from the ranks of the retired or other age groups to lend a helping hand. The opportunities to make a contribution are almost endless, but here are some examples:

- Reading to blind students
- Visiting shut-ins or helping with "meals on wheels"
- Joining the Peace Corps or VISTA
- Becoming a high school tutor
- Participating in a foster grandparents program
- Volunteering as a Red Cross helper or hospital aide
- Teaching art, music, or dance at a community or neighborhood center
- Cooking at a summer camp
- Playing games at an orphans' home
- Coaching a Little League team

People who keep active in their retirement years increase their chances for remaining healthy and living a long and productive life. Doing nothing is probably the worst possible choice, so a full range of volunteer opportunities needs to be provided for the leisure of those who have retired. Volunteering may be the best thing anybody at any age can do, whether it is delivering mail to patients in a hospital or teaching marketing skills to a group of mountain quilt makers in Appalachia.

A forgotten dimension of volunteering at any age is the valuable experience it provides as a training ground for later income-producing activities. In one family, for instance, a husband was partially disabled in his sixties and forced to take early retirement. He and his wife learned to quilt by going to classes and studying self-instructional materials. They eventually gained enough confidence in their quilting that they volunteered to instruct others in the basics of the craft. After several years of volunteering, they received numerous requests to conduct classes and workshops, using their particular method of instruction—for a fee. They eventually were able to realize a substantial income from their teaching program, as well as through the sales of their quilts in a ''cooperative group'' they helped to establish.

Another example of the volunteering aspect of leisure is the nationwide rescue squad program, which represents the best of the American tradition of giving time for others. An estimated 250,000 people volunteer their time each year in this program. There are four levels of Emergency Medical Technicians (EMTs). Each level has heavy requirements for initial entry. The EMT Paramedic, which is the most demanding stage, requires approximately 500 hours of training, plus fifty to seventy hours of continuing education every two years. This training is required just to begin to meet the emergency medical needs of the community. At this point, the EMT is expected to give at least six to fifteen hours of time per week to remain a part of the team, in addition to being on call for unusual emergency demands. Many EMTs are on call twelve to twenty hours per week. Often they work with local fire departments. Over 90 percent of all fire departments in the United States are run by volunteers.

Many EMTs regard this volunteer work as an excellent way to try out their interest in health careers and to determine whether they really like the more difficult aspects of medical treatment. Others have always wanted to work in a health-related occupation and joined the program in order to gain self-fulfillment and life satisfaction. But most of the EMTs are simply fulfilling a desire to help others.

After the EMTs attain a particular level of skill, they can take an instructor's course—enabling them to teach that material to other volunteers. They do not have to be active members of a rescue squad to teach EMT courses (or cardiopulmonary resuscitation and advanced first aid courses). The only requirement for maintaining certification is to teach a specified number of courses per year and to participate in a periodic refersher course. Consequently, an individual may volunteer leisure time in a teaching capacity alone.

The Virginia Tech Rescue Squad began in 1969 with four members. There are now about seventy members, who rotate day and night shifts balancing academic and rescue squad activity. Usually members remain with the squad for two or three years. Even during vacations, dedicated volunteers remain on duty so that a constant state of readiness is maintained. In general, students at Virginia Tech feel that this volunteer opportunity adds a great deal to their college experience.

In a book of readings entitled *America's Voluntary Spirit* (O'Connell, 1983), the contributors talk about America's third sector (other than public and private)—the independent or non-profit sector. Along with reports such as those by the Gallup poll and *Newsweek,* this book suggests that volunteerism will have a major impact on tomorrow's workplace. Increasingly, volunteer activity is looked on as an important try-out experience, and a job applicant's volunteer experiences are increasingly being considered along with his or her education and job experience. This trend certainly brings the connection between work and leisure into sharper focus as part of a larger career development plan.

There is even a push in Congress to get more recognition for the volunteer activities that are performed for the public good. The challenge to counselors is to find a way to invite people to volunteer for the sake of service to others, as well as helping them recognize at the same time the potential for helping oneself through awareness, exploration, and preparation for either work or leisure opportunities.

In and Out of the Work Force and the Workplace

Not too many years ago, a man or a woman starting out in a first or even a second job had reason to believe that "one life/one occupation" was a likely prospect over the next thirty to forty years. Today a young worker or a not-so-young worker returning to full-time or part-time employment may not stay on that job for the rest of his or her worklife. Some workers, of course, may remain in one job until retirement. But today, because of major and significant changes in the work force and the workplace, and in the larger society, more possibilities and options are open to or forced on workers. That is, a person may take a paid or unpaid sabbatical, be fired, quit to stay home with small children, or just decide to go on "breaktime," as Lefkowitz calls it.

The bases for those changes have been detailed in broad terms in Chapters Three, Four, and Five. The prospects for some quite different and unknown opportunities have been spelled out in Chapters Six, Seven, and Eight. It would belabor the point to go over these various prospects again here. Suffice it to say that workers of all ages face a somewhat uncertain future. This means that some contingency thinking about alternative scenarios is in order. We might mention here George Gallup's (1984) warning that we should always be preparing for our next job or occupation rather than simply wait for the merger, downsizing, or change of political climate to occur. Maybe the old admonition is right, "Better to be safe (prepared) than sorry!" Counselors therefore should be prepared to assist people who come to them for help by informing them about the role that leisure can play in the career development process.

That role for leisure can serve people well if they are in and out of the workforce for a variety of reasons. For example, as Ehrenreich (1987) contends, men in increasing numbers want to share home responsibilities and are willing to leave the work force from time to time to be at home. Thus, a stockbroker may leave work for a while to be with a growing family. At the same time, he may volunteer to teach an investment class at the YWCA in order to keep certain professional skills up to date. Or a machinist may get laid off and while unemployed take a lock-smithing course through correspondence study because of a past interest in tinkering with locks in leisure time. Some months later he may start part-time and then full-time work as a locksmith—not as a machinist. Or a high school graduate may get a job at a local hospital because of the experience she gained as a member of the local volunteer life-saving crew.

For many people, then, leisure and work may intermix over the course of their careers. These people might be influenced by some of the inspirational and self-help books currently available:

- *Late Bloomers* (Colman and Perelman, 1985)
- *Chop Wood and Carry Water* (Fields and others, 1984)
- *Breaktime* (Lefkowitz, 1979)
- *Work with Passion* (Anderson, 1984)
- *Do What You Love, The Money Will Follow* (Sinetar, 1987b)

Most of these books are available from the New Career Center in Boulder, Colorado, which specializes in creative books from small, sometimes unknown, publishers. Ten Speed Press of Berkeley, California, also publishes these types of books. *Chop Wood and Carry Water,* for example, invites the readers to take a fresh and creative look at themselves and the work and leisure options open to them. It is impossible to know with certainty how many individuals at various points in the career span are looking for the kind of fresh thinking and challenges presented in these sources. Counselors should surely know that these books are available and that there are individuals who are searching for answers to the kinds of questions these authors tackle head on.

What Should Counselors Do?

This section focuses briefly on some needed institutional responses to the changing role of leisure and work in America. So far, most agency or institutional programs have been passive or nonassertive at best. If the concepts set forth in this chapter are anywhere near the target, our major institutions and agencies will need to develop more active, assertive, positive programs; and counselors must help to bring about these changes. Some suggestions for action are spelled out below.

Encourage Parents to Promote Leisure in the Home. The core of leisure exists for most people in the home. For children it is the central place to learn both work and leisure values. Kelly (1982a, 1982b) and Rapaport and Rapaport (1975) supply ample evidence of the importance of the family and the need for early support for leisure awareness and exploration. The Research & Forecasts (1982) study further confirms that most leisure activity is centered in the home. How can parents promote leisure? First of all, parents can serve as role models for their children with respect to leisure attitudes and activities. If the parents have an active leisure life, emphasizing variety and intensity, they will serve as positive models. If parents have a passive leisure life, they will serve as negative models. For example, if the parents volunteer at a local senior citizens' center three days a week, the children will at least be aware of one leisure option involving significant members of the family; at best, the children also will be volunteers.

Second, parents can take full advantage of community opportunities involving families in the physical, creative, or intellectual aspects of leisure. For example, families can take part in local arts and craft shows, community children's theater, story hours at the local library, family fun runs. Parents can talk about *their* childhood leisure activities with the adults in their family. For a more detailed account of the role of the family in leisure

activities, see Hummel and McDaniels (1982). Counselors need
to take a much more active role in working with parents to invite them to support developmental leisure activities in the home.

*Help Schools and Youth Groups Become Involved in Leisure Activ-
ities.* Under the best conditions, the schools should adopt an
active leisure education program as advocated by Mundy and
Odum (1979); or they might consider the Leisure Education
Advancement Project (LEAP), available from the National Recreation and Park Association and described by Lancaster and
Odum (1976), or the "Life, Be in It" program, also sponsored
by the National Recreation and Park Association (1981). They
might also expand their career education programs to include
leisure as well as work. Unification of leisure and career education would best serve the interests of the young people.

Other school exploratory experiences could be adapted
at little or no cost. For example, some very successful "leisure
fairs" have already been held in elementary and middle/junior
high schools. At these fairs young people can get a first-hand
look at crafts *and* meet craft people. Or craft people can be
brought into the school for a day to demonstrate their craft (for
instance, painting, knitting, weaving, or carving). Another way
to introduce intellectual leisure activities is through a wide variety
of games—simple board games, card games, or more complicated
computer games using skills from different school subjects. The
objective is to allow students to explore games as a source of
fun and learning as well as basic educational skills.

Many young people belong to youth groups, which serve
significant leisure functions. In addition to their present activities, youth groups can teach youth to transfer leisure skills to
occupational settings. For example, in the many 4-H programs
involving animals, related jobs can be demonstrated. Outdoor
scouting experiences can be used to illustrate employment opportunities in forestry, wildlife management, farming, and various
aspects of agribusiness. Music, art, and drama clubs can accomplish the same objective by bringing in former club members
who work in set or costume design, music arranging, or art store
retailing. Since counselors have no "ax to grind" here, they

can be a very positive force in bringing about more positive involvement toward developmental leisure in schools. They can be assertive in holding on to what is good in current programs and improving leisure opportunities for students in and out of school.

Emphasize Leisure in the Workplace. Enlightened places of employment have sponsored progressive programs of industrial recreation for many years, and employer leisure programs have recently experienced a resurgence of activity. For example, Sentry Insurance provides a comprehensive recreation facility, including a gym, outdoor play, and jogging areas, and employees are urged to use this facility at appropriate times. This emphasis on the physical side of leisure is only one dimension of a concern for employee leisure in the workplace. Increasingly, employers are adding employee assistance, human resource development, or even employee career development programs. In most instances, these programs emphasize only the work aspect of the employee's life. A notable exception is the Employee Career Development Program at Virginia Tech. This program, now in its ninth year of operation, has a backlog of staff waiting to enter the regular six-week career development workshops. One of the premises of this program is the concept of $C = W + L$, and the participants' *leisure and work* roles are emphasized along with their roles as students and family members, as emphasized in Super's (1984) life career rainbow.

Many of the people who attend these career development workshops or take advantage of individual counseling express great satisfaction at having the opportunity to examine both their leisure and work roles and to relate both to their careers. Some workshop participants are satisfied with their jobs but feel that they need changes in their lives—because of aging, shifting economics, changing family responsibilities or work loads, or some other life transition. These participants are given information about leisure options and are helped to explore these options and to plan future activities. Other participants are genuinely unhappy with their jobs but feel that they are geographically place bound. These people are helped to explore all options—especially the leisure option. There has been a high degree of satisfaction with the work-leisure emphasis presented in this program. (For more details see McDaniels and Hesser, 1982, 1983; McDaniels and Watts, 1987.)

The growing number of counselors and counselor/consultants working in places of employment can do much to encourage attention to the $C = W + L$ concept. They can bring in examples of successful adult career transitions and point out the benefits of emphasis on helping the whole person versus just the "work aspect" of the employee.

Encourage Community Agencies to Assist in Leisure Development. One of the major ways that community agencies can contribute to people's leisure options is to provide extensive adult/vocational education opportunities. Too often these opportunities for adults are available only on a limited basis at odd hours and odd locations. Adults can expand their own enjoyment and increase self-satisfaction if they can develop sufficient skills from a leisure-learned activity to earn additional income on a part-time or full-time basis. Further, an expanding option for older adults is the Elderhostel program now available throughout the United States and overseas. Many of these program offerings are purely for pleasure, but some may be a vestibule to skill development and an eventual income source. Such a course, for example, might be in calligraphy or arranging wildflowers.

Community agencies can also assist in leisure development by providing ample opportunities for volunteering. This leisure acitvity can be a source of self-esteem and self-confidence for the volunteer. In addition, volunteers can test the particular places of employment and the employers; and the employers, in turn, can take a good look at the volunteers: Are they punctual, diligent, and conscientious? If the volunteers and the employer develop a mutual friendship, a part-time or full-time position may be in the offing.

Organized clubs can be excellent sources of leisure satisfaction. Clubs offer opportunities for joining together with others who share similar interests, such as Sweet Adelines or barbershop quartets, iris clubs, chess clubs, photography clubs, or racquetball clubs. In addition to the pure joy of close harmony (no pun intended) with others, there are always opportunities to write articles about different experiences, teach others how to achieve certain skill levels, or open a small neighborhood garden shop to sell exotic plants and shrubs.

Counselors in community agencies, especially mental health settings, need to be more aware of the potential healing power of satisfying work and leisure. Counselors need to be able to understand and promote better leisure activities for adults and youth, thereby helping them find entirely new areas of joy and fulfillment. When counselors can help individuals find meaningful leisure activities that are satisfying in their own right and a source of possible work, they will have rendered a very positive service for their clients.

Suggested Reading

Edwards, P. *Leisure Counseling Techniques*. (3rd ed.) Los Angeles: Constructive Leisure, 1980.

Edwards has operated Constructive Leisure in Los Angeles for a number of years. This manual spells out her theory and practice of leisure counseling. She is a frequent contributor to the literature in the leisure field (see, for example, Bloland and Edwards, 1981).

Kelly, J. R. *Leisure*. Englewood Cliffs, N.J.: Prentice-Hall, 1982.

Probably the best and most comprehensive book in the area of leisure. Kelly is a sociologist in the Leisure Behavior Research Lab at the University of Illinois, Champagne-Urbana. He has the freshest thinking in the field right now.

Lefkowitz, B. *Breaktime: Living Without Work in a Nine to Five World*. New York: Dutton (Hawthorn Books), 1979.

Case studies on 100 people who dropped out of the labor market. A readable and fascinating report on their plight. Lefkowitz is now associated with Daniel Yankelovich, frequently as his coauthor.

McDaniels, C. (ed.). Special issue on "The Role of Leisure in Career Development." *Journal of Career Development,* Dec. 1984.

Includes a strong article by Donald Super on "Leisure: What It Is and Might Be," as well as articles on leisure counseling; measurement of leisure interests; leisure and career development in the schools, for college students, and for adults; and leisure and leisure counseling from a recreation point of view. An excellent source of material on the $C = W + L$ concept.

Parker, S. *The Future of Work and Leisure.* New York: Praeger, 1971.

The author is a Britisher who has effectively tackled the tough job of making predictions about both work and leisure. Many of his forecasts have proved to be correct.

Roberts, K. *Leisure.* (2nd ed.) New York: Longman, 1981.

This short (140-page) paperback book by another Britisher reflects a good knowledge of the literature in this country and in Europe as well. A sociologist like Kelly, Roberts has keen insights into the leisure-work relationship.

10

Helping People
Put Their Leisure
to Work

This chapter focuses on what some call "the best of all worlds"—working at something one really enjoys. For many people that means putting their leisure to work. In the light of almost certain changes in tomorrow's workplace (the down sizing and general slowing of growth of large-scale employers), it means counselors helping their clients discover what they are good at and where they can try out their skills. More specifically, it provides suggestions on how counselors can help their clients become aware of and explore their leisure skills. The chapter also presents twenty illustrations of successful people who have put their leisure to work.

This book argues that we are in the midst of a major restructuring of work in the United States. This restructuring may not be as thoroughgoing as the Green Scenario suggests (Chapter Three) or as painful as the Red Scenario Forecasts (Chapter Five). But almost everyone agrees that tomorrow's workplace is going to be gradually shifting away from yesterday's pattern. Our contention has been that many members of the work force of the future will find promising opportunities in the three "wild cards" in the work game: (1) the entrepreneurship, (2) the small business, and (3) the work-at-home options. It is vital, therefore, that counselors begin to provide more information about options of this sort and inform people about how they can prepare themselves to become, for example, owners of small businesses. Hence, this chapter points out some of the ways in which people do get prepared for these newly emerging forms of work by learning about their leisure potential.

What Do You Enjoy Doing?

The place to look for the answer to this question is in one's leisure. Indeed, where else would one look? It is in their leisure hours that people from childhood to old age freely choose what they want to do. Leisure is the realm of freedom, of satisfaction, and of pleasure. It is in their leisure time that people choose what they want to do, with whom they want to do it, where they want to go, when they want to go, and how they find enjoyment. So, *why not work at what you enjoy?* In fact, many people do exactly that by finding work and leisure interests that are parallel.

Leisure-time activities contribute to personal development in many ways. Through such activities as running for student council, playing golf, sewing a new dress, or playing drums in a band, we can develop skills that will be useful throughout life. Such experiences give us insights into our interests and abilities and aid us in making career and other major decisions.

Taking part in leisure-time activities may also help us to discover useful and productive occupations. For example, skill and knowledge acquired playing tennis may lead directly to a career operating a sporting goods shop, teaching others how to play tennis, or working as a wholesale representative for a sporting goods manufacturer. Learning to sew shirts and blouses may lead to work as a tailor or seamstress, a job in fashion design or fashion merchandising, or a career in teaching sewing and other home economics skills.

Table 13 lists some of the leisure activities open to most high school students, college students, or adults and provides examples of occupations to which these activities may lead. In every case the list of career fields is suggestive, not exhaustive. Also, many of these fields have only a limited number of jobs;

therefore, the competition for positions in many of the occupations is keen. Perhaps the most obvious example, and well known to many, is the competition for jobs in professional athletics. For example, nearly 21 million boys play high school football, basketball, or baseball; but only 111,000 play in college, and only a couple of hundred turn professional each year in all these sports. Competition for other types of jobs may be somewhat less rigorous but it does exist. Despite the existence of competition, jobs or opportunities to start a business exist, and many people find satisfying careers in them each year.

Careers in some leisure-related fields, of course, may offer less than lifetime jobs, and career planning must include both immediate prospects and long-range job implications. Illustrative is the singer whose voice may fade long before the age of normal retirement or the professional athlete whose active participation may end in his or her twenties or thirties.

For some persons leisure activities and related jobs may suggest opportunities for part-time work built around a compatible main job. These include such jobs as church organist, summer camp worker, or free-lance writer or artist. In all fields, special opportunities exist in management-type jobs. For instance, a dancer may operate a dance studio, a musically inclined person may become manager of a symphony orchestra, or an actor may turn to running a summer theater.

Table 13. Leisure Activities and Related Occupations.

Leisure Activity	Leisure-Related Occupations
	Music
Singing	Choir director, entertainer, voice teacher, music teacher
Instrumental music	Director, performer, instrumental instructor, music group manager
Composing	Composer, arranger, music critic, record company employee
Dancing	Professional dancer, choreographer, dance teacher
	Art
Drawing	Artist, cartoonist, art teacher
Painting	Painter, painting instructor
Sculpting	Sculptor, art critic, art gallery employee

Table 13. Leisure Activities and Related Occupations, Cont'd.

Leisure Activity	Leisure-Related Occupations
Glass blowing	Glass blower, glass company employee, glass salesperson
Photography	Photographer, illustrator, advertising person
Pottery making	Potter, kiln operator, ceramic designer

Crafts

Needlepoint	Designer, shop operator, writer about crafts, craft wholesaler
Weaving	Professional weaver, teacher, designer, shop owner
Macrame	Teacher, professional macrame artist, designer
Woodcraft	Carver, wood furniture designer, furniture refinisher, cabinet maker, carpenter
Glass cutting	Laboratory equipment designer, glass designer, shop operator
Sewing	Tailor, seamstress, teacher, fabric store operator
Cooking	Chef, home economist, dietician
Baking	Baker, home economist, cooking writer or editor
Embroidery	Craft teacher, craft designer, craft shop operator

Outdoor Activities

Backpacking	Outdoor clothing store operator, camp director, travel guide
Sailing	Marina operator, sailmaker, waterfront director, sailor
Swimming	Pool operator, swimming teacher, recreation worker, waterfront director
Gardening	Farmer, farm store operator, agronomist, botanist
Bicycling	Cycle shop operator, bicycle repair person
Raising animals	Veterinarian, pet shop owner
Horseback riding	Veterinarian, animal caretaker, animal trainer, blacksmith
Camping	Camp director, camp counselor, youth agency worker

Individual and Team Sports

Baseball	Player, coach, teacher, camp director
Football	Trainer, professional player, coach, youth agency worker
Basketball	Player, coach, teacher, recreation aide
Hockey	Professional player, coach, teacher, skating rink operator
Bowling	Bowling machine repair person, bowling alley operator, bowling professional
Tennis	Teaching pro, tennis shop operator, tennis club operator
Golf	Teaching pro, golf shop operator, golf course superintendent
Archery	Teacher, sporting goods salesperson, camp operator
Skiing	Winter resort operator, instructor, ski shop owner
Track	Sporting goods store operator, outdoor facilities designer, wholesale representative
Sports (all)	Sports reporter, radio or television announcer

Table 13. Leisure Activities and Related Occupations, Cont'd.

Leisure Activity	Leisure-Related Occupations
	Out-of-School Community Activities
Boy/Girl Scouts	Scout leader, youth worker, social worker
4-H	Camp operator, teacher, extension agent
Boys/Girls Clubs	Teacher, recreation leader, social agency administrator
Tri-Hi-Y Hi-Y	YMCA-YWCA worker, youth agency worker, recreation department worker
Religious	Youth worker, minister, rabbi, priest, director of youth group
	In-School Extracurricular Activities
Art club	Artist, designer, photographer, teacher
Debate club	Lawyer, teacher, politician, announcer
Radio club	Electronics work, radio engineer, electrical engineer, military service, communications worker
Photo club	Photographer, photo shop operator, camera repair person
Health club	Nurse, physician, medical technician, dentist, orderly
Student government	Politician, lawyer, community leader, business manager
Newspaper	Reporter, journalist, printer
Choral club	Singer, music or voice teacher, arranger, music critic
Drama club	Actor, actress, director, set designer, drama teacher
Fellowship of Christian Athletes	Youth leader, religious worker, teacher
Future Farmers of America	Farmer, extension agent, farm business worker
Future Teachers of America	Teacher, counselor, youth worker
Future Homemakers of America	Home economist, interior designer, extension agent
Future Business Leaders of America	Secretary, accountant, clerk, typist, teller
Science club	Engineer, scientist, technician
Distributive education club	Salesperson, store operator, personnel worker
Industrial cooperative club	Electrician, mechanic, brick mason, engineer
Travel club	Travel agent, airline or railroad agent, salesperson

Leisure activities can be pursued throughout a lifetime without their actually leading to an occupation. Very few who enjoy playing football will be able to find full-time employment relating to football. They may, however, enjoy volunteer coaching or officiating in their hours off their wage-earning job. Many people take jobs out of economic necessity and obtain a sense of satisfaction and pleasure out of their leisure interests. Table 14 lists various leisure activities that may be pursued as leisure rather than as occupations, thus contributing to a satisfying life/career style.

Table 14. Part-Time Leisure Interests.

Initial Interest	Occupation	Leisure Activity
Animal raising	Licensed Practical Nurse (LPN)	Organizer of local American Kennel Club
Singing	Postman	Barber shop quartet
Macrame	Secretary	Teaching macrame at YWCA
Bicycling	Teacher	Family bicycle trips
Baseball	Plumber	Coaching Little League
Bowling	Construction worker	Company bowling league
Drama	Dentist	Act in local amateur plays
Sewing	Computer operator	Designing and sewing own clothes
Cooking	Assembly worker	Gourmet club member
Flower growing	Salesperson	Member of garden club

Kelly (1983), in his book *Leisure Identities and Interactions,* points out that through leisure some individuals build strong *identity, intensity, intimacy,* or *interactions.* In short, leisure can become the focus of one's life satisfaction. Some people live for their leisure, because through it they gain:

- *Identity* with something they do well and for which they get attention and self-actualization. For instance, a jogger who eventually competes in a marathon becomes known as the runner who works in the shipping department.
- *Intimacy* with an activity that they can relate to. For instance, a bridge player feels great after a weekend of winning hands at a regional tournament.
- *Intensity.* For instance, a musician's feelings after listening to or performing in a music festival over the Fourth of July holiday.
- *Interactions* with fellow volunteers. For instance, someone who actively campaigns for a political candidate shares common political beliefs with others in a primary election in Portsmouth, New Hampshire.

All these very positive involvements with leisure lead to what Marsha Sinetar (1987a) calls the actualized worker. These four leisure responses can, in the best of circumstances, be shared by individuals who put their leisure to work. So the counselor's role becomes clear: Encourage people of all ages to become knowledgeable about their leisure strengths and interests and to translate them into life satisfactions—part-time or full-time work, whatever seems to suit the person and the situation best.

Helping People Discover What They Are Good At

Leisure involvement and skills develop just as other aspects of human development do. The person (1) becomes aware of a leisure activity, (2) explores the activity, (3) prepares for greater involvement in it, (4) gains satisfaction from it, and in some instances (5) puts the leisure activity to work.

In the best of instances, the person will find an immediate relationship with a leisure activity. The classic illustration, of course, is the child prodigy who, it seems, has only to sit down at the piano and start to play or the genius who has an intuitive understanding of the game of chess. For the vast majority of people, however, finding out what they are really good at is a much more difficult task. While most people tend to pursue certain leisure activities that provide some of the responses that Kelly notes above, it is a slow, laborious process of trial and error to discover which specific activities could open up a career. Moreover, since a person can scarcely be expected to take part in a leisure activity that he or she has never heard of, the counselor's role is to invite the person to become aware of as many leisure activities as possible, to explore those in which he or she has some natural interest, and then to carry the activity as far as the person and situation suggest.

The dimensions of leisure activity grow out of the definition given in Chapter Nine. The key point here is to help people see leisure in the broadest possible way, including the following dimensions:

- Creative dimensions of leisure, such as all aspects of art, music, dance, writing, crafts, and drama.

- Physical dimensions of leisure, such as all aspects of running, jogging, swimming, bicycling, rowing, tennis, golf, and gardening.
- Intellectual dimensions of leisure, such as all aspects of card games, photography, languages, cooking, baking, and sewing.
- Social dimensions of leisure, such as all aspects of meeting and visiting with other people.
- Volunteering dimensions of leisure, such as all aspects of working for the Red Cross, hospitals, Boy and Girl Scouts, the YWCA and YMCA, Boys and Girls Clubs, and political parties.
- Combination of the above dimensions of leisure, such as volunteering to teach photography or coaching Little League baseball.

If people want to develop their skill in any of these areas, or want to know how strong their skills are, there are several ways to find out:

1. *Courses.* The person still in school can take a public-speaking course (if the person is interested in politics) or a semester of instruction in basketball, archery, fishing, poetry writing, teaching reading, or almost any other subject. If the person is out of school, courses ranging from art to zoology are available through correspondence study, adult education, free universities, or employer-sponsored classes.
2. *Clubs.* There are over 2,800 organized club groups in the United States. These clubs, which bring together people with similar leisure interests, serve people with such diverse interests as skiing, breeding canaries, or collecting stamps. If a person is interested in needlecraft, there are numerous clubs just waiting to show someone the finer points of the craft or help a beginner get started. Someone interested in flying can join the Academy of Model Aeronautics, which is the largest sport aviation organization in the United States, with over 2,000 local clubs and over 125,000 members. Or a person who enjoys painting might join with the 30,000 others in the National Society of Tole and Decorative Painters.

3. *Communities*. This setting offers almost unlimited oppor-
    tunities to become aware of and explore one's leisure in-
    terests. Take ballroom dancing, for example. In the 1940s
    it was a big hit; in the 1980s it is enjoying a mild comeback.
    A friend took ballroom dancing through the local recrea-
    tion department and liked it so well that he and his wife
    took several more rounds of lessons. They now are called
    upon frequently for ballroom dancing demonstrations and
    have been teaching for a commercial studio several times
    a year. They have even talked about dropping their regular
    jobs and trying to live off of their income from professional
    dancing—all from a recreation department class. The com-
    munity also may offer drama lessons and sponsor a little
    theater group or a summer stock series. Community-based
    team sports are legion. The individual who is not up to high
    school or college teams may find just the right opportunity
    to try out for a community-based soccer or volleyball team.

    These three options—classes, clubs, and community—are
rich resources for becoming aware of leisure interests and for
exploring those interests and preparing for further development
of skill in the area of interest. The byword may be—*give skill
a chance*. Encourage it and invite people to become aware of and
explore leisure through these three areas.
    The book *Amateurs* by Stebbins (1979) takes a fascinating
look at people who are "on the margin between work and
leisure"—somewhere between the novice or dabbler and the
paid professional. Stebbins lists some of the characteristics of
the amateur as confidence, perseverance, commitment, pre-
paredness, dedication, and identity. After studying three areas
in which amateurs can thrive—archeology, baseball, and theater—Stebbins concludes that amateurs pursue their interests
because they gain self-actualization, self-expression, enhanced
self-concept, self-gratification, self-enrichment, and genuine recreation. From a social standpoint, amateurs gain position,
positive social interactions, and a feeling of group accomplish-
ment through a team effort.

These gains are what people seek—and often do not find—through work. So as some, especially younger, workers seek deeper satisfaction from their work and not find it, possibly that fulfillment can be met through a variety of levels of leisure enjoyment and identity. Even if the individual is not quite up to putting his leisure to work, he can get enormous satisfaction from being an amateur, or at least a bona fide novice or dabbler. It is the thesis of this chapter that all three of these skill levels of leisure are important (to all but the most dedicated "workaholic") because they provide a variety of options to people involved in tomorrow's workplace.

Helping People Discover
Where to Try Out Their Skills

Once counselors have helped clients decide on the level of leisure skill they have, the clients may enjoy the activity so much that they want to try doing it part time for pay, or even full time. This is a good time to point out that *only quality sells*. A person may enjoy painting landscapes, but there is no point in plunging headlong into painting full time if there are no buyers for one's goods or services. There is a certain inaccuracy in the term *self-employed*. Unless a person is independently wealthy, he or she cannot really be self-employed. Someone else must eventually buy the goods or services produced by that individual. A dancer, for example, is only able to survive if an audience will pay to see his or her performance. A hat maker is only as successful as the buyers of the hats permit. There are, of course, some ways to find out whether a person is a dabbler/novice, an amateur, or a professional.

A person does not necessarily have to start her own business to put her leisure to work. Many outside interests could also be translated into part-time work or, even if the person is in school or has a job, to moonlighting for an employer. For example, the individual who has a leisure activity of flower growing and arranging may be anxious to start out on her own after several years of winning blue ribbons at flower shows and garden club competitions. A wiser transition, both to learn the business and to find out whether the leisure activity is as much fun for pay as it was for personal satisfaction, might be to work full or part time at a florist shop for a year or so. Or a jewelry maker or tennis player who wants to teach his skill to others might be urged to teach part time in a local recreation department or adult education program before starting out as a full-time teaching professional. The route from a beginning leisure interest to full-time employment is a long one and for most people involves many slow, halting, uncertain steps over many months or years. So there are a number of try-out efforts (part-time work, moonlighting after a regular job, working for someone else) that the counselor can suggest to the leisure enthusiast. The main idea is to help the individual seek options and opportunities at carefully measured levels of risk rather than blunder along on a trial-and-error basis.

A final suggestion involves the kind of thing Eisenberg (1982) brings out in his book *Learning Vacations*—that is, to explore leisure skills in a mentally enriching way in a relaxed atmosphere, perhaps on a college campus. Elderhostels, for those over 60 years of age, immediately come to mind in this regard, but colleges and universities offer many similar opportunities. It may be a writers' conference, an arts and crafts teaching festival, or a cooking/baking school. The range of options is almost unlimited. The counselor's challenge is to know about these options and point them out to the person who would be helped by knowing about them. (More about Eisenberg's book at the end of this chapter.)

Twenty Examples

To help illustrate the points stressed in this chapter, twenty examples of people who have put their leisure to work follow. The examples are divided equally between those who produce a product—a potter, for instance, or cribbage board maker—and those who produce a service—for instance, a gift shop owner or a travel agent. The examples are part of a collection of hundreds of similar case studies stored in my collection. Most of the examples are from personal knowledge; others are from newspaper and magazine clippings. Some of these people may not be involved at present in the work described, but they were when I knew about them. Of course, a number of similar illustrations appear in Part Three of this book (dealing with entrepreneurship, small business, and work at home). Each reader probably could cite just as many in every city and town across the United States. There are plenty of people out there who have put their leisure to work. These briefly noted cases are simply meant to serve as starter examples to give the reader some concrete cases to clarify the point.

Those Producing a Service

1. Leslie O. Carlin is a retired counselor-educator from Mount Pleasant, Michigan. Now he is a travel consultant. After years of dreaming of world travel, followed by a series of carefully planned summer vacation tours, for the past twelve years he and his wife have been part owners of a travel agency. The Carlins have led more than sixty groups (credit and noncredit) to over 149 countries around the world. Their dreams have come true because they have been able to turn a strong leisure interest in world travel into a full-time retirement business.

2. Ray Yoder operates "Painting Vacations" in Waynesboro, Virginia. For the past decade or so, he has harnessed a lifelong interest in art and put it to work helping aspiring artists develop their skill under his watchful tutelage. All ages (12–70) come to his workshops, which are held near his home in the Blue Ridge Mountains. Today Yoder is a nationally known art educator and award-winning water colorist. In 1986 he was rated among the top sixty painting-workshop instructors in the United States.

3. *Running News* is a newsletter published by the New York chapter of the Road Runners Club of America. For a year after he left his sales job of twenty-three years, Stan Singer, age 50, sold ads for the newsletter. An avid runner himself, who logged 70–90 miles per week, Singer now is the New York ad representative of the major magazine *Runner's World*. He finds working for this magazine a highly attractive way to combine avocation and vocation.

4. The top wedding director in Greensboro, North Carolina, is Louise Walters. She loves the social whirl of every wedding and making sure everything goes right—down to the very last detail. She has been doing this work for thirty-four years and still enjoys seeing things come off like clockwork. She wants the bride to be happy with herself and the community to know the wedding was a correct one. Her two sisters also direct weddings, and her daughter has helped to direct two already. This interest in the proper social graces keeps Louise Walters putting her leisure to work.

5. Blue Ridge Books is a new bookstore on the main street in Wytheville, Virginia. It is operated by Bob and Theresa Lazo. They have turned a lifelong fascination with literature and books into a profitable business. Before branching out on their own, they attended American Booksellers Association seminars and worked for a major chain bookstore. Now they believe that they have found the perfect kind of work.

6. Walt's Bike Shop in Columbia, Missouri, is the result of one man's enjoyment of bike riding and repairing and the need to earn a living. After graduating from high school and touring Europe on a bike, Walt Sanders decided that central Missouri could use a good sales and service bike shop. So he converted a barber shop into a bike shop and put his leisure to work. Now he is combining the best of the leisure and work worlds.

7. Dennis West of Salem, Virginia, has turned a hobby of collecting old records into a booming business called Heritage West Shop. He began record collecting in high school. Though he is just in his mid-thirties, he has been making a living selling records for over ten years. He sells vintage "hotwax" to customers in countries around the world. He estimates his inventory at half a million records. He sells rare 45s for as much as $1,000 a piece, but he sells hundreds of records for $1 a piece to people trying to get that certain missing tune for home use. He likes what he is doing, which is continuing a twenty-year interest in music and records into a solid business venture.

8. Sonja Keith is in her thirties and lives in Costa Mesa, California. Among local car buffs she is known as "the Cor-

vette Lady.'' She has parlayed a lifelong interest in buying old model cars and fixing them up for resale in her spare time into a profitable business. Over the years she began to specialize in Corvettes because of their high resale in Southern California. Eventually, she built up confidence in her ability to purchase and repair Corvettes and quit her job as an artist for *Road & Track* magazine. Now she tries to keep a fleet of twenty used Corvettes priced to sell from $4,500 to $65,000. She owns six of them herself and is happy working at a job that many would call a Corvette lover's dream come true.

9. The Purple Panache is located in Boston's restored Faneuil Hall Marketplace. It is owned by Louise Berenson, who until recently was an administrative assistant in a local hospital. Her hobby was collecting things in purple, her favorite color. Since it was such a problem finding things, she struck on the idea of opening a shop that sells only items in the color purple. The business sells purple pens, pencils, mugs, running suits, teddy bears, and the like. Her initial $3,000 investment has grown to a very profitable operation, which includes a mail-order division and a beginning franchising phase. She had no previous retailing or business experience and simply learned the business as she went along.

10. Ralph Miller has always loved the outdoors and animals. After years of hanging around race tracks and rodeos, he wound up in the Big Sky Country of Montana as a guide for horseback-riding groups in the back-country areas of Yellowstone National Park. He also owns enough horses now to have his own outfitting operation. Even though he earned his degree in veterinary medicine at Colorado State University, he still leads one- to two-week wilderness trips in the summer in the back country of Montana.

Those Producing a Product

11. Will Haddon is one of the most respected marine artists on the East Coast. It wasn't always that way. He used to be a traveling salesman who spent most of Monday to Friday on the road selling girls' gym suits. He had done a lot of draw-

ing as a boy, and when the long nights on the road got on his nerves, he turned to art again. He gradually began to sell his paintings in sufficient quantity to make the leap from painting in his leisure to painting as a full-time occupation. He does about 200 paintings a year and feels very lucky because he really likes the work that he does. He even likes Mondays.

12. Upholstery work has been a long-time interest for Alvin B. Harris of Norfolk, Virginia. Because of that interest, he worked as an upholsterer's apprentice and general helper before going to work at the U.S. Naval Shipyard during World War II. After the war he worked at the U.S. Naval Air Station as an electronics mechanic until he retired in the 1970s and went back to his long-time love of upholstery work. He opened his own shop and now works full time on his own terms at his own pace at the one interest that he has maintained for over fifty years. Now he helps students who are interested in on-the-job training to enable them to find out whether they too can develop a lifelong interest in upholstery.

13. Calligraphy is the ancient art of beautiful lettering and writing. Ann Van Tassell is an expert calligrapher in Blacksburg, Virginia. She took up the art because she wanted to improve her handwriting. She took art classes in high school, and soon family and friends were asking her to do invitations, gifts, and cards. As the demand grew, she simply decided "Why not work at what I love to do—calligraphy?" She now displays her work at area craft shows and fills special orders for all kinds of lettering and writing on certificates, awards, and the like. She is a member of the Virginia Mountain Crafts Guild and the Society of Scribes. She also finds time to teach others about this ancient art form in classes at the local free university.

14. Lots of people like to play cribbage. In San Diego the top players know that the best cribbage boards are made by Jacques West. He has a thriving business making customized cribbage boards. He is one of the growing number of retirees who become restless when their full-time work ends. He has always liked working with his hands and playing cribbage. Now he makes four or five cutomized boards per week and sells them for an average of $65 per board. He has the satisfaction of seeing a beautiful finished product at the end of the day.

15. Boone's Country Stores, in Burnt Chimney, Virginia, is where Randy and Elva Boone have their bakery shop. For over a decade now, they have been turning out some of the area's best and most sought-after bakery products. Their day starts at 4:30 A.M. and often lasts until 10 P.M. or later. Their four children, aged 7–14, also help with the business. Elva Boone started collecting recipes and baking after they opened the store. She enjoyed it so much that she carried more and more of her own products. Now, in addition to the family members, the business often employs four to seven outsiders at peak seasons such as the Christmas holiday. At its roots, though, the baking is a family affair and a labor of love.

16. Joan Raines worked in a New York City literary agency until the urge to indulge her "green thumb" finally overwhelmed her. It is estimated that 24 million adult men and women are gardeners in their leisure hours. She worked briefly on the grounds crew at the Bronx Zoo when she first enrolled in the nearby twenty-one-month program of classes and fieldwork at the New York Botanical Gardens' School of Horticulture. She now works on a rock garden at the Botanical Gardens and plans for the time when she will complete her studies and move on to work in some type of public garden, happy that she can now look forward to years of working at something she really likes.

17. Glass People of Bay Village, Ohio, is a business venture in which Carl Goeller put his leisure to work. He worked for fifteen years writing greeting cards but had always enjoyed tinkering with stained glass, and his wife enjoyed fashioning decorative leaded glass. About six years ago, the entire family decided to go into the stained-glass business on a full-time basis, working out of their basement. Sales rose from $6,000 to $300,000 a year. Everybody enjoys this work-at-home family business.

18. James and Barbara Guthrie live in Glenvar, Virginia, in Roanoke County. Their winery, called Fruit of the Bloom, is the largest nongrape winery in Virginia. They have what is called a farm winery, which means that they grow most of the fruit used in the production of their wide variety of fruity wines. They had been interested in wine making for years, and when the state of Virginia reduced the licensing for farm wineries from

$2,000 to $100 a year, they went into business for themselves. They have been growing more of their own fruit and expanding their business every year, and they enjoy creating, tasting, and producing quality wines each year.

19. Chippendale-style furniture has been the lifelong passion of Kern G. Weinhold of Ephrata, Pennsylvania. He thinks of himself as a cabinet maker. Although he has worked as a carver for a commercial airplane propeller manufacturer off and on over the years, he returns to his true love of cabinetmaking on a full-time basis whenever he can. He has many other leisure interests, such as buying and selling antiques, flying, photography, tennis, and local history. He is proudest, though, when he produces a piece of wooden furniture, which he identifies by the etching ''Made by Kern G. Weinhold, Ephrata, Pa.,'' followed by the date.

20. C&D Home Crafts in Roanoke, Virginia, is another family-run leisure activity that has turned into a successful business. The ''C'' is for Cheryl Sommardahl, who is a fabric painter. The ''D'' is for Don, her husband, who is a wood craftsman. Together they own a craft shop and school, in which both husband and wife have managed to turn a personal leisure joy into a thriving business. Cheryl started out doing custom-designed items for family and friends. Then she placed a few items around on consignment. Then the entire thing mushroomed. People wanted her to teach them how to do fabric painting and develop products as well. Thus, C&D Home Craft shop served to combine the couple's interests and needs at the same time.

What Should Counselors Do?

How, exactly, can counselors encourage people to become aware of, explore, and—if they are good enough—put their leisure to work? The following suggestions are put forth as options that do not cost any money and do not require another degree or even a licensure endorsement. These suggestions are merely starting points. There is much more that could and should be done in this area. There is the obvious need to carry out some research to determine what approaches to putting leisure to work are most effective and why they are effective. Again, what modifications are needed to approaches that do not work well? At any rate, here are some beginning ideas:

Future Leisure-Work Models. Look around your community, region, or state for people who have put their leisure to work. They do not have to be people who are making $100,000 a year selling handmade aprons. Just find some examples of individuals who have turned a leisure interest into a successful work option. Bring them in and let them talk about how the process started, how it grew and developed, how they got started making money, and what it means both affectively and cognitively to them. While they are with you, get the story down on audiotape or, better yet, get a good videotape for use later with those who might not have had a chance to see the "model" in person. Extensions of this idea would be to bring in clippings from area newspapers and magazines that highlight people such as the twenty in the previous section of this chapter.

Inventory Preparation Options. Emphasize as a part of the career development aspect of every counseling program the education-for-leisure options open to every person: traditional courses, such as art, music, foreign languages, drama, or public speaking; and the whole array of leisure and work options that flow from vocational-technical education in secondary schools, technical schools, community colleges, and private career schools. Here students can learn sewing and cooking for personal development and possibly for later development as a work skill; or they can learn about growing plants and animals for fun—but maybe for profit also in a landscape business or kennel; or they can learn carpentry/mechanical skills for do-it-yourself home repairs or, later, for work in some phase of the $28 million home improvement industry.

Adult education programs are open to people of all ages. Almost every town and city has many such programs, ranging from art to zoology, starting every few months and completing, at least some phase, in less than six months. Finally, a relatively unknown source of leisure exploration is correspondence study.

One main source of information on these programs is the National Home Study Council's (1987) *Directory of Accredited Home Study Schools,* which lists approximately 100 accredited home study programs. Another main source is *The Independent Study Catalog* (Peterson's Guides, 1986), which lists over 12,000 high school, college, graduate, and noncredit courses offered by over seventy accredited colleges and universities in the United States.

Discover Clubs and Community Agencies. Clubs can give individuals an opportunity to become aware of leisure options and find other people who share a common interest. Some examples are the American Harp Society, which has 3,000 members who are interested in the lure and literature of the harp; the North American Association of Ventriloquists, whose 1,700 members promote ventriloquism; and Unicorns Unanimous, which has almost 2,000 members interested in the cultural, mystical, and biblical lore of the unicorn. These are just a few illustrations from the current edition of *National Avocational Organizations* (Germain, 1987), which lists over 2,500 such groups. This book is a must resource for counselors to link up interested participants in a leisure activity and those from around the United States who share a similar interest.

Community resources can also help individuals become aware of, explore, and develop leisure talents. Often a school-age person will prefer to explore a leisure interest by joining a local church or community group rather than enrolling in a more formal educational program. Programs sponsored by recreation departments, cultural arts groups, and little-theater buffs may be a nonthreatening way to introduce a person to a leisure adventure that may some day be a source of great leisure/work satisfaction.

Suggested Readings

Eisenberg, G. G. *Learning Vacations: Mind-Expanding Recreation for Every Interest, Age, and Budget.* Princeton, N.J.: Peterson's Guides, 1982.

A real gem of a book covering all sorts of spectacular learning vacation opportunities—from traditional college and university offerings, including the popular Elderhostels, to explorations through archeological excavations and the world of gastronomy (food and wine courses at home and abroad). A top reference source for people of all ages who want to explore or develop leisure interests and skills on their vacations.

Gault, J. *Free Time: Making Your Leisure Count.* New York: Wiley, 1983.

The author is founder and director of "Uptime," a seminar and consulting firm specializing in leisure-time management in California. The focus of the book is on how to make leisure time more relaxing, entertaining, and personally enriching.

Germain, R. (ed.). *National Avocational Organizations.* (7th ed.) Washington, D.C.: Columbia Books, 1987.

This is *the* book for a guide to recreational, hobby, cultural, civic, and patriotic organizations. More than 2,800 organizations are listed. The variety of organizations boggles the mind but testifies to the richness and variety of American life. They are all here—sports, hobby, literary, historical, patriotic, artistic, and musical groups. They range from large and long-established groups such as the American Philatelic Society (stamp collecting), which dates back to 1886 and has over 56,000 members, to the Applelist, founded in 1980 with only 100 members who "seek to foster" the use and enjoyment of the Apple computers. An essential resource for counselors in the leisure area.

Kelly, J. R. *Leisure Identities and Interactions.* Winchester, Mass.: Allen & Unwin, 1983.

Kelly, a University of Illinois sociology professor, regards leisure not as just "an activity" but as an important source of personal identity and interaction throughout what he calls the individual's "life course."

Peterson's Guides. *The Independent Study Catalog, 1986–88.* Princeton, N.J.: Peterson's Guides, 1986.

This catalog lists over 12,000 high school, college, graduate, and noncredit courses offered by over seventy accredited colleges and universities. Courses range from accounting to marketing and foreign language to nutrition. An indispensable resource for anyone confined by choice or chance to correspondence study. Put together by the National University Continuing Education Association.

Stebbins, R. A. *Amateurs: On the Margin Between Work and Leisure.* Newbury Park, Calif.: Sage, 1979.

A sociologist, Stebbins explores the world of the amateur archeologist, baseball player, and actor. The author's solid research base results in a very interesting book that explores the in-between world of persons whose leisure takes them beyond novice/dabbler but, for a variety of reasons, not quite to the level of full-time professional.

11

Work and Leisure Counseling: A Life-Span Approach

The previous two chapters have brought out the emerging relationship between the various aspects of work and leisure. This was done so that we could arrive at a unified and expanded concept of "career." Clearly, the idea of Career = Work + Leisure over the life span has only marginal support from many people because they regard leisure in much the same way that it has been viewed for the past 100 years. In the first three parts of this book, a case was made for an evolving and changing workplace and work force of the future. Part Four has tried to make the case for a similar changing concept of leisure. That is, leisure is no longer simply a recreational pastime, but an important aspect of people's careers; therefore, the concept of leisure must be broadened to serve the needs of individuals throughout their life span as they struggle to find their way in tomorrow's workplace.

With this complexity of terms and conditions as background, this closing chapter will develop two main themes. It will first describe a life-span approach to work and leisure and then present seven principles that are essential to a unified career counseling approach to the life span.

A Life-Span Approach to Work and Leisure

This first section focuses on the interaction between work and leisure at various periods of the life span (career development is assumed to be part of the larger concept of human development). The well-known work of Erik Erikson, Robert Havighurst, Daniel Levison, and other human developmentalists undergirds the ideas expressed here. McDaniels (1973, 1976, 1977) has provided a basis for the role of leisure in career development. A more detailed study of a life-span approach to work and leisure can be found in *Leisure: Integrating a Neglected Component in Life Planning* (McDaniels, 1982). A notation on that monograph will be found at the end of the chapter. Readers should note also the important ideas of Rapaport and Rapaport (1975) in *Leisure and the Family Life Cycle*. They substantiate the significant influence of the family in the origin, development, and nurture of leisure interests, experiences, and activities. More recently Barnett and Chick (1986) have found that parents' leisure attitudes, satisfaction, and participation greatly influence their children's level of leisure involvement. Sociologist John Kelly of the University of Illinois has conducted extensive research on the influence of the family on leisure in the United States. For a detailed discussion of his concept of leisure and the "life course" (his term for life span), see *Leisure* (1982b) and *Leisure Identities and Interactions* (1983). Kelly emphasizes a three-stage life-course approach to leisure: preparation, establishment, and culmination. He describes each major stage by distinct leisure identities, interactions, and roles.

The six stages presented here could easily be combined into Kelly's three periods or modified to form four or five periods. Stages are not defined by hard-and-fast age barriers. They serve as guidelines for counselors, organizations, and agency planners as well as broad frames of reference for individuals. They are flexible time frames, not brick walls. Some individuals go back and pick up activities from earlier stages. Others, because of unexpected developments, jump stages and move toward earlier retirement.

Childhood (Birth to 13 Years): The Awareness Stage. This stage
of childhood is divided into preschool and elementary school
years. During the first five years, the home is the major influence
in children's development; during the next seven years, peers
and the school also become major factors. Childhood is an important stage because it provides opportunities for becoming
aware of available leisure activities and for discovering the level
of one's interest and skill in these activities.

In brief, the preschool years are important building blocks
in the establishment of leisure and work awareness. During this
stage, children can begin to learn about the wide range of leisure
and work activities, as well as their likes and dislikes: what is
fun and what is not; whom they like to be with during leisure
activities and whom they do not. They will also have an opportunity to observe the values of the significant adults in their lives
in relation to work and leisure roles.

The elementary school years, roughly ages 5 through 12,
are a time of expansive opportunities for leisure and work
awareness. Basic physical, psychological, intellectual, and social
dimensions and capabilities grow at a rapid pace during this
period, and new activities can be introduced easily and freely.
Usually, eye-hand coordination improves; manual dexterity and
small and large muscles come under control. Elementary school-
age children need to develop an awareness of a wide range of
leisure-related activities, events, and experiences. They need
encouragement and freedom to try out as many things as possible. They need to understand that not being good at everything
is normal. They can learn about their different abilities and interests through leisure. By encouraging the development of
leisure awareness, counselors can help children recognize their
multiple dimensions, including their intellectual, physical, creative, and social characteristics and interests.

This type of awareness is emphasized at a nearby elementary school, in what is called a spring camping weekend. From
Friday evening until the camp ends on Saturday night, each
child participates in thirteen activities, from chess to gun safety.
There are team and individual leisure learning situations. The

camping experience is now in its third year and gaining more support every year.

If all these dimensions are valued equally, then every child should enjoy some important, genuine success with leisure and work activities. The emergence, establishment, and continued development of the leisure self-concept is important during this time period. Ample opportunities to test and refine likes and dislikes contribute to a better self-understanding and self-concept.

Adolescence (13–18 Years): The Exploration Years. During adolescence most individuals mature physically, socially, economically, intellectually, and emotionally. All these traits play a role in the development and expansion of the leisure and work activities in which people may engage later in life. Adolescence is a time for continued awareness and beginning exploration of leisure. Kleibert, Larson, and Csikszentmihalyi (1986) found that leisure experiences during adolescence help individuals acquire necessary skills to handle the demands of adult leisure options.

The school should provide leisure exploration through both classroom and extracurricular activities. Opportunities for exploration exist in such subjects as home economics and industrial arts. Music classes are another area in which students can explore their work and leisure potentials, and the same is true of English classes, especially in terms of writing activities. High schools and colleges might use an "interterm" between semesters to give students an opportunity to explore lifetime leisure skills at school. Through extracurricular activities such as intramural and interscholastic athletics, as well as lifetime activities such as bowling, skiing, jogging, swimming, and hiking, both males and females can explore leisure interests. Equally important are competitive and noncompetitive activities in drama, public speaking, and art, through which students can move from awareness to exploration to preparation, if the skill and interest are present. Finally, all sorts of games—such as chess, backgammon, and bridge—can be explored to test interests and skills.

The family continues to be the single most significant influence on the leisure exploration of the adolescent. In cooperation with school and nonschool agencies, the family can provide an extremely wide array of exploratory leisure and work experiences. In large population centers, nonschool agencies such as the YMCA or YWCA, Boy and Girl Scouts, youth clubs, and 4-H are offering leisure exploration activities not provided by the schools.

The educational system is structured so that students are expected to make both educational and vocational decisions during adolescence. At this time, teachers and counselors should be helping students examine the relationship between leisure and work. Students can learn to relate leisure interests to an occupation. They can also learn to relate an occupation to their preferred leisure activities. However, before making a choice, students must be aware of available options. They must obtain information about the world of work and the world of leisure and learn how they may interact. Adolescence must be a time for exploring *both* areas of career development: work *and* leisure.

Young Adulthood (18–24 Years): The Preparation Stage. As young adults, individuals reach the crest of physical, intellectual, and social development. They have more freedom in making decisions about how to spend their time. Young adults probably have fewer financial responsibilities than older adults and less commitment to or investment in jobs; therefore, they have greater freedom to participate in leisure activities. Furthermore, education becomes a personal choice (leisure pursuit) for the first time; it is now an option, not a requirement. Adult education, higher education, vocational education, correspondence study, and the military are just some of the educational options open to young adults. The preparation stage is also a time for risk taking and exploration, a time for trying new things and testing new possibilities. Leisure activities can be a part of this exploration process. In the transition from school and parental influence to a life-style of personal choice, young adults will prepare for a lifetime of leisure and work activities. Young adults seeking employment may use the available time to prepare for productive work or to engage in leisure activities, or some combination of both.

In most communities the number of young adults continuing their education or working is about equal. For those in postsecondary education, the leisure options are quite different than for those working full time; however, interesting leisure opportunities exist in both educational and work settings.

For young college students, occupational choices can emerge from leisure interests in areas such as student government; music, art, and drama organizations; social groups; and intercollegiate athletics. Popular leisure programs have been reported by the Leisure Exploration Services (LES) at Southern Illinois University, the Leisure Resource Room at Texas Woman's University, and the Leisure Fair at the University of Oregon.

Young workers can continue leisure activities started in childhood or adolescence, or they can explore some new directions. This is a time of preparation for lifetime and life-style leisure activities when young people build on new interests or expand on older ones because of newly acquired money, time, or social approval. Also, young workers who are dissatisfied with their occupations can seek life satisfaction or develop new work skills through leisure.

Adulthood (24–40 Years): The Implementation Stage. Most adults in this age range are working full or part time. Their jobs may be instrumental in determining leisure pursuits and the time available for leisure. Job expectations can influence leisure; for example, an executive may carry on business while playing golf, or co-workers may expect a machinist to bowl or play softball on the company team. The types of company benefits or opportunities provided for leisure are also important. Chosen leisure activities may depend on whether the individual works alone or in a group. Paid vacations also may be a source of expanded leisure activities. Adults have the freedom to choose among leisure activities from archeological digs, singles camps, family vacations, camping, tours, fishing. The choice of leisure activities is now more than ever an individual decision.

A new potential for leisure comes to married adults through their families. Families can make leisure planning a part of their regular activities. Also, family-oriented leisure pursuits—such as growing an expanded garden, planting a tree farm, or forming a family musical group—can become a source of additional income. Men or women who remain at home caring for children may find useful opportunities for leisure activities through volunteering. Volunteer activities may help a person keep job skills current. In this period some adults quickly become disenchanted on the job, feeling that their work is dull, boring, or generally unfulfilling. For these adults, leisure may replace work as a major source of life satisfaction; and for a growing number of adults, it may be valued more highly than work. In adulthood, leisure may begin to bring a new meaning to life. For the most fortunate adults, work and leisure complement each other, both yielding equal satisfaction. For those who are not happy on the job, leisure may provide the principal meaning to life.

Midlife (40–60 Years): The Involvement and Reassessment Stage. At midlife most people are at the peak of development in many continuous leisure and work interests. Whatever a person likes to do, the person probably does it with some degree of expertise and may become a consultant or teacher to family and friends in leisure matters.

During the midlife stage, individuals may have a number of different experiences affecting their leisure. For example, during midlife a person may experience deepening job dissatisfaction, perceiving that a career plateau has been reached and that further promotions are unlikely. People can use leisure activities to provide alternate forms of life satisfaction. Individuals now may have more time for leisure activities because children are leaving the home or job responsibilities are lessening. More money may be available for leisure pursuits if the individual has reached the peak of earning power at the same time that family financial responsibilities have decreased.

Midlife is also the time when some people begin to prepare both psychologically and financially for retirement. Development of leisure interests that can be continued during retirement will provide continuity from a full-time work life to a full-time leisure life. Midlife is also a time to build possible part-time income-producing skills related to leisure interests.

Retirement (60+ Years): The Reawareness and Reexploration Stage. The retirement stage involves total identification with and fulfillment of the desire for leisure. Full-time work is or soon will be only a memory for many. Time is now available—vast amounts of time! For some people there is too much time. During retirement, leisure activities can provide alternative uses of time. Although there is an increase in discretionary time, income may decrease. The retired person's leisure activities may change because of reduced income; an individual may no longer be able to afford the things that he or she previously enjoyed. The availability of community resources can also affect the leisure activities of retired persons. Some communities have very few leisure activities for retired people. Others, especially retirement communities, provide a great many opportunities for the development and pursuit of leisure interests. Work-related volunteer activities, such as civic/service clubs, unions, professional associations, or other groups, may provide a new source of leisure satisfaction for retirees.

The best preparation for retirement is a carefully planned change over a period of years, eliminating the dramatic shock of full-time work one day to full-time leisure the next. If work has given the person satisfaction, planned leisure should provide the same satisfaction. The transition from full-time employment to retirement can be made more easily by individuals who have developed leisure interests throughout their lives.

Career Counseling for the Life Span

There are many types and varieties of counseling. One way to measure them is to look at the generic and specialized certifications and licenses available through the National Board of Certified Counselors (NBCC) and in the states that have licensure. For example, NBCC has a Nationally Certified Counselor (NCC); Virginia has a Licensed Professional Counselor (LPC); and NBCC also has available the Nationally Certified Career Counselor (NCCC). There does not appear to be any licensure available for one specializing in leisure counseling, though some people claim to provide such service and there are several books on the subject—for example, Loesch and Wheeler's (1982) *Principles of Leisure Counseling,* McDowell's (1976) *Leisure Counseling: Selected Lifestyle Processes,* and Edwards's (1980) *Leisure Counseling Techniques*—and a spate of journal articles, especially over the past ten to fifteen years. In other words, although there are obviously various specialties under the generic term of counseling, leisure counseling has not yet reached a level of recognition and respectability to warrant subspecialty status by the general counseling national organizations and state regulatory bodies.

Regardless of official recognition, counseling has a number of special purposes. One of those purposes can be leisure counseling, another can be work or vocational counseling, and still another can be career counseling. By definition, in this book and in other places, career counseling is a broader and more all-encompassing term of counseling than the other two. That, of course, is the point being stressed in this chapter: that counseling for the broadest and best prospects is what is needed—not a limited focus on work and occupation alone or leisure alone but a focus on both in the context of one's career.

Concentrating on the broadest possible concerns in the career development of individuals across the life span, it is argued here, will serve the best purposes for a changing workplace. Narrow preparation and experience may turn out to be of limited value in an uncertain workplace, whereas a person who has confidence in both work and leisure areas can face the future with a measure of assurance that there are satisfactions in life ahead built on solid preparation for an evolving world of work and leisure throughout the life span. To help counselors and others accomplish this goal, seven principles toward a unified career counseling approach are offered here.

Stress Both Continuity and Change in Future Occupations. Richard Bowles, at the World Future Society August 1983 special conference on "Working Now and in the Future," charged that the "sloppy talk" about the future has paralyzed people with fear about the possibility of overwhelming change without pointing out the continuity. There will still be a need for farmers, mechanics, clergy, physicians, and lawyers. It is fair to present possible changes, but we must also refer to the constant. People need a sense of constancy to give them a sense of security.

Emphasize the Best and Broadest Preparation Possible, Along with Marketable Skills. Basic command of fundamental reading, writing, mathematical, and communication skills is necessary for performing current *and* future occupations. In addition, though, marketable skills are increasingly required for the occupations of the future. It is not an either/or situation. Both are needed to meet the flexible changes expected in any future scenario. In addition, the broad preparation should include areas such as art, music, and physical education, to develop attitudes for work or leisure satisfaction.

Be Aware of All the Educational and Occupational Options/Information Systems. The emerging state career information delivery systems offer promise for coordinating state and local data into more manageable terms and, just as important, disseminating the data to all who need the information in the state. Full advantage should be taken of the services provided by these systems as well as those available from commercial systems such as Guidance Information Systems (GIS) or Discover.

Encourage Development of Leisure and Work Interests and Abilities. When considering their careers, individuals often think only of work interest and abilities. Counselors and others need to encourage the development of leisure interests and abilities as well. These areas of potential may provide a surprising array of opportunities that individuals may not have considered, especially in a career-change situation.

Bring Out a Life-Span Approach to Career = Work + Leisure (C = W + L). If people are encouraged to look at their career as incorporating both work and leisure over the life span, they can take a broader approach to planning. This concept has been discussed in detail by McDaniels (1982, 1984a, 1984b). In essence, a career is viewed as an interaction of work and leisure with varying degrees of importance at various times in the life span.

This approach emphasizes the similarities in work and leisure, *not* the differences.

Emphasize Life Satisfaction from a Broad Range of Both Work and Leisure Options. Some people live for their leisure. Lefkowitz (1979), in his book *Breaktime,* showed that individuals can get great satisfaction from their leisure—more than they did from their work. If people can seek satisfaction widely rather than narrowly, they can face life's challenges more confidently. People need to be challenged to think of a broad range of work and leisure options—not work alone.

Help People Find, Prepare for, and Engage in Work and Leisure Options They Really Like. In an uncertain future, which may have frequent career transitions, individuals will need to be given the skills to discover all their talents and abilities and the full range of options open to them. They can help themselves through a variety of career transitions if they learn about themselves and can use their work and leisure options to help them make career decisions.

Suggested Readings

Edwards, P. *Leisure Counseling Techniques.* (3rd ed.) Los Angeles: Constructive Leisure, 1980.

Patsy Edwards has operated the entrepreneurial business called Constructive Leisure in Los Angeles for a number of years. This manual spells out her theory and also provides practical applications. She is a frequent contributor to the literature in this field (see, for example, Bloland and Edwards, 1981).

Kelly, J. R. *Leisure.* Englewood Cliffs, N.J.: Prentice-Hall, 1982.

Probably the most comprehensive book in the area of leisure. Covers all major topics related to leisure. Well written and well organized for easy reading.

Loesch, L. C., and Wheeler, P. T. *Principles of Leisure Counseling.* Minneapolis: Educational Media Corp., 1982.

This book provides a framework for effective leisure counseling. After an overview of leisure and leisure counseling, guidelines for individual, group, and developmental leisure counseling are presented. Information on available leisure counseling assessment instruments and an extensive bibliography are also included. A very useful book for professional counselors in a variety of settings. Could also serve as a text for a graduate course in leisure counseling.

McDaniels, C. *Leisure: Integrating a Neglected Component in Life Planning.* Columbus, Ohio: National Center for Research in Vocational Education, 1982.

Considers leisure as an integral part of life planning according to six life stages: childhood, adolescence, young adulthood, adulthood, midlife, and retirement. Each stage is treated individually, indicating the most positive features of leisure at that stage and explaining how various institutions can help a person take advantage of the opportunities of that stage. Suggestions for action by vocational educators, adult educators, and others are included.

McDowell, C. F., Jr. *Leisure Counseling: Selected Lifestyle Processes.* Eugene: Center for Leisure Studies, University of Oregon, 1976.

Probably the best book of its type. Written by a person with a recreation background, but with a very broad perspective of various life-style processes. Solid treatment of both the theory and the practice of leisure counseling.

References

Administrative Management Society. *1986 AMS Flexible Work Survey.* Willow Grove, Pa.: Administrative Management Society, 1986.

Albus, J. S. "Robots in the Workplace: The Key to a Prosperous Future." *The Futurist,* 1983, *18* (1), 22–27.

Albus, J. S. "Robots and the Economy." *The Futurist,* 1984, *19* (6), 34–40.

American Federation of Labor–Congress of Industrial Organizations. *The Future of Work.* Washington, D.C.: AFL-CIO, 1983.

American Society for Training and Development. *Serving the New Corporations.* Alexandria, Va.: American Society for Training and Development, 1986.

Anderson, N. *Man's Work and Leisure.* Leiden, Netherlands: E. J. Brill, 1974.

Anderson, N. *Work with Passion: How to Do What You Love for a Living.* New York: Carroll & Graf, 1984.

Applegath, J. *Working Free.* New York: AMACOM, 1982.

Arden, L. *The Work-at-Home Sourcebook: How to Find "At Home" Work That's Right for You.* Boulder, Colo.: Live Oak Publications, 1987.

Armstrong, J. S. *Long-Range Forecasting: From Crystal Ball to Computers.* (2nd ed.) New York: Wiley-Interscience, 1985.

"Asian, Native Americans Top Minority Entrepreneurs." *USA Today,* Dec. 5, 1986, p. A-11.

Asimov, I., and others. *Work in the 21st Century.* Alexandria, Va.: American Society for Personnel Administration, 1984.

Atkinson, W. *Working at Home: Is It for You?* Homewood, Ill.: Dow Jones–Irwin, 1985.

Bailey, G. *Maverick: Succeeding as a Free-Lance Entrepreneur.* New York: Franklin Watts, 1982.

Barnett, L. A., and Chick, G. E. "Chips Off the Ol' Block: Parents' Leisure and Their Children's Play." *Journal of Leisure Research,* 1986, *18* (4), 266–283.

Behr, M., and Lazar, W. (eds.). *Women Working Home: The Homebased Business Guide and Directory.* Edison, N.J.: Women Working Home Press, 1981.

Best, F. (ed.). *The Future of Work.* Englewood Cliffs, N.J.: Prentice-Hall, 1973.

Best, F. *Flexible Life Scheduling.* New York: Praeger, 1980.

Best, F. *Work Sharing: Issues, Policy Options and Prospects.* Kalamazoo, Mich.: Upjohn Institute for Employment Research, 1981.

Best, F. "Technology and the Changing World of Work." *The Futurist,* 1984, *18* (2), 61–62, 64–66.

Bienstock, H. *New and Emerging Occupations: Fact or Fancy.* Columbus: National Center for Research in Vocational Education, Ohio State University, 1981.

Birch, D. *Job Creation in America: How Our Smallest Companies Put the Most People to Work.* New York: Free Press, 1987.

Bloland, P. A., and Edwards, P. "Work and Leisure: A Counseling Synthesis." *Vocational Guidance Quarterly,* 1981, *30* (2), 101–108.

Bluestone, B., and Harrison, B. *The Deindustrialization of America: Plant Closings, Community Abandonment, and the Dismantling of Basic Industry.* New York: Basic Books, 1982.

Bluestone, B., and Harrison, B. *The Great American Job Machine: The Proliferation of Low Wage Employment in the U.S. Economy.* Washington, D.C.: U.S. Congress, Joint Economic Committee, 1986.

Botkin, J., Dimancescu, D., and Stata, R. *The Innovators: Rediscovering America's Creative Energy.* New York: Harper & Row, 1984.

Brabec, B. "Button Hobby Becomes Family Business." *National Home Business Report,* 1986a, p. 22.

Brabec, B. *Homemade Money.* White Hall, Va.: Betterway Publications, 1986b.

Bureau of the Census: *Statistical Abstract of the United States 1988* (108 edition). Washington, D.C.: U.S. Government Printing Office, 1988.

Bureau of Labor Statistics. "Bureau of Labor Statistics' 1970–1980 Projections: How Accurate Were They?" *Occupational Outlook Quarterly*, 1982a, *26* (3), 20–21.

Bureau of Labor Statistics. "Emerging Occupations: Not Every Acorn Becomes an Oak." *Occupational Outlook Quarterly*, 1982b, *26* (3), 12–13.

Bureau of Labor Statistics. "Spotlight on Service: Where the Jobs Are." *Occupational Outlook Quarterly*, 1985, *29* (2), 2–25.

Bureau of Labor Statistics. *Employment Projections for 1995: Data and Methods.* Washington, D.C.: U.S. Government Printing Office, 1986a.

Bureau of Labor Statistics. *Occupational Outlook Handbook, 1986–87.* Washington, D.C.: U.S. Government Printing Office, 1986b.

Bureau of Labor Statistics. *Occupational Projections and Training Data, 1986 Projections.* Washington, D.C.: U.S. Government Printing Office, 1986c.

Bureau of Labor Statistics. Special issue of *Monthly Labor Review* (containing projections to year 2000), Sept. 1987.

Bureau of Labor Statistics. *Occupational Outlook Handbook, 1988–89.* Washington, D.C.: U.S. Government Printing Office, 1988.

Bureau of Labor Statistics. *Labor Force Statistics Derived from the Current Population Survey, 1948–87.* (Bulletin 2307) Washington, D.C.: U.S. Government Printing Office, 1988b.

Bureau of Labor Statistics. *Projections 2000.* (Bulletin 2302) Washington, D.C.: U.S. Government Printing Office, 1988c.

Bureau of Labor Statistics. *Employment and Earnings,* 1988d, *35* (12), 8.

Bureau of Labor Statistics. *Employment and Earnings,* 1988e, *35* (3), 82–97.

Casale, A. M. *USA Today: Tracking Tomorrow's Trends.* Kansas City: Andrews, McMeel & Parker, 1986.

Center for Education Statistics, U.S. Department of Education. *Trends in Adult Education.* Washington, D.C.: U.S. Government Printing Office, 1987.

Cetron, M. J. "Getting Ready for the Jobs of the Future." *The Futurist,* 1983, *17* (3), 15–22.

Cetron, M. J. *Jobs of the Future*. New York: McGraw-Hill, 1984.

Cetron, M. J., and O'Toole, T. *Encounters with the Future: A Forecast of Life in the 21st Century*. New York: McGraw-Hill, 1982.

Chelte, A. F., Wright, J., and Tausky, C. "Did Job Satisfaction Really Drop During the 1970's" *Monthly Labor Review*, 1982, *105* (11), 33–38.

Colman, C., and Perelman, M. *Late Bloomers: How to Achieve Your Potential at Any Age*. New York: Macmillan, 1985.

Cornish, E. *The Study of the Future*. Bethesda, Md.: World Future Society, 1977.

Cornish, E. (ed.). *Careers Tomorrow: The Outlook for Work in a Changing World*. Bethesda, Md.: World Future Society, 1983.

Cornish, E. (ed.), *The Computerized Society: Living and Working in an Electronic Age*. Bethesda, Md.: World Future Society, 1985.

Csikszentmihalyi, M. *Beyond Boredom and Anxiety: The Experience of Play in Work and Games*. San Francisco: Jossey-Bass, 1975.

de Combray, N. "Volunteering in America." *American Demographics*, 1987, *9* (3), 50–52.

de Grazia, S. *Of Time, Work, and Leisure*. New York: Twentieth Century Fund, 1962.

Didsbury, H. F., Jr. (ed.) *The World of Work: Careers and the Future*. Bethesda, Md.: World Future Society, 1983.

Drucker, P. F. *Innovation and Entrepreneurship: Principles and Practices*. New York: Harper & Row, 1985.

Dumazedier, J. *Toward a Society of Leisure*. New York: Free Press, 1967.

"Economic Forecasts Vary for USA's Regions." *USA Today*, June 29, 1987, p. 4–B.

Edmondson, B. "Colleges Conquer the Baby Bust." *American Demographics*, 1987, *9* (9), 26–31.

Edwards, P. *Leisure Counseling Techniques*. (3rd ed.) Los Angeles: Constructive Leisure, 1980.

Ehrenreich, B. *The Hearts of Men*. New York: Doubleday, 1987.

"Eighth Annual Franchise 500." *Entrepreneur*, Jan. 1987, pp. 98–183.

Eisenberg, G. G. *Learning Vacations: Mind-Expanding Recreation for Every Interest, Age, and Budget*. Princeton, N.J.: Peterson's Guides, 1982.

Ely, V. K. *Teacher's Guide for Entrepreneurship Education.* Alexandria, Va.: American Vocational Association, 1983.

Fain, T. S. "Self-Employed Americans: Their Number Has Increased Between 1972–79." *Monthly Labor Review,* 1980, *103* (11), 3–8.

Feingold, S. N. "Emerging Careers: Occupations for the Post Industrial Society." *The Futurist,* 1984, *17* (3), 20–35.

Feingold, S. N., and Miller, N. R. *Emerging Careers: New Occupations for the Year 2000 and Beyond.* Garrett Park, Md.: Garrett Park Press, 1983.

Feingold, S. N., and Perlman, L. G. *Making It on Your Own.* Washington, D.C.: Acropolis Books, 1985.

Feldman, B. *Homebased Businesses.* Los Angeles: Till Press, 1983.

Fields, R., and others. *Chop Wood and Carry Water: A Guide to Finding Spiritual Fulfillment in Everyday Life.* Los Angeles: Tarcher, 1984.

Filbee, M. *Cottage Industries.* North Pomfret, Vt.: David & Charles, 1982.

Franslow, A. M., and Compton, C. W. *Entrepreneurship: A Senior High School Home Economics Career Exploration Unit.* Ames: Iowa State University Home Economics Education, 1982.

Gallup, G., Jr. *Forecast 2000.* New York: Morrow, 1984.

Gault, J. *Free Time: Making Your Leisure Count.* New York: Wiley, 1983.

Germain, R. (ed.). *National Avocational Organizations.* (7th ed.) Washington, D.C.: Columbia Books, 1987.

Gilder, G. *The Spirit of Enterprise.* New York: Simon & Schuster, 1984.

Gillespie, G. A. (ed.). *Leisure 2000: Scenarios for the Future.* Columbia: Department of Recreation and Park Administration, University of Missouri, 1983.

Gillis, P. *Entrepreneurial Mothers.* New York: Rawson Associates, 1984.

Ginzberg, E. *Good Jobs, Bad Jobs, No Jobs.* Cambridge, Mass.: Harvard University Press, 1979.

Goldstein, A. *Starting on a Shoestring.* New York: Ronald Press, 1984.

Goldstein, H., and Fraser, B. "Computer Training and the

Workplace: A Little Goes a Long Way." *Occupational Outlook Quarterly,* 1985a, *29* (4), 24–29.

Goldstein, H., and Fraser, B. *Training for Work in the Computer Age: How Workers Who Use Computers Get Their Training.* Washington, D.C.: National Commissions for Employment Policy, 1985b.

Greenberg, P. D., and Glaser, E. M. *Some Issues in Joint Union-Management Quality of Worklife Improvement Efforts.* Kalamazoo, Mich.: Upjohn Institute for Employment Research, 1980.

Groller, I. "A Couple of Business Partners." *Parents,* Jan. 1985, pp. 72–75.

Harman, W. W. *An Incomplete Guide to the Future.* New York: Norton, 1979.

Harman, W. W. *Global Mind Change: The Promise of the Last Years of the Twentieth Century.* Indianapolis: Knowledge Systems, 1988.

Harrington, P. E. "The Enrollment Crisis That Never Happened: How the Job Market Overcame Demographics." *Chronicle of Higher Education,* Apr. 8, 1987, pp. 44–45.

Harrison, P. (ed.). *America's New Women Entrepreneurs.* Washington, D.C.: Acropolis Books, 1986.

Hayes, G., and McDaniels, C. "The Leisure Pursuit of Volunteering." *Parks and Recreation,* 1980, *15,* 54–57.

Hedges, J., and Taylor, D. "Recent Trends in Worktime: Hours Edge Downward." *Monthly Labor Review,* 1980, *103* (3), 3–11.

Helmer, O. *Looking Forward: A Guide to Future Research.* New York: Russell Sage Foundation, 1983.

Henderson, H. *Creating Alternative Futures.* New York: Putnam (Perigee Books), 1980.

Herbert, R. F., and Link, A. N. *The Entrepreneur.* New York: Praeger, 1982.

Hirschhorn, L. *Beyond Mechanization: Work and Technology in a Postindustrial Age.* Cambridge, Mass.: MIT Press, 1984.

Howard, R. *Brave New Workplace.* New York: Viking Penguin, 1985.

Hummel, D., and McDaniels, C. *Unlocking Your Child's Potential.* Washington, D.C.: Acropolis Books, 1982.

Hunt, H. A., and Hunt, T. L. *Human Resource Implications of Robotics.* Kalamazoo, Mich.: Upjohn Institute for Employment Research, 1983.

Hunt, H. A., and Hunt, T. L. *Clerical Employment and Technological Change.* Kalamazoo, Mich.: Upjohn Institute for Employment Research, 1986.

Industrial Union Department of AFL-CIO. *Crossroads for America.* Washington, D.C.: Industrial Union Department of AFL-CIO, 1987.

Johnson, W. B. *Workforce 2000.* Indianapolis: Hudson Institute, 1987.

Kabl, A., and Clark, D. E. "Health: Cross Roads over the Horizon?" *Occupational Outlook Quarterly,* 1985, *29* (2), 4–11.

Kalleberg, A. L., and others. *Indianapolis/Tokyo Work Commitment Study: Preliminary Results.* Bloomington: Institute for Social Research, University of Indiana, 1983.

Kaplan, J. R. *Leisure: Theory and Policy.* New York: Wiley, 1975.

Kelly, J. R. "The Centrality of Leisure." *National Forum,* 1982a, *62,* 19–21.

Kelly, J. R. *Leisure.* Englewood Cliffs, N.J.: Prentice-Hall, 1982b.

Kelly, J. R. *Leisure Identities and Interactions.* Winchester, Mass.: Allen & Unwin, 1983.

Kent, C. A., Sexton, D. L., and Vesper, K. H. *Encyclopedia of Entrepreneurship.* Englewood Cliffs, N.J.: Prentice-Hall, 1982.

Kinstone, B. *The Student Entrepreneur's Guide.* Berkeley, Calif.: Ten Speed Press, 1981.

Kiplinger Washington Newsletter. *The New American Boom.* Washington, D.C.: Kiplinger, 1986.

Kleibert, D., Larson, L., and Csikszentmihalyi, M. "The Experience of Leisure in Adolescence." *Journal of Leisure Research,* 1986, *18,* 169–176.

Kuttner, B. "The Declining Middle." *Atlantic Monthly,* 1983, *252* (1), 60–72.

LaBier, D. *Modern Madness: The Emotional Fallout of Success.* Reading, Mass.: Addison-Wesley, 1986.

Lancaster, R., and Odum, L. "Leisure Education Advancement Project." *Journal of Health, Physical Education and Recreation,* 1976, *47*, 43–44.

Lefkowitz, B. *Breaktime: Living Without Work in a Nine to Five World.* New York: Dutton (Hawthorn Books), 1979.

Levitan, S. A. "Beyond 'Trendy' Forecasts." *The Futurist,* 1987, *21* (6), 28–33.

Levitan, S. A., and Johnson, C. M. "The Future of Work: Does It Belong to Us or to the Robots?" *Monthly Labor Review,* 1982a, *105* (9), 60–72.

Levitan, S. A., and Johnson, C. M. *Second Thoughts on Work.* Kalamazoo, Mich.: Upjohn Institute for Employment Research, 1982b.

Loesch, L. C., and Wheeler, P. T. *Principles of Leisure Counseling.* Minneapolis: Educational Media Corp., 1982.

Long, W. "The Meaning of Entrepreneurship." *American Journal of Small Business,* 1983, *8* (2), 47–56.

MDC. *Shadows in the Sunbelt.* Chapel Hill, N.C.: MDC Inc., 1986.

McCarthy, M. E., and Rosenberg, G. S. *Work Sharing Case Studies.* Kalamazoo, Mich.: Upjohn Institute for Employment Research, 1981.

McDaniels, C. "Vocation: A Religious Search for Meaning." *Vocational Guidance Quarterly,* 1965, *14* (1), 31–35.

McDaniels, C. "The Role of Leisure in Career Development." In *Fifth World Congress, ACTES Proceedings.* Quebec, Canada: International Association for Educational and Vocational Guidance, 1973.

McDaniels, C. (ed.). *Leisure and Career Development at Mid-Life.* Blacksburg, Va.: Department of Counselor Education, Virginia Polytechnic Institute and State University, 1976. (ERIC NO ED 155–577)

McDaniels, C. "Leisure and Career Development at Mid-Life: A Rationale." *Vocational Guidance Quarterly,* 1977, *25* (4), 356–363.

McDaniels, C. *Leisure: Integrating a Neglected Component in Life Planning.* Columbus: National Center for Research in Vocational Education, Ohio State University, 1982.

McDaniels, C. "The Role of Leisure in Career Development."

Journal of Career Development, 1984a, *11* (2), 64–71. (Note: The December 1984 issue of *JCD* is a special issue in which all articles are devoted to the role of leisure in career development.)

McDaniels, C. "Work and Leisure in the Career Span." In N. C. Gysbers and Associates (eds.), *Designing Careers: Counseling to Enhance Education, Work, and Leisure.* San Francisco: Jossey-Bass, 1984b.

McDaniels, C., and Hesser, A. "Career Services for Adult Workers at Virginia Tech." *Career Planning and Adult Development Newsletter,* 1982, *4* (11), 1–2.

McDaniels, C., and Hesser, A. "Outplacement: An Occasion for Faculty Career Development." In *Outplacement Counseling.* Ann Arbor, Mich.: ERIC/CAPS Clearinghouse, 1983.

McDaniels, C., and Watts, G. "Cooperation: Key to Employee Career Development Program." *Career Development Quarterly,* 1987, *36* (2), 170–177.

McDowell, C. F., Jr. *Leisure Counseling: Selected Lifestyle Processes.* Eugene: Center for Leisure Studies, University of Oregon, 1976.

Manly, K. "Hotel Business Checked Out, so Exec Checked In." *USA Today,* Aug. 4, 1987, p. B-4.

Meier, G. S. *Job Sharing.* Kalamazoo, Mich.: Upjohn Institute for Employment Research, 1978.

Meier, G. S. *Worker Learning and Worktime Flexibility.* Kalamazoo, Mich.: Upjohn Institute for Employment Research, 1983.

Moore, G., and Hedges, J. "Trends in Labor and Leisure." *Monthly Labor Review,* 1971, *94* (2), 3–11.

Morehouse, W., and Dembo, D. *The Underbelly of the U.S. Economy: Joblessness and Pauperization of Work in America.* New York: Council on International and Public Affairs (a series of seven Special Reports, October 1984-February 1988, No. 7).

Morf, M. "Eight Scenarios for Work in the Future." *The Futurist,* 1983, *17* (3), 24–29.

Mundy, J., and Odum, L. *Leisure Education: Theory and Practice.* New York: Wiley, 1979.

Murphy, J. *Concepts of Leisure.* (2nd ed.) Englewood Cliffs, N.J.: Prentice-Hall, 1981.

Naisbitt, J. *Megatrends.* New York: Warner Books, 1982.

Nardone, T. "Looking at the Future." *Occupational Outlook Quarterly,* 1984, pp. 14–19.

National Commission on Jobs and Small Business. *10,000,000 Jobs.* Washington, D.C.: National Commission on Jobs and Small Business, 1986.

National Home Study Council. *Directory of Accredited Home Study Schools, 1987–1988.* Washington, D.C.: National Home Study Council, 1987.

National Federation of Independent Business. *Small Business in America.* San Mateo, Calif.: National Federation of Independent Business, 1981.

National Recreation and Park Association. *Life, Be in It.* Alexandria, Va.: National Recreation and Park Association, 1981.

Neulinger, J. *Introduction to Leisure.* Newton, Mass.: Allyn & Bacon, 1981.

"The New Volunteerism." *Newsweek,* Feb. 8, 1988, pp. 42–43.

Nollen, S. D. *New Work Schedules in Practice.* New York: Van Nostrand, 1982.

O'Connell, B. (ed.). *America's Voluntary Spirit: A Book of Readings.* New York: Foundation Center, 1983.

Office of Technological Assessment. *Automation and the Workplace: Selected Labor, Education, and Training Issues.* Washington, D.C.: U.S. Congress, Office of Technological Assessments, 1983.

Office of Technological Assessment. *Technology and Structural Unemployment: Reemploying Displaced Adults (Summary).* Washington, D.C.: U.S. Congress, Office of Technological Assessment, 1986.

Olmstead, B., and Smith, S. *The Job Sharing Handbook.* Berkeley, Calif.: Ten Speed Press, 1983.

O'Toole, J. *Making America Work.* New York: Continuum, 1981.

"Our Endless Pursuit of Happiness." *U.S. News and World Report,* Aug. 10, 1981, *90* (6), 58–67.

Overs, R., Taylor, S., and Adkins, C. *Avocational Counseling Manual.* Washington, D.C.: Hawkins & Associates, 1977.

Paradis, A. *Planning Your Career of Tomorrow.* Lincolnwood, Ill.: National Textbook Company, 1986.

Parker, S. *The Future of Work and Leisure.* New York: Praeger, 1971.

Pascarella, P. *The New Achievers: Creating a Modern Work Ethic.* New York: Free Press, 1984.

Peevy, E. "Leisure Counseling: A Life Cycle Approach." Unpublished doctoral dissertation, Virginia Polytechnic Institute and State University, 1981.

Personick, V. A. "The Job Outlook Through 1995: Industry Output and Employment." *Monthly Labor Review,* 1983, *106* (11), 24–36.

Personick, V. A. "A Second Look at Industry Output and Employment Trends to 1995." *Monthly Labor Review,* 1985, *108* (11), 26–41.

Peterson's Guides. *The Independent Study Catalog, 1986–88.* Princeton, N.J.: Peterson's Guides, 1986.

Pieper, J. *Leisure: The Basis of Culture.* New York: Pantheon, 1964. (Originally published 1952.)

Pollock, M. A., and Berstein, A. "The Disposable Employee Is Becoming a Fact of Corporate Life." *Business Week,* Dec. 15, 1986, pp. 52–56.

Rapaport, R., and Rapaport, R. *Leisure and the Family Life Cycle.* Boston: Routledge & Kegan Paul, 1975.

Research & Forecasts, Inc. *Where Does the Time Go? The United Media Enterprises Report on Leisure in America.* New York: United Media Enterprises, 1982.

Research & Forecasts, Inc. *The Miller Lite Report on American Attitudes Toward Sports.* Milwaukee: Miller Brewing Company, 1983.

Riche, R. W. "Higher Technology Today and Tomorrow: Small Slice of Employment Pie." *Monthly Labor Review,* 1983, *106* (11), 50–58.

Roberts, K. *Leisure.* (2nd ed.) New York: Longman, 1981.

Rosenthal, N. H. "Is the Middle Class Shrinking?" *Occupational Outlook Quarterly,* Fall 1985, *29* (3), 15–17.

Rosow, J. W. "Quality-of-Work-Life Issues for the 1980s." In C. Kerr and J. W. Rosow, (eds.), *Work in America: The Decade Ahead.* New York: Van Nostrand Reinhold, 1979.

Rosow, J. W. "Personnel Policies for the 1980s." In C. S. Sheppard and D. C. Carroll, (eds.), *Working in the 21st Century.* New York: Wiley, 1980.

Roth, D. M. "The Franchise 50." *Venture,* Feb. 1987, p. 38.

Rumberger, R. W. *The Job Market for College Graduates, 1960–*

1990. IFG Project Report No. 83-A3. Stanford: Institute for Research on Educational Finance and Government, Stanford University, 1983.

Schumacher, E. F. *Small Is Beautiful: Economics as if People Mattered.* New York: Harper & Row, 1973.

Schumacher, E. F. "Good Work." In D. W. Vermilye (ed.), *Relating Work and Education.* San Franchisco: Jossey-Bass, 1977.

Schumacher, E. F. *Good Work.* New York: Harper & Row, 1979.

Sears, S. "A Definition of Career Guidance Terms: A National Vocational Guidance Association Perspective." *Vocational Guidance Quarterly,* 1982, *31* (2), 137–143.

Seltz, D. D. *A Treasury of Business Opportunities for the 80s.* (3rd ed.) Rockville Centre, N.Y.: Farnsworth, 1984.

Silvestri, G. T., and Lukasiewicz, J. M. "Occupational Employment Projections: The 1984–95 Outlook." *Monthly Labor Review,* 1985, *108* (11), 42–57.

Silvestri, G. T., and others. "Occupational Employment Projections Through 1995." *Monthly Labor Review,* 1983, *106* (11), 37–49.

Sinetar, M. "The Actualized Worker." *The Futurist,* Mar.–Apr. 1987a, pp. 21–25.

Sinetar, M. *Do What You Love, The Money Will Follow.* Boulder, Colo.: New Career Center, 1987b.

Small Business Administration. *The State of Small Business: A Report of the President.* Washington, D.C.: Small Business Administration, 1986.

"Small Business in America" (a poster). Washington, D.C.: The NFIB Foundation, 1981.

Solomon, S. *Small Business USA.* New York: Crown Publishers, 1985.

Stebbins, R. A. *Amateurs: On the Margin Between Work and Leisure.* Newbury Park, Calif.: Sage, 1979.

Stern, B., and Best, F. "Cyclic Life Patterns." In D. W. Vermilye (ed.), *Relating Work and Education.* San Francisco: Jossey-Bass, 1977.

Stewart, J. F., and Boyd, D. R. "Education and Entrepreneurial Training: A Definite Must." *Minorities and Women in Business,* May-June, 1986, pp. 26–28.

Super, D. E. "Leisure: What It Is and Might Be." *Journal of Career Development,* 1984, *11* (2), 71–80.

Supple, T. S. "The Coming Labor Shortage." *American Demographics,* 1986, *8* (9), 32–37.

Tinsley, H. E. A., and Teaff, J. D. *The Psychological Benefits of Leisure Activities for the Elderly: A Manual and Final Report of an Investigation.* Carbondale: Department of Psychology, Southern Illinois University, 1983.

Tinsley, H. E. A., and Tinsley, D. J. "A Holistic Model of Leisure Counseling." *Journal of Leisure Research,* 1982, *14* (2), 100–116.

Toffler, A. *Future Shock.* New York: Random House, 1970.

Toffler, A. *The Futurists.* New York: Random House, 1972.

Veblen, T. *The Theory of the Leisure Class.* New York: Viking Press, 1935. (Originally published 1899.)

Vesper, K. H. *Entrepreneurship Education, 1985.* Wellesley, Mass.: Babson College for Entrepreneurial Studies, 1985.

Virginia Employment Commission. *Virginia 1990: Occupational Employment Projections.* Richmond: Research and Analysis Division, Virginia Employment Commission, 1985.

Virginia Occupational Information System. *Virginia Occupational Demand, Supply, and Wage Information.* Charlottesville: Virginia Occupational Information System, Tayloe Murphy Institute, University of Virginia, 1986.

Wehmeyer, L. B. *Futuristics.* New York: Franklin Watts, 1986.

Weinstein, R. V. *Jobs for the 21st Century.* New York: Macmillan, 1983.

Worthington, R. "At-Home Factories Help Farmers." *Kansas City Star,* June 7, 1987, p. E-1.

Yankelovich, D. *New Rules: Searching for Self-Fulfillment in a World Turned Upside Down.* New York: Random House, 1981.

Yankelovich, D., and Lefkowitz, B. "American Ambivalence and the Psychology of Growth." *National Forum,* 1982a, *62* (3), 12–15.

Yankelovich, D., and Lefkowitz, B. "Work and American Expectations." *National Forum,* 1982b, *62* (2), 3–5.

Index